Elizabeth Anne Galton (1808-1906)
A Well-connected Gentlewoman

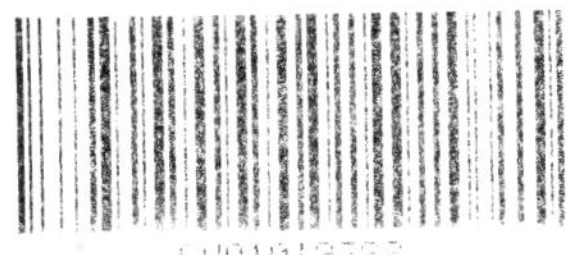

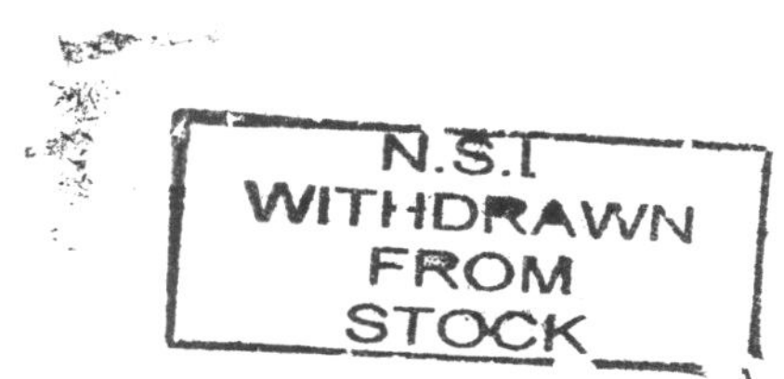

Elizabeth Anne Galton (1808-1906)

A Well-connected Gentlewoman

Edited by

ANDREW MOILLIET

ISBN
1 901253 36 8
First published November 2003

Published by:
Léonie Press
an imprint of
Anne Loader Publications
13 Vale Road, Hartford,
Northwich, Cheshire CW8 1PL, Gt Britain
Tel: 01606 75660 Fax: 01606 77609
e-mail: anne@leoniepress.com
Website: www.anneloaderpublications.co.uk
www.leoniepress.com

Printed by:
Anne Loader Publications
Collated and bound by: B & S Swindells Ltd, Knutsford
Covers laminated by: The Finishing Touch, St Helens

Elizabeth Anne Galton, aged 35, from a painting by Easton

CONTENTS

List of illustrations vii

Preface ix

Galton Family Tree xii

Darwin Family Tree xiii

Wheler Family Tree xiv

Moilliet Family Tree xv

Chapter 1 - Introduction and early childhood 1

Chapter 2 - School days (1818-1824)............ 30

Chapter 3 - Birmingham and some travels (1824-1829) 40

Chapter 4 - Some London connexions (1829) 72

Chapter 5 - Birmingham (cont) and more travels (1929-1832) 78

Chapter 6 - Leamington (1832-1838) 90

Chapter 7 - The Coronation of Queen Victoria (1838) 119

Chapter 8 - Royal Leamington Spa (1838-1839) 127

Chapter 9 - A Scottish pilgrimage (1839) 133

Chapter 10 - Royal Leamington Spa, cont (1839-1845) 139

Chapter 11 - Early years of married life (1846-1857) 160

Chapter 12 - Final entries (1857-1865) 186

Epilogue - The Diamond Jubilee (1897) 197

Postscript - by her daughter Mrs Lucy Studdy 202

Index 213

List of illustrations

Frontispiece - Elizabeth Anne Galton, aged 35
Samuel Tertius Galton xvi
Frances Anne Violetta Galton (née Darwin) xvi
Edward Wheler xvii
Millicent Adele Bunbury (née Galton) xvii
Elizabeth Anne Galton, aged 96 years xviii
The drawing room at Dudson 3
Sketch from Grass walk at Dudson 3
"Duddeston House" 4
Dudson Pool 4
Samuel Galton Jnr 11
Erasmus Darwin 11
Radbourne, Derbyshire 11
Puzzle letters 46-49
Galtons Bank 54
Galtons and James Bank cheque 54
The Larches 59
Sampler sewn by Elizabeth Anne Galton 59
Menu from dinner given for the Duke of Wellington 83
Family reunion in 1837 113
Claverdon 113
Ury - the residence of the Barclay family 136
Bertie Terrace, Leamington 178
Mrs Samuel Tertius Galton at Bertie Terrace 178
Sophia Galton and Adele Galton 193
Emma Sophia Galton 204
Darwin Galton 204
Erasmus Galton 204
Sir Francis Galton FRS 204

Preface

Elizabeth Anne Galton (Mrs Edward Wheler), who lived from 1808 to 1906, was the eldest of the nine children of Samuel Tertius Galton, a well-to-do Birmingham banker who retired to Leamington in 1832. Although he joined the Church of England when he married, Samuel Tertius came of an old Quaker family which had been prominent in Birmingham affairs for three generations and had many local connections. He was related to a number of influential people, most of them Quakers: Barclays, Frys, Gurneys, Hoares, Bevans, Lloyds, Buxtons, Trittons, and Hanburys. Elizabeth Anne therefore grew up in the midst of people of some importance, many of whose immediate forebears had helped to make the Industrial Revolution. This gave her an excellent opportunity of meeting and talking to important people, as well as of observing upper-middle-class life in England in the first half of the nineteenth century.

Fortunately, Elizabeth Anne took advantage of these opportunities, keeping a diary and preserving correspondence and other family papers, all of which augmented a naturally retentive memory. Towards the end of her long life, she put much of this information on paper, in the "Galton Book" which is now in the Galton Laboratory at University College, London, and in the reminiscences which she dictated to her daughter, Mrs Lucy Studdy. With the disappearance of the male line of Elizabeth Anne's family, these reminiscences have descended to us through her sister Lucy Harriot (Mrs James Moilliet). It seems to us that, with suitable editing, they are of sufficient general interest to be worth a wider circulation.

Our interest in Elizabeth Anne Galton and her circle is enhanced by what we might call her "scientific connections". Her youngest brother, Sir Francis Galton, FRS, is generally regarded as the founder of the science of eugenics (a word which he coined), and he also made important contributions to statistics, meteorology, scientific geography, and biometrics (including the use of fingerprints and personal measurements for purposes of identification). In the same generation, her first cousin, Sir Douglas Galton, achieved distinction as an engineer. She shared a common grandfather (Erasmus Darwin, FRS, the moving spirit in the famous Lunar Society of Birmingham) with her half-cousin, the great Charles Darwin, and her paternal grandfather, Samuel Galton, Jr, the friend and protector of the chemist, Joseph Priestley, was also a "Lunatick." Elizabeth Anne was no scientist herself, but these illustrious men and their friends appear from time to time in her memoirs, often in a very human light.

It is not surprising, in view of her family connections and of the times in which she lived, that Elizabeth Anne Galton was keenly interested in matters of family and genealogy; this interest is clearly one reason for her recording her reminiscences. Her interest in "family" was compounded of an objective interest and a genuine affection. Although she could not help being a bit upset when her Aunt Sophia married her grandfather's steward, or when a cousin eloped with a private soldier, she is careful to point out that her aunt's marriage was a happy one, and that the private soldier in question was a "respectable Scotchman". She is also quick to express her admiration for people who made their own way in life. Her own very happy marriage, to a husband of "good family" but limited means, meant that, with the passage of time, she came less and less in contact with prominent people. This, and the fact that she felt no need to record events after her children were grown, probably explains why her story "tails off" during the 1860s.

The task of editing these reminiscences has not been easy and was initially undertaken in conjunction with my late father, J.L. Moilliet. I have recently re-edited the earlier version which was issued for private family circulation only, by including many more items from the original reminiscences. They were recorded in chronological order, without any attempts at arranging their contents, and contain a great deal of trivial matter. Embedded in these trivia, however, are many amusing anecdotes and other items which give us a picture of life in the early nineteenth century. We have tried to pick out these items, leaving enough other material to make them intelligible. Explanatory footnotes and interpolations (the latter in square brackets) have seemed appropriate in some places, as have a few insertions from other papers left us by Elizabeth Anne and her daughter. We have also had to alter the position of a few passages, supply chapter headings, and introduce some pauses, in order to make her easier to follow. For the rest, however, we have refrained from tampering with the original and have allowed Elizabeth Anne to tell her own story, which we think gives a social document of some interest and value.

We are indebted to the late Mrs Joyce Pearson for permission to reproduce part of a letter from the late Hesketh Pearson to his mother, and we are also grateful to various friends and relatives who have given us their candid opinions as to whether or not some of the passages are worth including.

The illustrations are mostly from old drawings and photographs which had been pasted in the original manuscript, most of them being very faded and yellow with age.

We have indexed this book as completely as possible, quoting dates of birth and death where known. We have also compiled family trees for Elizabeth Anne's nearest relatives, in some cases leaving off the names of the people she does not mention. On both the family trees and in the index, where we know that people were not called by their first name, we have underlined the name by which they were usually known. We have been unable to identify some of the people who appear in this book. If anyone can help with further information (such as dates of birth or death, or corrections) we would be very pleased to hear from them.

Andrew Moilliet
Diana Moilliet
Bramhall, 2003

GALTON FAMILY TREE

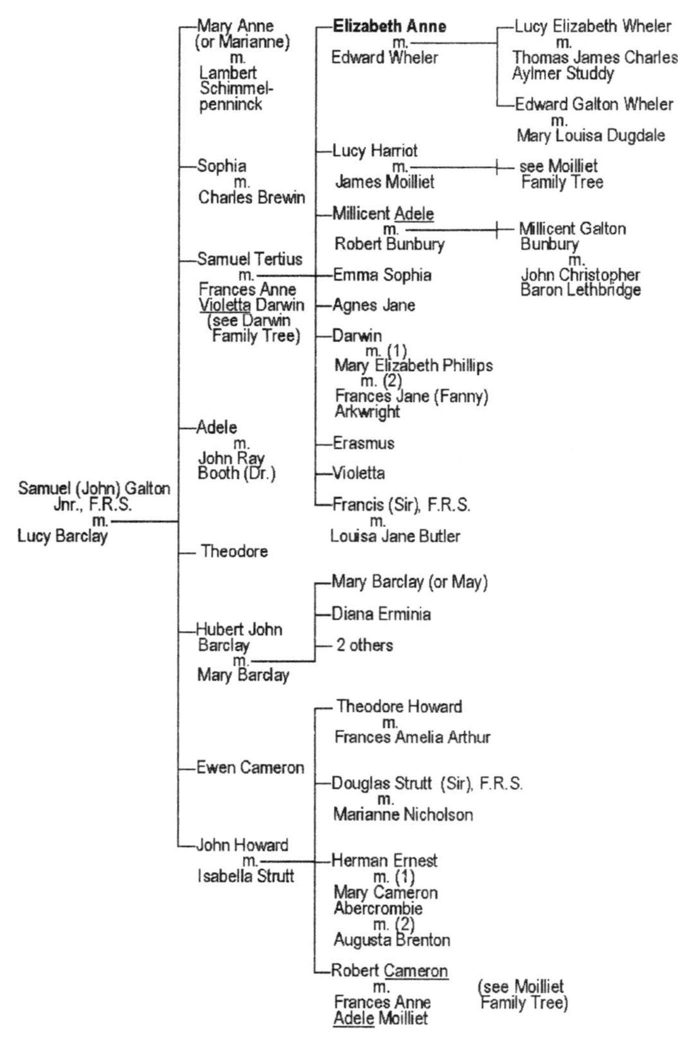

DARWIN FAMILY TREE

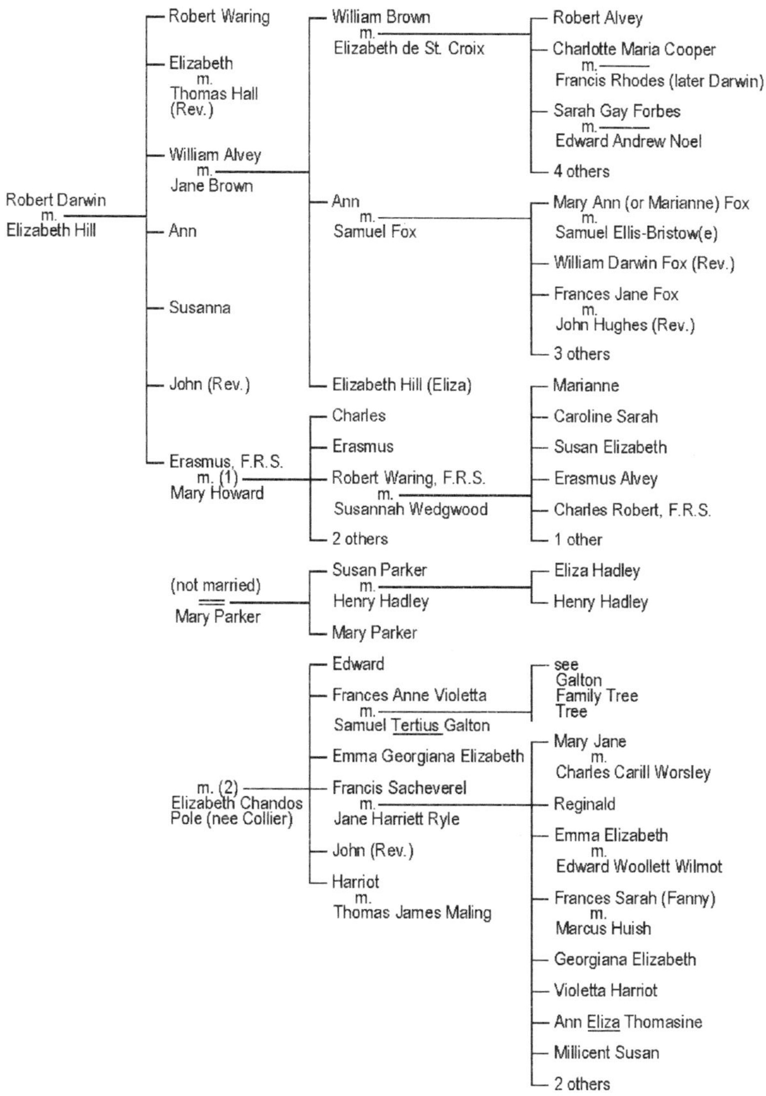

WHELER FAMILY TREE

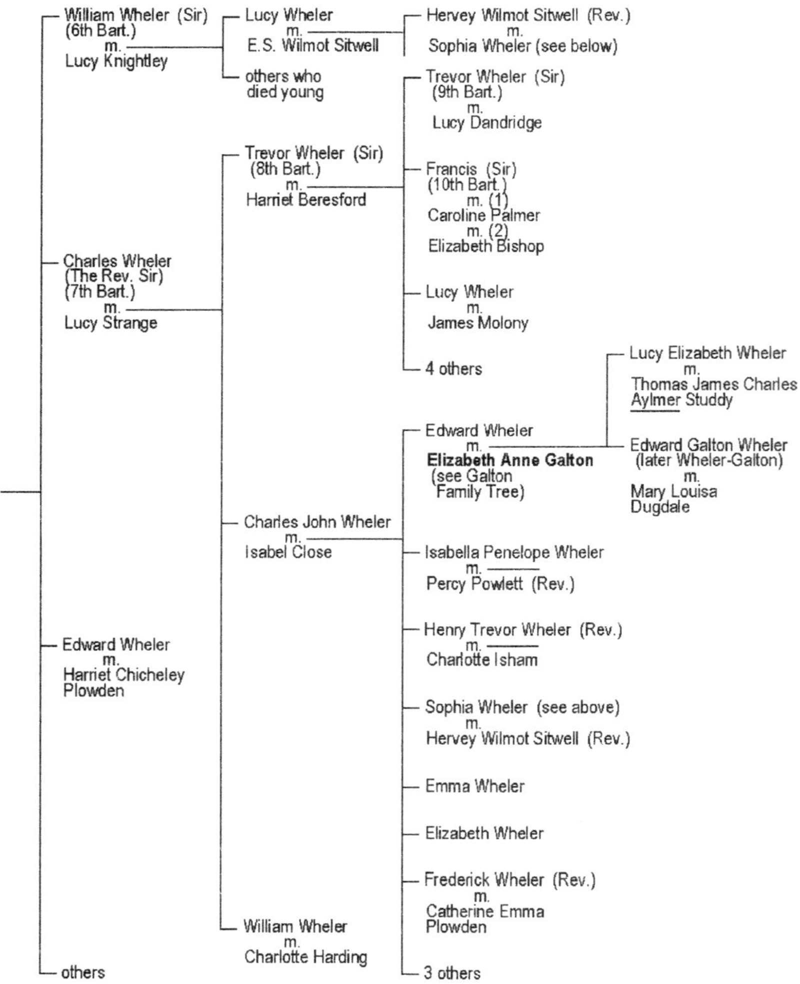

MOILLIET FAMILY TREE

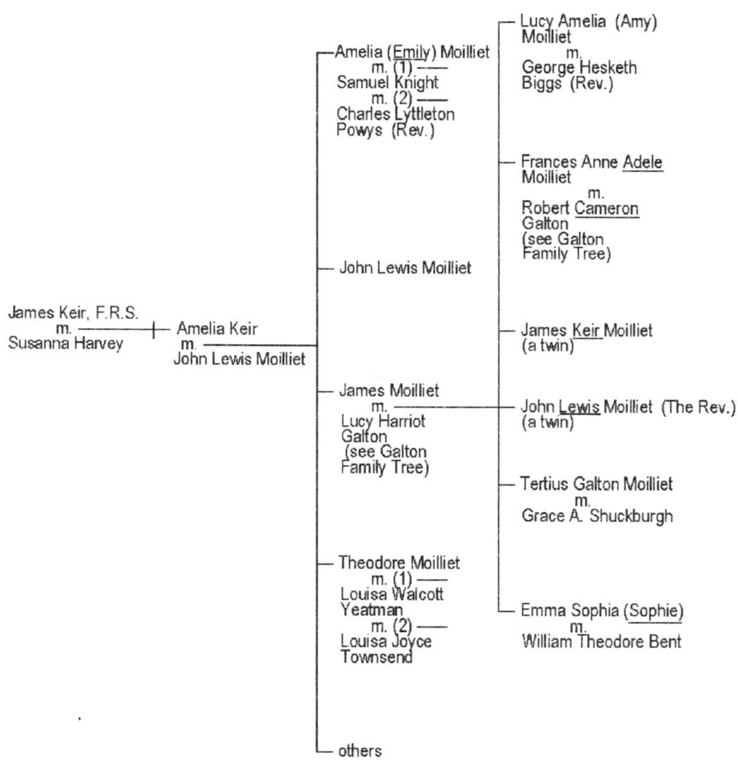

Samuel Tertius Galton,
Elizabeth Anne's father

Frances Anne Violetta
Galton (née Darwin)
Elizabeth Anne's mother

Edward Wheler
Elizabeth Anne's husband

Millicent Adele Bunbury (née Galton) Elizabeth Anne's sister

Elizabeth Anne Galton, aged 96 years

Chapter 1

Introduction and Early Childhood

My children urge me to write a History of My Life. I was born on 19th. February, 1808, at Ladywood, one mile from Birmingham, now (1895) in the middle of the town. I was the eldest child, and have often been told that the snowstorm was so severe and the snow lay so deep on the day I was born, that Dr. Barr, the Surgeon who brought us all into the world except Francis, had to make his way with difficulty over the field to attend my Mother.

My Father and Mother were married in March 1807. Ladywood was a nice small house, with a field in front, through which was a public footpath, another field at the side of the house, and a garden at the back, at the bottom of which was an empty greenhouse with hot-house attached, and this greenhouse was our out-of-door playroom. Through it we went into the orchard, where we had our swings. Our ring in front had two gates, one to a lane up to the Canal Bridge, and from there through a narrow secluded lane to the Crescent. The other gate led through an Avenue in our field to another road to Birmingham. The field next to ours was called the Pest Field, where all who had died of the Plague in 1666 were buried, and we were told it was not allowed to be ploughed in consequence.

The Galton family was originally Dorsetshire, and came from near a hamlet called Galton. They had much property in Dorsetshire and were allied to several County families (see the "Galton Book"). They were Quakers, and for that reason they could not, before the middle of this century, enter into a profession or go to College, on account of the oaths which they would not take. They were therefore all in business and made good fortunes.

My Great-great-uncle John Galton and his brother Samuel (my Great-grandfather) came to Birmingham in about 1770 and set up a business there with one of the Farmer family, whose sister was Samuel's wife, my Great grandmother. Her niece, my Grandfather's first cousin, married Mr. Charles Lloyd of Bingley. My Great-grandfather and his son, my Grandfather, had one of the largest manufactories in the Town for guns (a curious business for Quakers*) and for many years supplied the Tower with guns. I have often heard my Father say that, during the war, guns were made in Birmingham at the rate of one a minute on average, besides many parts of guns sent to London.

My Great-grandfather was a good Christian and a thorough gentleman. He always drove with four horses as was the custom, and used to wear a muff and clogs when he went to a Quaker meeting. Every morning a row of baskets full of fruit or vegetables was placed in the hall, and he put a paper in each with the name of the family to whom it was to be sent. At my Great-grandfather's death, my Grandfather and Father wound up the gun business and set up a bank in Steelhouse Lane, in which he and his three sons were partners with Mr. Paul Moon James, who married Olivia, a daughter of Charles Lloyd**, as working partner. [See illustration on p.54.]

*

After my Great-grandfather's death, my Grandfather and Grandmother lived at Dudson, or Duddeston, three miles from Ladywood and one mile from Birmingham; a very pretty country place, with grounds remarkably well laid out – the house large and handsome. It was part of the Aston Hall Estate, and when my Great-grandfather settled in Birmingham, he took a ninety-nine year lease of it, which my Grandfather renewed. There were two large pools where we used to watch and feed the swans. At the sale of the Aston Hall property my Father bought Dudson, which is now built upon,

**Her grandfather, Samuel Galton Jr, was sternly called to account for all this by the Birmingham Meeting, though he remained a Quaker all his life.*

*** Charles Lloyd was one of the great figures in the early history of Lloyds Bank; c.f. R.S, Sayers, Lloyds Bank in the History of English Banking, Oxford, 1957, p. 26.*

The drawing room at Dudson (Duddeston), from a sketch by Lucy Harriot Galton, 1827. (Compare the relative austerity and elegance of this interior with the "fussiness" of the drawing room on page 178.)

Sketch from the Grass Walk, Dudson, 1827

"Duddeston House" from a drawing by E.S. Galton

Dudson Pool

and is now very valuable property.

My Grandfather had five sons. My Father was the eldest; the second, Theodore, from all accounts was one of the most amiable, charming, and handsome young men, beloved by all who knew him. He travelled with my Uncle Francis Sacheverell Darwin to Spain, Italy, Greece, and other places. When he was twenty-four, he caught the plague at Smyrna and died at Malta, to the inexpressible grief of his family and friends. Had he lived, he was to be in partnership with Mr. Moilliet* who calls one of his sons after him. Another son, Cameron, a very nice boy, died at eight years old, his illness caused by the cruelty of the boys at Dr. Valpy's school at Reading. Hubert and Howard were the younger sons of my Grandfather and were some years younger than the rest.

My Grandfather had three daughters. The eldest, Marianne (Mrs. Schimmelpenninck**) was very clever and talented, and wrote several clever books, but unfortunately was a great mischief-maker, causing such annoyance and quarrels in the family, and among all their acquaintances from her habit of distorting truth so as to give a false impression, that at last it was settled by her parents and family that all intercourse with her must cease, so that I did not know her. My aunts Sophia (Mrs. Brewin) and Adele (Mrs. Booth) were most kind to us, more like sisters than aunts. My Grandmother Galton was a very clever, beautiful woman, very dignified and queen-like in her manner. Her Father was Robert Barclay of Ury, and her Mother daughter of David Barclay of London. The Barclays are a very old family, and she was doubly descended from Barclay the Apologist***. Her Father and her half-brother, Captain Barclay

**John Lewis (Jean-Louis) Moilliet, banker, merchant and philanthropist of Birmingham and Geneva (1770-1845), whose family frequently appear in these pages. The banking business which he acquired and built up was amalgamated with Lloyds Banking Company in 1865 (c.f. Sayers, op. cit., p. 220).*

***Mrs Schimmelpenninck is chiefly remembered today for her scurrilous attacks on Erasmus Darwin; see Hesketh Pearson's Doctor Darwin and Desmond King-Hele's Erasmus Darwin, She appears again on p.105 of these reminiscences.*

****Robert Barclay (1648-1690) of Ury, author of An Apology for the True Christian Divinity Held by the Quakers (1678), one of the standard expositions of Quaker beliefs.*

Allardice of pedestrian fame (see p.105) were great agriculturists, and did much to improve farming in Scotland. They were also remarkable for their great strength.

Her maternal Grandfather, David Barclay, entertained George I, George II and George III at his house in Cheapside, where they came to show themselves in the City. The day before the Royal Party arrived, they sent a set of dinner napkins and other things for their use, which they left behind as remembrances. I have the dinner napkins with the Royal Arms on.

We children were often sent to Dudson when my Father and Mother went from home, and liked to see my Grandfather feed his dogs. But the great delight was speaking through the speaking trumpet in the library to the maids in the kitchen. Everything was very quiet and regular at Dudson; a good deal of state was kept up. We were never allowed to pick a flower, or any fruit, doors were to be shut, and no noise. My Grandfather was very fond of birds, and kept several to watch their habits. He wrote a book upon birds, which was thought much of at that time. He put boxes with overlapping lids and bottles, in which hung little buckets the size of a thimble, hanging by a light chain outside the windows, and our amusement was to watch the wild birds nodding up the lid of the box with their heads to get the seed, and drawing up the bucket with their beak and foot. One bird, I think a Tom-tit, had only one leg, and yet managed to get it very cleverly.

My Grandfather was a very clever scientific man, and was a member of the Lunar Society.

[This is perhaps the chief claim to fame of Samuel Galton Jr, FRS (1753-1832), though he was also the inventor of the colour top, usually attributed to Thomas Young, which demonstrates that white light can be synthesised from the primary colours. The Lunar Society, nicknamed "the Lunaticks" by Samuel Galton's butler, met informally at the full moon, so that members could travel home afterwards in (comparative!) safety. It played an important part in the scientific and industrial development of the Midlands; see R. E. Schofield, The Lunar Society of Birmingham, Oxford, 1963.]

My Mother was the eldest daughter of Dr. Erasmus Darwin by his second marriage. The Darwins came from Elston in Nottinghamshire. My Mother remembered her Grandmother Darwin very well, as she used to go to Elston every Christmas with her Father and all the family. Her Grandmother lived to the age of ninety-five, and to the last day of her life she got up to feed her pigeons. When her grandchildren came to Elston, she used to come into the nursery at six o'clock in the morning. Her maid placed a pillow on the window seat (all windows in those days had window-seats which opened with a lid, and were very useful), on which she sat to see the children dressed. She had four sons, Robert Waring the eldest, William Alvey the second, John the third, and Erasmus the youngest. She had three daughters, Elizabeth married the Rev. Thomas Hall, Susanna died unmarried, and Ann lived to a great age. Her eldest son Robert never married. He was brought up as a Barrister, but never practised. He died in 1816, as I shall mention bye and bye.

The second son William Alvey was brought up to the Law. He married Miss Brown, and had one son William Brown Darwin, who married Miss St. Croix. They had a large family who all died young of consumption, except two daughters. Charlotte the eldest, inherited Elston and married Mr. Rhodes, who took the name of Darwin, and they have a large family. Sarah, the other sister, married Mr. Noel, and had several children. Their brother Robert just lived to be twenty-one, and left Elston to his sister. Had he died a few weeks before it would have come to my Uncle Dr. Robert Darwin of Shrewsbury. William Alvey Darwin had two daughters, Ann the eldest married Mr. Fox of Derby (whose first wife was a Miss Strutt). The other, Eliza, died single. Mrs. Fox had five daughters and one son, with whom we were very intimate, constantly visiting each others' houses. Mr. and Mrs. Fox lived at Osmaston Hall, near Derby, which belonged to Sir Robert Wilmot, whose wife was Miss Howard, niece to my Grandfather's first wife. Mrs. Fox's eldest daughter, Marianne, married Mr. Ellis-Bristow, and had two sons and a daughter. She died early. Frances Jane, the youngest but one, married Mr. Hughes, Rector of Penally. His first wife was Miss Bilsborough of Derby, and she had one son, George, who married and died lately.

My Grandfather, Dr. Erasmus Darwin, was a celebrated physician, poet, and philosopher, and was fond of science and mechanics. He and Mr. William Strutt, and Whitehurst, a clock-maker, invented many things. One was a watch to watch the watchman; the hands were stationary, and the dial moved round. There was a little peg over each figure on the outside of the dial, which could be pushed down between five minutes, but at no other time. So by seeing in the morning what pegs were standing up, it was known when he had not done his duty. My Grandfather was the first, I believe, that sunk an Artesian Well near his house in Full Street, Derby. He originated all the ideas that Charles Darwin had time and talent to work out. [Perhaps this excess of filial piety can be forgiven! For an objective summing-up of the contributions of Erasmus Darwin, FRS, (1731-1802) to the theory of evolution which made his grandson famous, see Desmond King-Hele, Erasmus Darwin, Macmillan 1963. Erasmus Darwin was perhaps the moving spirit in the Lunar Society, though his contacts with it became infrequent after his removal to Derby in 1781.]

Dr. Darwin was a very benevolent man, and extremely kind to the poor. Once when he was going to visit a patient at Margate (my Father's elder sister) he slept one night at Newmarket, and found the town in great excitement, the Races going on. In the night he saw someone open the door and a man come into his room. He started up and asked his business, and the man said in a low voice: "Hush, Dr. Darwin, I am not come to rob you. You were very kind some years ago to my wife, attending her in her long illness without a fee, and I determined to return your kindness if it ever came in my power, and I can do so now. Tomorrow, such-and-such a horse is the favourite and everyone is betting on it. I am to ride the horse, and we have settled he is not to win, so you may bet what you please against him and make your fortune." My Grandfather thanked him and left early next morning. On his return he had the curiosity to enquire what horse won and heard that, to the astonishment of all, and the ruin of many, the favourite had lost the race.

Another time my Grandfather was riding home, through a forest, when a man rode quickly up to him. My Grandfather said: "A fine night!" The man made no reply, but fell back a little. Presently he rode up again and passed my Grandfather, who again made some remark to him. He said nothing, but rode away quickly. A few days after, a man was taken up for robbing a gentleman at the same place in the forest. My Grandfather, thinking it must be the same man that passed him, went to the jail and, recognising him, asked how it was he had not robbed him. He replied: "I intended to do so, but when you spoke I thought it was your voice, and the second time I passed you I was sure of it, and nothing would induce me to do you harm, as you were so kind in bringing my Mother through a long illness without charging a penny, and so I rode on."

*

My Grandfather married first Miss Howard of Lichfield and had three sons. Charles, the eldest, was a remarkably talented young man, who distinguished himself though so young. He died when only twenty-one from a wound when dissecting a child. My Grandfather never got over his death, it was such a grief to him. Erasmus, the second son, was in the Law, very clever and witty. He drowned himself during temporary insanity.

Robert, the youngest, set up as a physician at Shrewsbury when only twenty-one years of age and got into a very good practice at once. His Father gave him twenty pounds, telling him to send for more when he wanted it. His Uncle also gave him twenty pounds, and from that time he never asked for more, but got on rapidly. He married Susan, the eldest daughter of Mr. Wedgwood the potter, and had four daughters and two sons. Charles Darwin was his second son. We often went to stay at Shrewsbury and our cousins came to stay with us. My Uncle Robert Darwin was a very large man, weighing from twenty-five to thirty stone, six feet two inches high, very active for his size, full of anecdote, and very fond of his garden, which was very pretty, with small orchard trees on the lawn, the ground sloping down to the River Severn.

My Grandfather Darwin married, secondly, the widow of Colonel Pole of Radbourne, and she was my Grandmother. She was a remarkably beautiful woman and very agreeable. She had four children by

Colonel Pole, Sacheverell, Elizabeth Anne, and Millicent and German (twins). German died as an infant.

Sacheverell, who married Miss Wilmot, a very beautiful woman, and had a large family. Reginald, Rector of Radbourne, died single. Mary married Captain, afterwards Admiral, Lord Byron, and had a family. German, Anne and Charlotte, all died young of consumption. Elizabeth Anne Pole, married Colonel Bromley, who was a natural son of Lord Montfort. She had seven daughters, with whom we were very intimate, often going to stay at Abberley with them and they with us. Jemima, the second daughter, became the second wife of Admiral Maling, and Mercy married the Rev. Mr. Cocks. Colonel Bromley was quartered in Worcestershire with the Militia, and a Mr. Bromley, no relation, who lived at Abberley, took such a liking to him, and especially to my Aunt, that at his death he left Abberley and all his fortune to them. Millicent, the youngest daughter of Colonel Pole and my Grandmother, married Mr. John Gisborne, and had a large family. The Gisbornes are an old Derbyshire family, Mr. Gisborne's eldest brother lived at Yoxall and wrote several books. Colonel Pole had a natural son, Mr. Edward Pole, who was much beloved by the family, Poles and Darwins. He was Rector of Radbourne, and married a Miss Bingham.

Dr. Erasmus Darwin, by his second marriage to Mrs. Chandos-Pole, had three sons and three daughters. The daughters were remarkably beautiful, the sons tall and large. My Mother used to say that five of her brothers were over six feet two, and large powerful men. Edward, the eldest of the second family, lived at Mackworth, near Derby. He was an invalid and could not walk, when I knew him. The second son was Francis Sacheverell, afterwards Sir Francis. He practised as a physician at Lichfield for some time and married a Miss Ryle. They had a large family. We much enjoyed going with my Father to breakfast at Lichfield, setting off very early in the morning, and playing with our baby cousins.

My Grandfather's third son was John, and he was Rector of Elston, the family place of the Darwins. He died when I was very young, and I scarcely remember him.

My Grandfather had three daughters by his second marriage,

Samuel Galton Jnr

Erasmus Darwin

Radbourne, Derbyshire

Violetta my Mother, Emma, and Harriot, all (especially Emma) extremely beautiful and agreeable. Emma was very kind to us children, and we used to like going to her little charity school at Morley to teach the children and to learn from them how to plait straw and make bonnets,

My other Aunt, Harriot, was seven years younger than my Mother; she was a very clever girl and taught herself Latin and Greek, took great interest in the poor, and set up the little school which at her marriage my Aunt Emma continued. My Aunt Harriot taught the children herself, and when the small-pox was about, she vaccinated them all herself. She married Captain, afterwards Admiral Maling and had no children, but brought up one of her husband's nephews.

[Excerpt from a letter from Miss Harriot Darwin to her sister, Mrs Samuel Tertius Galton, dated October 31, 1811, announcing her engagement to Captain Maling:

"*...I hope my dear Violetta you will not consider this on either side as a transient watering place attachment, I assure you we feel reciprocally the same affection towards each other that would have been the result of an acquaintance for years — My dear Friend feared there might be some objections made to our marriage on the part of his family, but my uneasiness on this account has been entirely removed by very kind & affectionate letters to me both from his mother & sisters — I assure you I have fixed my choice upon one of the most amiable & liberal men in the world, he is quite idolized by his own family — & I trust that as soon as he is known to my family he will be as much beloved by them.... You will be anxious to know something of his family, fortune, &c. I am a little frightened at his family as I suspect some of them are rather fine, Lady Mulgrave is one of his sisters, another married Mr. Ward who is a Member of Parliament, another Colonel Welsh who has a sinecure of 2000 a year — he has seven sisters and two brothers — In regard to his fortune, he is much poorer than he would have been had it not been for his excessive liberality, however he has quite enough to satisfy me, enough to live in the manner I have been accustomed to, that is to say, to keep our saddle horses & pair of carriage horses — We are to live in*

Buckinghamshire 30 miles from Town — Captain Maling has very good prospects in his profession as he expects in four or five years to be admiral — his connections being so good he has great interest — Lord Mulgrave is in the Admiralty."

The gallant Captain duly arrived to carry off his bride, and obviously made a very favourable impression by his good looks, his manners, and the magnificent diamond ring, wedding ring, and a particularly hideous diamond brooch from his mother, with some of the Captain's hair woven into it. Emma Darwin was able to report all this in a letter dated November 12, 1811, in which she gave further particulars of his fortune:

"He is the eldest Son & has about 1500 per annum, but 'tis a very increasing property, and his profession will bring in 7 or 800... he has two servants & three horses here, green livories and cockades. I think my dear Nibs I have been tolerably minute...."

But to resume Elizabeth Anne's memoirs....]

My Aunt Maling went to the Mediterranean in her husband's ship, but had to be sent at a moment's notice on shore at Minorca in an open boat, an engagement with the French being imminent. She was some time at Minorca, where she astonished the Natives by riding on a side-saddle and gained their pity, they supposing the poor young lady had only one leg. While she was there (1814) Admiral Maling sent her word that Bonaparte was beaten and peace proclaimed. She immediately looked out for some white ribbon which she had, made a large bow which she fastened to her English footman's hat and another bow on his coat, and sent him with the news to the old Duchess of Orléans, who was living in Minorca. On hearing the news, the Duchess clasped the footman in her arms with joy, much to his discomfiture. Her letters while abroad were most amusing and interesting.

*

We frequently went to stay with my Grandmother Darwin at the Priory*, the most pleasant cheerful house I ever was in; we called it

"Happiness Hall". We were allowed to do what we liked, and pick fruit to our heart's content. The Priory was a very pretty place with two small pools and a stream running down.

We used to meet Mr. and Mrs. Hadley, their son Henry, and their daughter Eliza. Mr. Hadley was the principal surgeon in Derby. Mrs. Hadley was one of the kindest and most excellent persons one could meet with, and was the beloved friend of every member of the family. She and her sister, Miss Mary Parker, were the natural daughters of my Grandfather Darwin. He had them well educated, and they set up a school at Ashbourne, where my Mother and Aunts (the Sitwells) and most of the young girls in Derbyshire were educated.

We also met Dr. and the Miss Bents, Miss French, Poles and Sitwells, who were constant visitors there; also Sir Francis and Lady Darwin and their children, and the Gisborne family and others.

At Breadsall Church the large Prayer Book, which the Rev. Mr. Dewe used, had a blank space left, where the Sovereign's name should be in the prayers, and from the date, it was printed when Queen Anne was dying and it was uncertain who would succeed her.

*

As I said before, I was the eldest child of my parents, and was born on the 19th. February 1808. My sister Lucy Harriot was born on the 8th. May 1809. She was a very delicate child for the first two years, always apparently in pain, after then she suddenly recovered and was a very lively, merry child, remarkably good-tempered and loving. Millicent Adele was born on 21st. July 1810, a very quiet child. After she had the whooping cough at two years old, it was discovered that her spine was far from straight, and from that time she had to lie down for five hours a day. Her bones being weak, she had not the same strength we had, in spite of which she was utterly fearless. Emma Sophia, my next sister, was born on 17th. October 1811. She was always a strong child and very helpful,

Agnes Jane was born on 4th. February 1813. Just before her birth,

**Breadsall Priory, near Derby, where Erasmus Darwin moved shortly before his death. It is referred to several times in these reminiscences.*

Sally our nurse married Benjamin our man-servant, and left. My Mother engaged another nurse, who it was found afterwards had been nursing children with whooping cough and had caught it. She gave it to us all, and the poor baby died after much suffering the following May. I was almost five when she was born and remember her. When we recovered, we all went for some weeks to Malvern Links, which we much enjoyed.

My brother Darwin was born on 18th. March 1814; I remember his birth well. My Mother gave me a box with a key in which, while she was ill, I was to put in all bills, and every day I went to give out what stores the cook wanted. I used to stand on a footstool to make tea, which amused all our friends. When my Mother recovered, we all went to Great Malvern, where we were very happy, picking the violets and wild flowers in the hedges, and going every day to Saint Anne's well for water. Lucy and I rode two donkeys, we named them Thunder and Lightning, and we got my Father to ride his horse behind us, which set the donkeys galloping.

I remember when we were going to Malvern passing a butcher's shop which was shut up, and my Mother telling us that the butcher had been sold up because he could not pay £30 (I think it was) which he owed, and the reason was that Lord Foley, who owed him £300, would not pay his bill. It made an impression I have never forgotten of the cruelty of not paying one's debts as soon as owing.

When I was five years old, I remember seeing a balloon go up from Vauxhall near Dudson. Balloons were then new, and some years before the time I am writing about, Mr. Baker of Birmingham, hearing that one was going up from Paris, got a large piece of torn paper and wrote some French words upon it, as if it were part of the French balloon, and left it on the ground. The hoax took so well, it was long before he dare confess the truth.

I remember the Battle of Leipsic (1813), when a subscription was raised for "the distressed Germans"; Lucy and I gave sixpence each and felt we had materially helped them,

The year 1814 was the year of the Peace, and my Father was High Bailiff of Birmingham that year, which was something like a Mayor now. There was a High Bailiff and a Low Bailiff, and they managed the affairs of the Town. He gave, as High Bailiff, a grand dinner at the Royal Hotel to Lord Hill and Lord Combermere. He invited Dr. Parr* of Hatton, among others, who accepted on condition that a sucking pig, of which he was very fond, should be placed before him. Many amusing tales were told of him. Once when Dr. Butler, the Headmaster of Shrewsbury School, came to see him at Hatton and went to Church with him on Sunday, Dr. Parr preached a very learned sermon with a long Greek quotation, which the villagers could make nothing of. Dr. Parr concluded with, "Now none of you can understand this, but there" (pointing to Dr. Butler, on whom every eye turned) "there sits a man who understands every word!"

My Father went to London to present the address of congratulations from the Town of Birmingham to the Prince Regent on peace being declared, alas for so short a time. We were greatly interested in my Father's court dress. There were illuminations everywhere; all the dogs were named Blucher or Platoff, boots were called Wellingtons, and so on, and the joy general.

*

When I was six years old, my education began in earnest. I could read well at three years old and could write at five, but now I began French with Mr. Jaegier [Jaeger?] and German and music with my Mother, and my Father, every morning before breakfast, taught me arithmetic, which he did most thoroughly. He taught the two daughters of our washerwoman with me, Sarah and Harriet Bromley. Harriet Bromley had a marvellous memory for mental arithmetic, and at ten years old she once multiplied a line of thirty figures in her head mentally; I could never do more than three. My Father used to have her do sums mentally for Mr. Horner** and other friends, and as they always gave her a shilling apiece, she got a nice little sum in the Savings Bank. At six years old, Lucy and I had twopence a week, but had to keep an account of what we spent. I never remember the time

Dr Samuel Parr (1747-1825) was noted as a wit, scholar and conversationalist.

***Leonard Horner (1785-1864), brother of Francis Horner, the distinguished Whig MP. Both brothers were friends of Samuel Tertius Galton.*

when I did not keep accounts, and I have found the advantage of it through life.

At this time I went to Church with my Father and Mother. [Samuel Tertius Galton left the Society of Friends when he married, and became a member of the Church of England.] Christ Church, or as it was called, the Free Church, was lately built and the whole body of the Church was free, and we sat in the gallery. At that time and long after, the pew openers were called Beadles and wore a sort of livery and carried a long pole or staff, with which they tapped naughty children's heads or those who were asleep. One of them always walked before the clergyman as he entered or left the Church. I went to Church in much fear of the Beadle; once I thought I had been pretty good, when to our horror he came to our pew and, bending down to say something to my Father, laid his stick along the back of our pew, so as nearly to touch me.

My Brother Erasmus was born on 31st. May 1815, and as soon as my Mother was able to travel, we set off to go to the Isle of Wight, where we saw the sea for the first time. We stopped at Stratford to see Shakespeare's house, then a small butcher's shop. We went to Oxford next, where we slept. At breakfast the next morning the waiter rushed in, throwing up his hat and exclaiming, "Boney's beat, Boney's beat!", the news of the Battle of Waterloo having just arrived.

We children were much interested during this journey in hearing the watchmen calling the hour at night and seeing the huge wagons with eight horses each, each horse having a bell attached to its head, which made a very pretty sound. Everything was so new to us. Erasmus, the baby, slept at night in the great trunk, which was his cradle when from home. Bassinettes were not known until years later.

We slept at Southampton and went next day in a sailing packet to Ryde. An Alderman and his wife came on board, bringing several hampers of provisions, believing it would be a long voyage, When told we should be there in three hours or so, he ordered the hampers to be unpacked and invited all the passengers to enjoy the good things he had provided at Ryde.

The intense excitement was to see Bonaparte arrive in *H.M.S. Bellerophon*, as the ship was expected every hour, but to everyone's disappointment, he had been transferred to H.M.S. Northumberland off Plymouth, and sent off at once to St. Helena. While off Plymouth, the Captain received, among other orders, word that the Emperor was to be addressed as "General Bonaparte." Nobody liked to be the first to address him, so the Captain asked Mr. (afterwards Lord) Lyttelton, a very agreeable, genial man and a thorough gentleman, to come on board and be introduced to the Emperor, as he would manage it best. He went, breakfasted with Boney, and made himself most agreeable, and after some time addressed him naturally as "General". Bonaparte gave a little start, but bore it well.

The mourning all over England for the many that fell at Waterloo was so general that it was determined to have no illuminations, as after other victories.

We stayed a few weeks at Ryde and then returned home. There was great distress in the country; for the next two years trade was very bad, and the winters were severe. I remember my Mother advertised for a housemaid and had seventy applications — how different to now!

*

This year (1815) my Uncle Hubert Galton married his cousin, Mary Barclay of Clapham. They lived at Hockley Abbey, a house near Birmingham, for a few years and then went to Warley*, an estate my Grandfather bought about three miles from Birmingham, on the Hagley Road, and on which he built them a house.

My Grandfather and Grandmother and Aunts used to come and see us about twice a week, and we used to go often to see them. My Grandfather always drove "Unicorn," with several dogs following. In those days most of the better families drove four-in-hand. The roads were so bad, and there were deep ruts in all the lanes; streets and many footpaths were paved [i.e. cobbled, *pavé*] and very unpleasant to walk on. People carried everything on their heads — milk pails, bundles, etc., There were little carriages drawn by dogs, and one often

**Now a park in Birmingham, approached from Hagley Road by Galton Road, while nearby is Barclay Road!*

saw a little dog leading a blind man, which it did very carefully. [This passage suggests that guide dogs for the blind, so familiar today, were an old institution which had declined during the nineteenth century.]

At six in the morning when we travelled, we saw at the corners of the streets a man with a sort of tin urn and cups, selling saloop to workmen as they went to work; I never could make out what "saloop" was. There were no match boxes, but a round tin box in which was put a piece of linen, which was set on fire, and then immediately a flat tin lid was put upon it to extinguish the fire. Then when a flint and steel were struck together, sparks flew out on the tinder and smouldered, and a brimstone match would then take fire. Rush lights were used for night, put in a round tin a foot high with holes in the side to let out the light. Miss Strutt of Derby, Mr. William Strutt's daughter, a great invalid, first thought of the present nightlights. She got a chandler to make a long thin candle, which she marked in inches; when she found how much was burned in the night, she got pieces made of that length.

In those days we often saw dancing bears, shown led about by a cord.

Travelling was very expensive. It was thought "infra dig" for ladies to travel in a stage coach, and posting with a pair of horses cost one and sixpence a mile and threepence a mile for the postboy, something to the hostler, and one or two turnpikes to pay each stage. When the railway from Leamington was opened, if I asked a lady if she was going by train, she generally drew herself up and replied, "Certainly not! I never went in a stage coach, and I shall therefore never go in a railway carriage." I was also often amused at the fright of passengers going for the first time. They sat trembling, expecting to be shot along at once at rapid speed, and they were surprised at starting slowly and never feeling how quickly they went.

*

We had a nursery governess to teach us, but my Father always taught me before breakfast, and I much liked my lessons with him, he explained so thoroughly. Lucy was not fond of her lessons and could not keep her attention fixed, but was most lovable and merry. From her earliest childhood she had a wonderful eye for perspective (see page 3), and when she was five or six years old, when she wanted to explain anything, she always drew it in good perspective.

When I was eight years old, my Mother was confined of Violetta, her eighth child, on 11th. June 1816, a most lovely child. She died at Tenby the following January.

My Grandmother, Mrs. Galton, undertook as soon as I was eight to direct my reading, and I used often to go to Dudson for her to examine me on what I had read. She gave me De Lessep's Travels to read, I had to find all the places mentioned in the map, and to know something about them, and I had to read the history of any bird or animal mentioned in Smith's Cabinet. It was very thorough teaching; I have the book in which she marked what I had to read, and where to refer, for it would be very useful to those who teach.

At this age I began to suffer from severe inflammation of the eyes, and for four years wore a shade and was often for weeks together in a dark room, so that all my teaching had to be carried on by reading to me. My Father and Mother were unremitting in teaching me, that I might not lose anything I had learnt. I learnt to knit without looking, which was my only amusement.

We had a very happy childhood: my Father and Mother were so kind and just, with no favouritism and all treated alike. We were taught to give up to the youngest, and next to Adele, "because she had to lie down," so there was no jealousy of the eldest, which I have so often seen in families. We all took our turn, and the only difference I had as eldest was a constant reminder that I had to set a good example to the others. We were so many that we never wanted playfellows. Sometimes we spent a day at Smethwick with the young Moilliets. Mr. Horner (brother to Mr. Francis Horner) was a great friend of my Father's. He and Mrs. Horner often came to stay with us. Their eldest daughter, Mary, was my age; both daughters had been brought forward in their education and both were held up as examples to each other. She was always a friend of mine and became wife to Sir Charles Lyell [the famous geologist].

Whenever we children quarrelled and went to my Father or Mother to complain, he used to send one into one corner of the room, and the other into the opposite corner, and at the word of command they had to rush into each other's arms: this made us laugh and ended the dispute. My Father was a true peacemaker and always turned the matter off playfully. He was fond of science and took much interest in new improvements*. He liked measuring hills and mountains with his portable barometer, which we always took on a journey, When we went to Derby, he always pointed out to us a small viaduct which we passed, as a work of art. How much would he be amazed at those which are now built by the railways!

My Father taught us Natural Philosophy out of Mrs. Marcet's books**. We had an orrery, solar microscope, pantograph, camera obscura, and magic lantern, all of which we enjoyed seeing. He had a large telescope, through which we could see the Planets, Jupiter's moons, etc. My Mother was an excellent manager, and made us all useful and tidy, and never allowed us to be idle for a minute.

*

About this time Mrs. Stock, a very clever woman, came to stay at Dudson. She was very deep in phrenology, which was beginning to be the fashion. In every house you saw a plaster head, marked with all the different organs. She called upon my Mother and asked to see her children, so we four little girls were sent for, and she examined our heads carefully, and my Mother said she certainly told all our characters very truly. She said Lucy had a large organ of liberality and would give away her last sixpence. This of course we did not hear; as we were running out of the room, Mrs. Stock called Lucy and said "Good-bye, little stingy girl." Poor Lucy, when she got into the playroom, burst into tears and said, "Mrs. Stock says I am stingy; I won't

Among his interests was scientific economics; in 1815 he published a chart showing the correlation between banknote circulation, the rate of foreign exchanges, and the prices of gold, silver, and wheat. His son, Sir Francis Galton, inherited these talents in a greatly augmented form.

**Mrs. Marcet's <u>Conversations on Chemistry</u> etc., written in dialogue form, were much used in scientific education of the young. Among her distinguished "pupils" was the great chemist Sir Humphry Davy.*

be stingy, I will cure myself." Soon after, the nurse came to my Mother and said: "I wish, Ma'am, you would speak to Miss Lucy; she is very unhappy and is giving away everything to the maids and to me, for fear she should be stingy." Mrs. Stock was delighted when she found her prophecy so soon fulfilled. [It is not clear whether this story is told as an example of the accuracy of phrenology, or of the dishonesty of some phrenologists.]

While speaking of phrenology, I must mention another case, When my Brother Francis was a boy of twelve or thirteen at King Edward's School in Birmingham under Dr. Jeune, the Headmaster, one of the Professors from Oxford or Cambridge came to Dr. Jeune to examine the boys. The day before, he had told Dr. Jeune he was fond of phrenology and would like to examine the boys' heads, to see whether he was right in the opinion he had formed of their talents before the next day's examinations. He went into the schoolroom and kept Francis a long time. When he had gone round to see them all, he called Francis again to feel his head and said to Dr. Jeune, "This boy has the largest organ of causality I ever saw in any head but one, and that is the bust of Dr. Erasmus Darwin."

"Why," said Dr. Jeune, "this boy is Dr. Darwin's grandson!" [One feels that Francis Galton himself would have attributed this correlation to hereditary biometrics, rather than to any validity of the so-called science of phrenology.]

When Francis was an infant of a few months old, Mr. Owen of Lanark examined his head and said it was a peculiar one, and that he would not be a common character. Mr. Owen stayed in our house once when we were children. He was, as I remember him, a mild, pleasant man, always talking of his crotchets. He had plans for making a Utopia of the world, and was sure they would soon be adopted everywhere, as they were in his place in Lanark. One thing I remember: we were to wear only one garment, so as to dress quickly. Of course none of his plans came to anything. [Perhaps a rather summary dismissal of the great reformer's career?]

*

In the autumn of 1816, my Great-uncle Robert Darwin of Elston died at the age of ninety-two. He was the head of the family and a bachelor. He was educated as a barrister, but in making his will there was a flaw, which gave rise to a lawsuit which lasted some years. There were eight codicils, and in some of them in dividing his fortune equally among his nephews and nieces, he used the expression "my brothers or their issue." Now issue means grandchildren as well as children. It was well known that his brothers' children only were meant, but it turned out that parents could not give up their children's rights, and they must go to law. In one case the money would be divided equally among nine persons, in the latter case among thirty or more.

Lord Eldon was Lord Chancellor, and the suit began at the end of 1818, and was not totally concluded at the beginning of 1822. The children very properly lost their cause. As we children were disputing our parents' claims, it was necessary we should have someone else to act as our Guardian, so in joke, my Father called us all in and made us all six stand in a row and told us that the Lord Chancellor, for whom he had the highest reverence, had sent word that he and Mama were not considered by him as able to take proper care of us, so Uncle Howard was chosen. A loud roar from all the six was the consequence, and we declared that we wouldn't have Uncle Howard, nothing should make us give up Papa and Mama. At this very awkward moment, Mr. Ingleby*, the lawyer, was seen approaching the house, when we were to give him our consent to have our Uncle as guardian. We were hastily soothed, and the matter explained to Lucy and me, and we were sent into the nursery to explain to the little ones that we were not to be taken away from Papa and Mama, and that we were only to say that Uncle Howard might take care of some money for us. We were then sent for into the Drawing-room, with very red eyes, and gave our consent, the little ones making Mr. Ingleby promise that the Lord Chancellor should not take us away from our parents.

*

**Clement Ingleby was a distinguished Birmingham lawyer, who seems to have acted for many of the families mentioned in these reminiscences. His son was a well-known Shakespearean scholar and critic.*

In November, 1816, we all went to Tenby for three months, and very much we enjoyed it. As we were a large party to travel, seven children and servants, my Father hired an old stage coach, which carried us all. Stephen the coachman drove a brake full of luggage with our horses. My Father and maids went outside the coach, and he pulled my little brothers through the window in turns to sit on the box with him, to their delight, to watch the four. It was a long journey, two and a half days, setting off at six in the morning, but through a beautiful country. My Father was very fond of the sea, and took us long walks on the sands, and helped us to collect shells, of which there was a great variety. He was an excellent walker and never tired; his friends used to complain that, when they were quite done up, he was quite ready to set off again. He inherited it from his Barclay ancestors.

We lived at Milford House, overlooking the North Sands. Tenby was a very primitive place then. All the inhabitants spoke English, though only ten miles off only Welsh was spoken. The women wore jackets and men's hats, only under the hat they wore a frilled cap. All the carts were drawn by two oxen and two horses. All grocery, coal, and everything was brought to Tenby by two packets from Bristol, the *Betsey* and the *Dove*, which were due once a fortnight, but as they depended on the wind, they were often many days late. I remember one lady, giving a tea party, requested her guests to bring each a teaspoon of tea with them, as there was none left in the shop. Another time the coal ran short, for the Welsh coal was so hard that it would not burn without English coal. The kitchen fires were made up every morning with coal and culm (small anthracite coal), mixed and made into little balls and placed close together on the fire, which then lasted all day. Great were the rejoicings when the *Betsey* or the *Dove* appeared in sight. Being so large a family the Tenby shops were delighted at our arrival, and a butcher from Pembroke set up his shop at Tenby for our custom. The Druggist (there was but one) went every Saturday to Pembroke and did not return till Monday, during which time no medicine could be got.

There was a very pleasant society, and people met in an evening for tea and to play cards for a trifle.

In January 1817 my little Sister Violetta was taken ill and died after a few days' illness, to our great grief. She was buried in the Church at Tenby. It is a fine old Church, but what is unusual, there are a great many steps up to the Communion Table, and my little sister is buried in the corner on the right hand side of these steps.

There was a new coinage at this time. The old coins were worn quite thin, and the edges were so sharp that it was considered lucky by the poor to lance their children's teeth with a crooked sixpence. The new coins looked very pretty, and sovereigns were coined instead of guineas.

*

My Father was much interested in the account he heard of the landing of the French, about twenty years before, at Fishguard in Pembrokeshire, which was still talked about at Tenby. He used to tell us children all about it, which I remember was as follows:

Lord Cawdor was away with most of the military and Lady Cawdor was alone, when they came to tell her that some French ships were coming to land their troops. There were very few soldiers in the town, but she called them together, when the thought luckily struck her to gather all the women, who wore hats and red cloaks, and to place them on the heights, where they looked like soldiers. The few Military were then sent down to the shore, showed the French the preparations that were made to receive them, and said that, if they ventured up the hill without laying down their arms, they would be fired upon from the heights. Seeing so formidable a force, they laid down their arms and surrendered. Three hundred men were escorted up the hill, and were much disgusted when they found the enemy was a parcel of old women. A book has been written lately, giving a rather different account, and saying that one thousand four hundred men landed. It is now nearly a hundred years ago.

There was no coach to Tenby; a man rode in with the mail every day. One day he was very late, and as there was much disturbance in the country and a revolution was feared, all the gentlemen turned out when they heard the horn, to know the cause of the delay. This however turned out to be that the floods were so much out near Llandilo that the ford could not be crossed for some time.

In 1816 the Princess Charlotte married Prince Leopold, and my Father went to Court to present the Address of Congratulations from the town of Birmingham.

*

My Father suffered from a peculiar Hay Asthma all his life, from the age of nine years. He inherited it from his Grandfather. It used to come on quite suddenly in June, when the elderflowers appeared, and lasted six weeks, when it left him as suddenly. During that time, he could hardly get his breath, and the perspiration ran down his face. He seldom got any sleep until the morning. When he got well, his clothes hung upon him like rags, he was so thin. From eating nothing, he then became ravenously hungry till he recovered his usual size and strength, which he soon did.

Whenever he left home, he used to write us letters in poetry, which we much appreciated, and when we were very young he used to illustrate them with pictures, very well done. We have none of the latter left; we wore them out reading them. He and my Mother were capital at telling us tales, when we all sat round them to hear, my Mother on the small sofa which I have, and we children seated on the cushions or footstools to listen to Tommy Bobbin or to my Father's graphic account of Red Riding Hood.

Somewhere about this time, my Father and Dr. Delys became interested in a deaf and dumb girl, her name I think was Jane Williams, about ten or twelve years old. Her mother brought her to Ladywood, to show how intelligent she was, and how well she understood anything taught her by signs. My Father, Dr. Delys, and Mr. Alec Blair in consequence exerted themselves and the result was the Deaf and Dumb School at Edgbaston, which has answered so well. We used to go to the yearly examination, which was very interesting. Once a gentleman wrote on the blackboard, "God is good, God is just, why then did He make you deaf and dumb, while I can speak?" The little girl thought for a moment and then wrote, "Even so, Father, for it seemeth good in Thy sight." Many of their answers were very good.

I have mentioned Dr. Delys. He was a Frenchman of high birth. His father, Marquis Delys, escaped during the French Revolution with his child, and died in a small place in Wales, leaving his little boy friendless. A lady, Mrs. Brookes, took compassion on the child and adopted him. He was educated as a physician and practised in Birmingham. He married a Miss Ledsam, and left a son and two daughters.

About this time Velocipedes came into fashion. My Father set up one, but tried it only round the garden. There were no treddles, but it was worked along by the feet on the ground.

*

We knew Mr. Boulton, the son of Mr. Watt's partner*. He went on with the works at Soho, and made most of the steam engines and was constantly improving them. In former days they coined copper at Soho, and called them tokens; I have many of them, and they are now rare. When old Mrs. Boulton died, every workman at Soho, some hundreds in number, had a new suit of mourning given him. Messieurs Boulton and Watt were very kind, allowing anyone, if they were not manufacturers in the same line, to see their works at Soho. One day a Frenchman called and asked to see the works, assuring them that he had nothing to do with business. He went over the works, asked many questions, and seemed most interested. Mr. Boulton, who was with him, said he was sorry that he could not show him some part of the works, which were not at work just then, but that as the gentleman was going to France he could see nearly the same thing at M.'s manufactory. Vanity triumphed over prudence, and the Frenchman exclaimed, *"Moi, je suis Monsieur!"* He had come to spy their secrets. So from that time the works were not shown to strangers.

I do not remember Mr. Watt. I have often heard my Father say that

**This is of course a reference to the great inventor James Watt (1736-1819), perfector of the steam engine, and his partner, Matthew Boulton.*

when a young man called to show what he thought to be a wonderful invention, Mr. Watt would take him into his workroom, where his numerous discarded inventions were, and ask the young man which was the same as his, and he would then kindly explain why it would not do, or how it could be done better. Mr. Watt identified himself in whatever he was doing, entering into it with his whole mind. The same while listening to a novel, he realised it all. A tale I have heard of him that, going to a theatre to see a tragedy, he realised it so completely that when the cruelty of the heroine was enlarged upon, he forgot it was a play and exclaimed in a loud voice, "Why does she not go to a magistrate?"

When going to Shrewsbury we passed through the coal country at Wolverhampton and Bilston, and it was interesting to watch the steam engines at work, the old ones heaving and groaning, doing the work so slowly, the newer and improved ones at double the pace, and working so easily and cheerfully.

*

My Grandfather lived for some years at Great Barr, about four miles from Birmingham, and very near Oscott, which he rented from Sir Joseph Scott. Oscott was the college to which all the best Roman Catholic families sent their sons, and as Mr. Potts, one of the priests there, was always invited to bring one or two of his pupils with him to dine at Dudson, my uncles became acquainted with many of the leading Roman Catholic families. They were a remarkably gentlemanly set of boys.

Mr. Alexander Blair was a great friend of my Father's, and a very clever man. He was a younger son of Mr. Blair, who was in business, and lived at Castle Bromwich near Birmingham. Alec, afterwards Dr. Blair, was a very studious boy, and never took to business, but occupied himself with literature. He was remarkably short sighted, and we children were always afraid he would cut his nose off, he bent his head so low to see what was on his plate. He was very intimate with all the Moilliet family, with whom he often stayed. He lived to much above ninety-five.

In November, 1817, we paid one of our happy visits to the Priory, and while there the news came of Princess Charlotte's death, after giving birth to a stillborn son. The grief throughout the country was very great. She was much beloved, and had lately married so happily. I remember my Mother and Aunt cried when they heard the sad news.

Some time later my Grandmother Galton, who had been in declining health for some time, also died. In one of my last lessons with her, I had read about the sable, whose fur lies equally well stroked either way. Just before her death she sent me a present of a sable ruff and tippet, and smiled with pleasure when my Father told her that the first thing I did was to stroke the fur both ways.

We returned home on the day of Princess Charlotte's funeral, and at every stage we listened to the muffled peals. My Father went to London again to present the condolences of Birmingham on the Princess's death.

Chapter 2

School Days (1818-1824)

After my Grandmother's death in February 1818, I was sent to school at Miss Byerley's, at Barford near Warwick. There were six Miss Byerleys who taught. Their father married a Wedgwood, a sister I think of the great potter. I was at the school for a year, but was often sent home on account of my eyes, which were often inflamed. I did not learn much at the school, because I was too forward for the lower classes and too young for the upper ones. I never learnt arithmetic or geography after my Father taught me, as I knew more than any of the girls, and my parents wished me to spare my eyes. Marianne and Sarah Priestley, granddaughters of Dr. Priestley, were at Barford with me, and were my particular friends. Dr. Priestley was a friend of my Grandfather's, and a member of the Lunar Society. After the Birmingham riots my Grandfather often sent him money. At one time there was the question as to whether he could come with safety to Birmingham to see his friends, or whether he would be mobbed or ill-used. My Grandfather wrote to say that if he would come, he would meet him on his arrival, and walk with him through the town, and should be glad of the opportunity of showing his esteem for him. Dr. Priestley, however, did not come, but settled in America.

I was at school also with Anne, Susan and Agatha, the three daughters of Mr. Charles Lloyd of Bingley, and through Mrs. C. Lloyd, my third cousins. They were day scholars and lived in Barford with their Grandfather, Mr. Whitehead, and I often spent my half holidays with them. Mr. Whitehead had another daughter, Mrs. Greaves, mother of the Mr. Greaves we knew here of Barford, and The Cliff, Warwick.

In the Spring of 1818, my Aunt Emma died at the age of thirty-four, after a long and painful illness, to the great sorrow of my Mother and all who knew her. She was very beautiful, agreeable and amiable and most kind hearted. She was buried at Breadsall.

*

At the beginning of 1819, when I was eleven, we had a governess whom we all cordially disliked. She made a favourite of Lucy, and disliked Adele and myself, because she had to read to me, and Adele, lying down, gave her more trouble in teaching. She had a habit of leaving halfpence about and in an open drawer, and our young maid Harriet Bromley told us once how cruel it was to put temptation in her way, and how once she could not resist taking some, but how her conscience would not let her rest, and she put the money back. It has been a lesson to me through life never to leave temptation in the way of children or servants.

I remember well the birth of our Queen Victoria, and the joy that it caused.

All this year I was seldom out of a dark room with constant leeches round my eyes; when I went out I wore green spectacles. My eyeballs looked like red-hot coals, and I was not allowed to do anything but knit, without looking. All were very kind to me, and would read to me with just one ray of light let into the room to enable them to see. The doctors then told my parents that they could do no more, and that I must go blind. In despair, as a last resource, they sent for a Dr. Hodgson*, a young surgeon just settled in Birmingham with first-rate testimonials, especially as an oculist. I was his first patient. He took off the hot green spectacles, put a large blister on one side of my head and an issue in my arm, and sent me out of doors to play with the others. From that time my eyes gradually got better, and in a few months were quite well, and I have always had excellent sight.

At the end of this year, my youngest Uncle, Howard Galton, mar-

**Joseph Hodgson (1788—1869) was a physician of some note, who made his reputation in Birmingham, after an unsuccessful start in London. He returned to London in 1849.*

ried Isabella, eldest daughter of Mr. Joseph Strutt of Derby.

*

In January 1820 George III died, and the same week the Duke of Kent also died, from sitting in wet shoes, and George IV was so ill that for some days he was not expected to live. The Duke of York was unpopular, and the country was very unsettled. Many large Radical meetings were held in Birmingham, headed by Attwood, Schofield, Major Cartwright, Hunt, and others, which kept people in constant anxiety. I remember our horror at the Cato Street conspiracy, when at a Cabinet dinner the ministers were to have been murdered.

At the time, we were staying in Tenby, and my Father had to leave us and go home for a fortnight to the Bank. He had always promised that when I was twelve (which I just was) I should have a watch. On his return, how great was our delight when he produced four watches, which my Grandfather had sent as a present to each of my sisters and myself, and to which Aunt Sophia put a pretty watch ribbon and a seal with our name on. I have my watch now. It was then considered a small watch as compared with others.

At Tenby on Shrove Tuesday the old custom of football was kept up and it was dangerous to walk in the town. On that day Lucy and I, with someone to guide us, walked to Saundersfoot for shells, the return trip being about thirteen miles in all, since we had to come a roundabout way to escape the football; very tired and ravenously hungry we were. The game was always played between All Saints and St. Peters. It was the great day of the year, and many gentlemen took sides. The crowd was so great that after the ball was first thrown up, it rarely touched the ground, but was pushed by the hand towards one or other of the two churches.

We returned from Tenby in the Spring of 1820, and in June left Ladywood, which we had outgrown, and went to live at the Larches, one mile from Birmingham on the Warwick road (see p.59).

*

I have never mentioned that the fields next to ours at Ladywood belonged, with others, to the King Edward's Free School in Birmingham; a large stone, like a gravestone, was in the fields stating the fact. King Edward VI endowed Birmingham and (I think) King's Norton each with a similar sum of money to keep a free school. King's Norton put their money in the funds and received every year twenty pounds interest. Birmingham put theirs in buying land near the Town, which is now built upon and yields so large an income that it supports many other schools in the town.

*

The Larches was a very nice house. There were two larch trees, one on either side of the front door, and they were I believe some of the first brought to England. The house, which had been Dr. Priestley's (and was then called Fair Hill) was burnt during the Birmingham riots, and nothing was left but one room, his laboratory, which was over our stables. When it was rebuilt, Dr. Withering the botanist lived there, and there were many nice flowers remaining which he had planted. My Father rented the house from his son, Mr. Withering.*

My Father bought two small Welsh ponies for my brothers. Large droves of Welsh ponies used to come periodically to be sold at Birmingham, also large droves of turkeys from Wales, driven with a red rag upon a pole. We used to buy some and fatten them for Christmas; they were miserably thin when they came.

*

In the Autumn of 1820, my three cousins from Shrewsbury, Marianne, Caroline, and Susan Darwin, came to us to attend the Birmingham Music Meeting, which was held in October every third year. My Mother took Lucy and me to hear the 'Messiah', which was

**The reader will recognise the great chemist, Joseph Priestley (1733-1804), and William Withering (1741-1799), famous for his work on digitalin (foxglove) for the treatment of heart diseases. Both were members of the Lunar Society.*

a great treat. The performances were then held in St. Philip's Church, in those days called the "New Church." The front seats in the gallery were reserved for the President and Nobility. On this occasion, a by no means gentlemanly-looking man, rather shabbily dressed, a manufacturer, appeared at the Church door and said he wished to sit in the front seat in the principal gallery. The Steward told him it was impossible, as only those of the highest rank sat there. He still insisted, and the Steward refused. He then drew out of his pocket a cheque for one hundred pounds and said, now would they give him a seat? The bribe succeeded: the Steward went to the noble ladies in front and stated the case. They were much amused, and begged he might come, which he did, and the Hospital got the cheque. The ladies were most affable. He was delighted, and for several Music Meetings afterwards the same thing occurred and he gave one hundred pounds to sit with the nobility.

When we had friends staying with us, my Father used to take them to see the various manufactories: papier maché, brass, glass, and many others. The principal one was Sir Edward Thomason's*, which had a world-wide reputation, as almost everything was made there: jewellery, plate, plated goods, medals, wire, etc. Sir Edward was an amusing person, full of vanity at being visited by Crowned Heads and everyone of distinction, foreign and English, who came to see his manufactory. When the company had gone round all, he would open a door, where Lady Thomason would be seen seated at a table, on which was a handsome collation. While partaking of it, Sir Edward would descant on all the presents he had received from all the Crowned Heads and distinguished Nobility, and describe his going to Court to show the Prince Regent his medals, &c. He invented a corkscrew, by which a cork could be drawn quite easily, and was highly flattered by hearing that the King of Abyssinia, wanting a corkscrew, called for his "Thomassine."

Mr. Ostler's manufactory of glass beads, seals, dolls' eyes, &c., was an interesting one to see. He told us that at one time his trade was

**Sir Edward Thomason (1769—1849) was a well—known manufacturer and inventor, who had been apprenticed to the great Matthew Boulton. He received eight foreign orders of knighthood, and was vice-consul in Birmingham for no less than eight foreign governments. See also p.82.*

declining and very bad, when one of his workmen thought of Paul Pry for a seal, with the motto "I hope I don't intrude." It sold immensely and brought all round. In those days we always sealed a letter with wax and a seal with some device or motto and had a large number. I often wish I had made a collection of the mottoes. Wafers were used to fasten notes to tradesmen. Mr. Ostler told us that he had an order for five hundred pounds' worth of doll's eyes, from one firm, each eye costing not quite a farthing.

*

In the spring of 1821 the Emperor Napoleon died at St. Helena. The news was announced to George IV: "Sire, your greatest enemy is dead." "What! Is she dead?" exclaimed the King, hoping it was his wife!

In the Summer, the King was crowned, and we all six went to Mr. and Mrs. James at the Bank [Galton and James] to see the illuminations, and Mr. James gave us each a medal. Queen Caroline, who was prevented from attending the ceremony, suffered so much from disappointment that she died soon after...

*

At the beginning of 1822, my sister Adele, then eleven years old, who had lain flat for five hours a day on account of her weak spine, was recommended to lie down entirely for two years. She lay quite flat on her back without a pillow. In the day time she was shoved on to a board, on which she could be carried about the house, or put on a sort of brake to be wheeled about in the garden. She lay down most patiently for two years, and her spine became quite straight, but as soon as she got up and began to walk, the curvature returned as much as ever, from want of marrow in her bones, and all her life she was obliged to lie flat most of the day. She bore the trial with the greatest patience and resignation.

On the 16th. February, 1822, my youngest brother Francis* was born. He was six years younger than the youngest of us, and never was a baby more welcomed. He was the pet of us all, and my Mother was obliged to hang up her watch, that each sister might nurse the child for a quarter of an hour and then give him up to the next. He was a great amusement to Adele, as soon as he could sit up. At five or six months old he always preferred sitting on her couch to be amused by her. She taught him his letters in play, and he could point to them before he could speak. Adele had a wonderful power of teaching and gaining the attention without fatiguing. She taught herself Latin and Greek, that she might teach him. She never made him learn by heart, but made him learn his lesson bit by bit, eight times over, when he could say it. He could repeat much of Scott's "Marmion," and understood it very well. By the time he was five, he often amused us by his apt quotations – and, all this taught him by a girl not twelve years old when he was born.

*

I was now fourteen and Lucy thirteen, and as our Governess had left us, it was thought better that we should go to school. In October, therefore, my Father and Mother took us to Bath, to a school kept by the five Miss Fourniers.

[A prospectus which was issued when Elizabeth Anne's daughter Lucy entered the school in 1861, informs us that:

"The Miss Fourniers receive a limited number of Young Ladies for Board and Education, on the plan which they have successfully adopted for many years, combining the personal comforts of a private family, with the advantages derived from association in study with eligible Companions. The French language is taught by a Protestant Parisian Lady resident in the house. Instruction in Geography, Astronomy, Composition, &c, by Mr. Morris Junr. Terms Eighty Guineas the Year."

**Sir Francis Galton, FRS (1822-1911), statistician, biometrician, founder of the science of eugenics. He also made important contributions to scientific geography, meteorology, and the development of the fingerprint method of identification, and was one of the last survivors of the great Victorian men of science. See D.W. Forrest, Francis Galton: The Life and Work of a Victorian Genius, Elek, London, 1974.*

Optionals included Piano Forte (Ten guineas the Year from Mr. Roeckel, but only eight from Mr. Macco – was Italian music already eclipsed by German?), Italian from Signor Moscardi and German from Dr. Koch (each Ten Guineas the Year – parity!), and English Literature from Mr. Morris (only two guineas!). Day pupils were not received.]

There were about twenty to twenty-five girls, many of them very nice ones. We were well taught and very kindly treated. Captain and Mrs. Byron (afterwards Lord and Lady Byron*) lived a few doors from the school in Lansdowne Crescent and used to invite us to spend the afternoon with them, which was a great pleasure to us, and playing with their little children. Mrs. Byron was a Miss Pole, half-niece to my Mother and so our first cousin.

I ought to mention that, in travelling, trunks were generally tied on behind the carriage or put in the boot, where they were not on springs and, unless very tightly packed, would arrive reduced to tinder. Two straps were therefore nailed inside the trunk, halfway down. Three pieces of wood about one and a half inches wide, with thick webbing between to join them, were put on top of the clothes, and strapped down tight with the straps, so that nothing could move.

In those days Bath was a very fashionable place and crowded in the Season for the waters and amusements. Many old ladies lived in Bath, it being a warm place, and they used to meet in the evening to play cards. They went about in sedan chairs, carried by two men with long poles. A sedan chair just carried one person; it was carried into the hall, and when the hall door was shut, the lady got in and was carried into the hall at her friend's house, so there was no fear of her catching cold. It opened at the top, and then in front to get in and out.

In Lent, all the ladies in Bath used to dress in black, and on Easter Day came out in a new coloured dress. It had been the custom everywhere, but was dying out. The cries at Bath were amusing: "mew" for milk – everything carried about had its cry, and some were musical. Our school was in Lansdowne Crescent, at the top of a steep hill. It was the fashion then for ladies to pinch in their waists, and coming up the hill they seemed scarcely able to breathe.

Footnote: **George Anson, Seventh Baron Byron, first cousin of the poet.* *See also p42.*

When my Father and Mother left us at school, they went to High Ham and Loxton (Somerset) to see my grandfather's farms, and when on Loxton Hill they saw a steam packet for the first time, coming up the Bristol Channel. I remember well the sensation the first steam packets, the *James Watt* and the *Soho*, caused, each steaming against wind and tide and arriving punctually. People thought it was not canny!

*

In December 1823, Captain Maling was appointed to *H.M.S. Cambridge*, eighty-two guns, to the South American Station, and my Aunt Maling decided to go with him. They took out a great number of passengers, consuls and their families, to be dropped at different ports. It was an interesting voyage, and my Aunt's letters were most amusing and clever. They passed a large American ship. The Americans were still sore against the English, so my Uncle Maling desired the band to strike up "Hail Columbia" as they passed by, which gave intense pleasure to the United States when they heard it. At that time, Bolivar and Rodil were fighting near Callao, and the *Cambridge* remained to protect our people, but to take neither side; all however preferred Bolivar.

*

There was a terrible murder at the end of this year: a Mr. Weare was murdered by three men, Thurtell, Probert, and Hunt, for his money. It created a sensation, as Thurtell was of a highly respectable family in Norfolk. Thurtell was hanged, but the other two men turned King's Evidence and got off, but I think were both convicted afterwards for other crimes. It was said that Thurtell's parents were never told how he died, but believed his death was from natural causes.

At this time Mrs. Byron was confined of Georgina (afterwards Mrs. Morewood) and Lord Byron the Poet died, so the title came to his Cousin Captain, now Lord, Byron.

In January 1824, Lucy and I paid visits to our cousins the Foxes at

Osmaston (Derbyshire) and to Mrs. Hadley in Derby, also to my Uncle Darwin in Shrewsbury, and then returned to school. At school this year we acted two of Madame Genlis' plays, "L'Enfant Gatée" in which I acted the Aunt, and "Les Deux Flacons", in which Lucy and Emma (who came with us to school this time) took parts, and it all went off with much success.

In June 1824, my Father and Mother came to take us home for the holidays, and I left school with great regret, being now sixteen and a half. It was a great grief leaving the Miss Fourniers and my school-fellows, all of whom had been so kind to me.*

** Lucy appears to have cared less for the school; according to the diary of her daughter Sophia, admittedly written many years later, she found the atmosphere "worldly." Too many French plays, however carefully chosen?*

Chapter 3

Birmingham and Some Travels (1824-1829)

In July 1824, as soon as my father had recovered from his asthma, we went to Ramsgate with my Mother, my Father following a short time after. We stopped on the road to see Oxford, and then drove through the Parks of Haythrop and Ditchley to Blenheim. Driving through one of the Parks in our carriage with all our luggage, we came to a haha, with a gate at the bottom. The Post Boy found the gate locked, to his horror. It was impossible to back the carriage, as it was so steep, and banks on each side. We all got out, when to our dismay the driver turned the horses' heads towards the bank and gave them a very sharp cut with the whip, and they actually pulled the carriage up to the top. The Post Boy said no one would believe the horses could have done it, but there was no other way. We saw Blenheim and went over Windsor Castle on our way, and arrived at Ramsgate.

The Duchess of Kent and her two daughters, Princess Feodora and the little Princess Victoria, aged five, were staying at Ramsgate, and we used every day to see the little Princess riding her donkey, which her Uncle the Duke of York had given her.

The Archbishop of Canterbury, Manners Sutton, was also at Ramsgate, with his eight daughters, all dressed to a pin alike, and all walking out together. The Archbishop of York, Vernon Harcourt, had eight sons, and Queen Charlotte made some epigram, suggesting that the eight sons should marry the eight daughters, which made them so shy at meeting that it defeated her object.

While we were at Ramsgate, Lucy, Adele, and I were confirmed by the Archbishop.

Just before we left Ramsgate, my Father, to give us a treat, took us all in a steam packet to Calais, and back the next day. Francis, who was two years old, had learnt several French sentences, and much amused the French people by repeating them when they talked to him. We had a very rough passage returning.

*

When we left Ramsgate, we stayed a week in London, as my Father and Mother wished to consult the leading surgeons on Adele's case. They consulted Brodie, Sir Astley Cooper, Ward, and Earle; all, especially Sir Astley, were most kind and interested. When they heard that my Mother was daughter to Dr. Erasmus Darwin, it was with difficulty my Father could make them take a fee; Sir Astley almost embraced my Mother, he was so pleased to see a daughter of Dr. Darwin. My Father took Lucy and me all over London, seeing sights. He always admired the London bridges, and took us over and under them. The old London Bridge was then standing, and rash people used to shoot under it, which was very dangerous; the arches were so small that the water was higher on one side, at high tide, than the other. Waterloo Bridge was the first flat bridge, and was considered a wonder in consequence.

One night we went to Vauxhall, which was like Fairy Land lighted up. I remember Carlton Palace, where the Prince Regent lived, then standing at the bottom of what is now Regent Street. It had several columns in front (now the portico of the National Gallery), which were apparently of no use.

We also saw Exeter Change, a large house where wild beasts were kept in small pens where they could only turn around. There was an immense elephant, one of the tallest known. Some years afterwards he became savage, and as he was too tall to get out of his cage, they tried to poison him, but though they gave him an immense amount of arsenic, it had no effect upon him. I think he was shot at last with great difficulty. We went to the Tower, where the lions and the other wild beasts were kept. There were no zoological gardens then, and the poor animals were sadly cooped up in small dens.

*

While we were in London, Lord and Lady Byron came to Town. He had just been appointed Captain of *H.M.S. Blond*, to take the remains of the King and Queen of the Sandwich Islands back to their home. The King and Queen with their suite came to England some months before and were delighted with everything they saw, and with their reception, and collected all sorts of things to take back with them. They ate much trash and sweet things. Soon after their arrival, they took the measles and their state, from the way they had lived, was such that there was no hope from the first. They both died, and our Government was anxious to send the coffins back, and the rest of the Islanders, so that their friends might know that they had been well treated, and the cause of their Sovereigns' death. The suite were Monsieur and Madame Boki, the Governor or Prime Minister, and some others, about eight in all. Lord Byron amused us much, telling us about them. The vessel was loaded with their collections; a quantity of ripe cherries that they were very fond of, plants and trees, and at last, when the ship could hold no more, a great cartwheel appeared, which Lord Byron had slung outside the ship.

The Sandwich Islanders ate enormously during the voyage, wishing to get as fat as possible. Madame Boki ate the whole of a large cheese for her lunch. The Governor died on board, and Lord Byron was so afraid they would kill themselves with eating, and none left alive to arrive, that he put them on an allowance while in the Tropics. The eight people ate sixty pounds of meat every day, besides other things!

Just before Lord Byron sailed, his Mother-in-law, Mrs. Pole, sent him a large cask of water from Malvern Wells. He was rather annoyed, being already so loaded; however, not wishing to offend her, he took it, and said it was the greatest comfort. When all other water went bad, this remained perfectly pure and good for the whole voyage. Lady Byron went only as far as Rio and then was obliged to return on account of her health. She used to pay Madame Boki a visit often, and one day, when they were in the Tropics and it was very hot, she found Madame with her petticoats drawn up over her knees, and her legs in a bucket of water to cool.

Lord Byron was very well received by the Sandwich Islanders. He and the officers attended the funeral of the King and Queen. He had many presents given him: one was a very handsome large cloak, lined with small feathers, I think only two from each bird, so it must have caused the death of many hundred birds.

While we were at Ramsgate, Darwin fell ill of smallpox; he was ten years old and had been vaccinated when a baby. It was a surprise to the Doctors, as it was the first case they had known of smallpox after vaccination. He had it very severely, and his constitution was much shattered for some time after, but he was not marked. My sisters and I were vaccinated in consequence.

*

In the beginning of the year 1825, I "came out," being seventeen in February. My first dinner party was at Dr. John Johnstone's, at the Monument, near Birmingham. (The Monument was a tall tower, built against a house some years before, by a madman who took it into his head that there would be another deluge, and that he would be safe at the top of the tower.)

Dr. John Johnstone came in late, saying that he had just come from Dr. Parr, who was dying. I was very shy and nervous, as this was my first party, and one great trouble was that of being asked to drink wine. A gentleman would call across the table, "Miss Galton, may I have the pleasure of drinking wine with you?" It would be the height of rudeness to say "No, thank you." Wine was then poured into his glass, and into mine, each bowed to the other, and drank more or less. I had a great dislike to the taste of wine and only took a drop each time, and as it was essential that some should be put into my glass each time, I was obliged to take some, or it would have overflowed.

A lady would be asked five or six times during dinner. The host was expected to drink wine with all the ladies, and most of the gentlemen, at the table. My Father used to have a decanter filled with toast and water, the colour of sherry, when he had a dinner party. The wine was placed on the table, not handed around, and gentlemen helped themselves. Some years after, a Roman Catholic Priest, an Irishman, Father Mathew*, went all over the country preaching total abstinence from wine, and taking the pledge. In consequence, to our great comfort, drinking healths ceased and wine was handed round by the butler instead of being put on the table before dessert.

Dinner parties were at five o'clock, 5.30 was very late. The guests came very hungry, as luncheon was merely a few sandwiches, and a dinner then was very different to now: soup and fish, next a joint at the bottom, calf's head or veal at the top, fowls on one side and ham on the other, and then four entrées at the corners, or two entrées and two vegetables, an epergne in the middle, filled with flowers. All the dishes on the table at once; second course, game and seven or eight sweet dishes. Everything was carved by the person who sat opposite the meat that required carving.

In February, I went to my first public ball in Birmingham, held at the Royal Hotel. The Hubert and Howard Galtons came in honour of the event. I led off in a country dance, but was somewhat taken aback by being desired to "call the dance," viz, to tell the band what tune to play; however, a young friend prompted me, and "Lady M'Donald" was called, and I much enjoyed the evening.

*

We used often to go to Heathfield to drink tea with old Mrs. Watt and her sister Miss McGrigor. Mrs. Watt was widow of Mr. Watt, the inventor of the steam engine. She was bent and crippled with rheumatism, but very cheerful. Everything at Heathfield was in perfect order, not a leaf to be seen on the lawn, and yet no one ever saw a gardener about. Mrs. Watt was Scotch, and went to Scotland every year, posting all the way. She never would tell us on which day she meant to travel, but always appeared at Church the Sunday before. In her crippled state, sitting at Church was very painful to her, and she seldom left the house. My Grandfather and Aunts often drank tea with her. In

**According to the Dictionary of National Biography, Father Theobald Mathew (1790-1856) played a large part in reforming social customs on both sides of the Atlantic.*

those days we dined at 4 o'clock or thereabouts, and so had plenty of time to go out to tea at seven or eight o'clock.

*

[In the summer of 1825, Miss Sophia Galton (later Mrs Brewin) wrote the puzzle letter to her niece, Miss Emma Sophia Galton (Elizabeth Anne's sister) which is reproduced over the next few pages. The account of "taking the waters" on page 3 of the letter is as follows; readers may care to decipher the other pages!

"Now I must tell you how we spend our day – I am called at seven – come down at half past eight with my Bonnet and Shawl – your Grandpapa & I sally forth to the Great Pump room, where, whilst he takes his pint of water, I amuse myself with every variety of making ugly faces – for few of the company take the waters here, with[out?] some variation of Countenance, & not often expressive of pleasure or satisfaction – In the Pump Room is a band of musicians – when the Pint has been swallowed, we join the Company on a well rolled, broad gravel walk between an avenue of young Lime trees, which will, no doubt, ten years hence afford an agreeable shade – all the fashion, beauty, and ugliness of Leamington Spa assemble, in the first place to give full effect to the virtue of the Waters – secondly to talk over the amusements of the evening preceding & to devise some for the ensuing day – After fee-feeing for an hour with all the acquaintances we meet we return home with a good appetite for breakfast – after this meal I write letters and receive morning calls till about one o'clock when we generally, if the weather is not too hot, walk for an hour; or return any calls that we may owe. At two o'clock we drive out – We have once made the tour of the pretty drives & shall begin it again today. We return in time to dress for dinner – At five we join the dinner table, which consists of between forty and fifty persons – there have already been many departures & new arrivals – for we have reached the middle of the table, which said Table now reaches from one end of the room to the other, leaving only room for the Servants to pass & repass – Since we were here last year Mrs. Williams has lighted her Dining & Drawing rooms with Lamps which

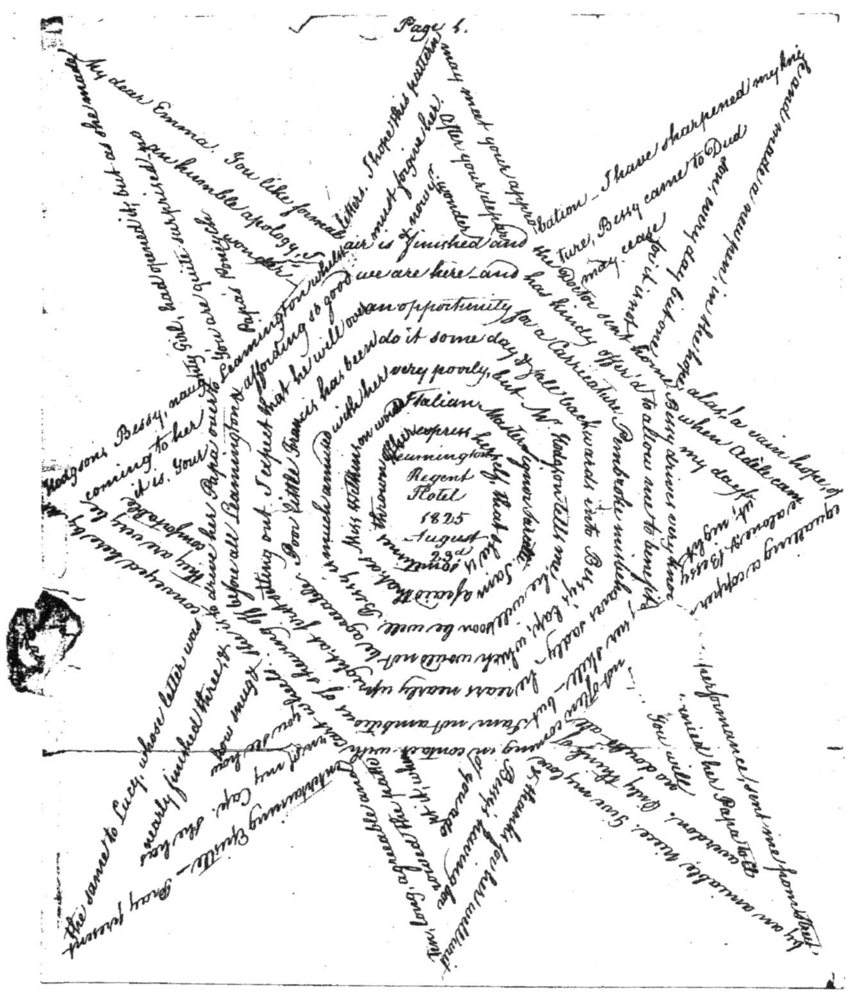

Page 1.

Leamington
Regent
Hotel
1825
August
25th

Puzzle letter from Miss Sophia Galton to her niece, Miss Emma Galton, August 25th., 1825 (page 1).

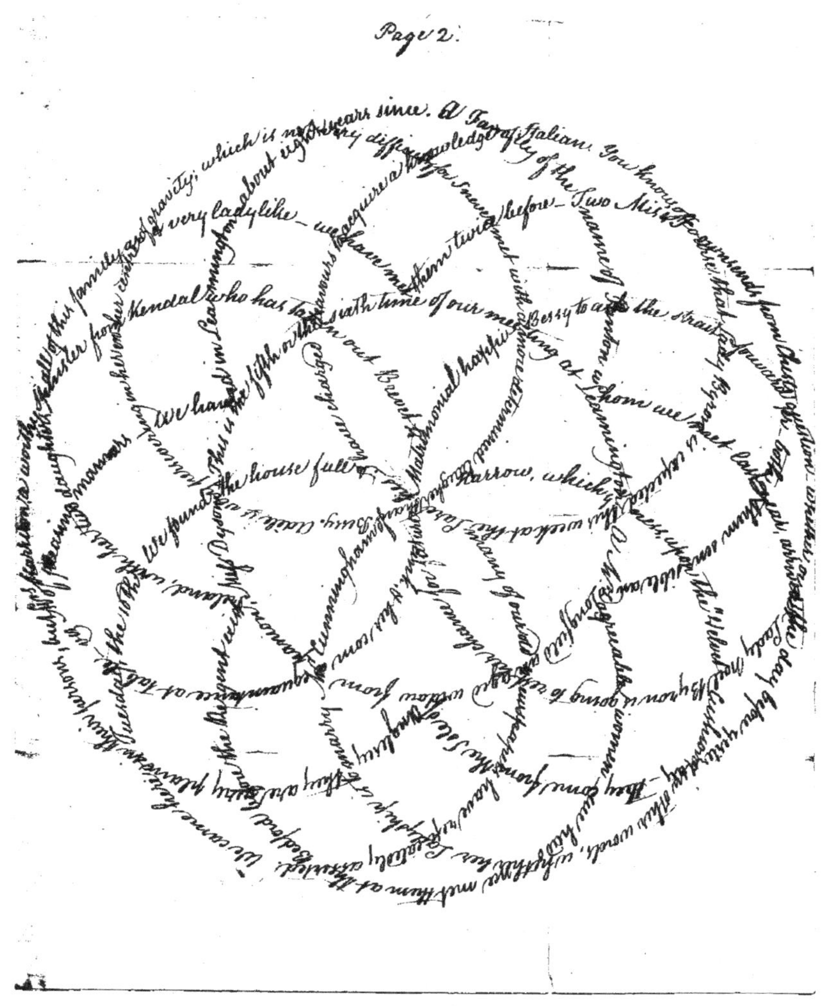

Puzzle letter from Miss Sophia Galton to her niece, Miss Emma Galton, August 25th., 1825 (page 2).

1825
Aug
25th

Puzzle letter from Miss Sophia Galton to her niece, Miss Emma Galton, August 25th., 1825 (page 3).

very bad one — And the Surgeons anticipated a recurrence
of the disorder. Augt 25th Last evening I received very
melancholy news of poor Sarah — St Anthony's fire prevailed in the Hospital which made Mr Vaux anxious that
Sarah should be removed from the danger of taking it
She returned to the Cottage last Friday — She was dreadfully
sick all the way — her sickness continued till Monday
morning when she was seized with a shivering fit —
she rapidly got worse & expired yesterday morning —
She died very happy in her mind, which is a great comfort to myself & her other friends — Her remains will
be interred on Saturday — Her bodily sufferings have
been dreadful — In her I lament the loss of a faithful
honest & attached Servant — Give my love to Lucy & Emma — Present my Comps to Miss Forbes & believe me, my dear Emma yr Affecte Aunt Sophia Galton

Puzzle letter from Miss Sophia Galton to her niece, Miss Emma Galton, August 25th., 1825 (page 4).

adds greatly both to the comfort, light and handsome appearance of the rooms. We expect yr. Uncle & Aunt Hubert with May and Di to spend a few days here ... "]

*

In the Spring of 1825 we went to the Priory to my dear Grandmother Darwin. My Father gave her a telescope, through which she could see who was coming down the hill, nearly a mile off, to call upon her, and this gave her great pleasure. It always stood on a little table in the window.

We found several Uncles, Aunts and Cousins to meet us. The Darwins were all good conversationalists, and most cheerful and pleasant were these meetings — Hadleys, Bents, Sitwells, Miss French and others coming to see us..

From the Priory we went to Mr. and Mrs. Fox at Osmaston, and went with them and my cousins to the Hunt Ball. The eldest Miss Arkwright (Fanny's sister) and the eldest Miss Fitzherbert (afterwards Mrs. Wright of Osmaston) came out at the same Ball, and we were introduced to each other. Miss Fitzherbert's Mother had been an old friend of my Mother. They were born on the same day. She was a Beresford, who lived at Ashbourne, so that my mother saw much of her when she was at school. My little sister Agnes was named after her. My Mother met many old friends of her youth at this Ball. I remember being very much surprised at seeing a tall aristocratic looking man walk in, in what was thought to be a footman's livery, though very unlike a footman in manner. My cousins whispered that it was the Duke of Devonshire, in his Windsor uniform. We returned home after very pleasant visits. We used to go twice a week to Dudson, and often to the Hubert Galtons at Warley, and to the Howard Galtons at Springhill. In June Adele and I went to the Miss Fourniers for a week, and I had much pleasure in seeing them and many of my old school fellows again. Lucy and Emma returned with us for the holidays. Lady Byron and the Darwins from Shrewsbury came to visit us and in October my Father and Mother again went to the Priory for the Derby Music Meeting. Marianne, Susan, Caroline and Erasmus

Darwin, and Sir Francis and Lady Darwin came also, and very much we enjoyed going to see all the performances, which finished with a ball. At this Music Meeting the person who most engrossed everyone's attention was Mrs. Coutts, widow of the rich banker. Mrs. Coutts was a Miss Mellon, an actress, whom my Mother remembered having seen in her school days, acting in a barn at Ashbourne. The actresses were so poor that they put flour on their arms and hands to look like gloves! Mr. Coutts fell in love with her, to the great annoyance of his three daughters – Lady Burdett, Lady Guildford, and the other whose name I forget. After the Music Meeting was over Mrs.Coutts drove to Ashbourne to show her friends where she had acted many years before. She soon after married the Duke of St. Albans, and we saw them some years after, driving in a carriage and four at Worthing. After her death the Duke married Miss Gubbins. Mr. Coutts left his immense fortune to his widow, and at her death she left it all to Miss Burdett (who took the name of Coutts).

On the 7th. of November, we heard that Lucy was ill with rheumatic fever. My Mother and her maid went off at once to Bath and took Lucy to a lodging, with a nurse to help. One night she seemed more easy and fell asleep. My Mother, worn out with sitting up and with anxiety, said she would go to bed, giving the nurse strict injunctions to call her if necessary. Scarcely had my Mother fallen into a profound slumber, when she was aroused by the nurse saying "Oh, Ma'am, the young lady is dying." My Mother rushed to the room and found Lucy in a comfortable sleep, just as she had left her, and asked why she had been disturbed. "Why, Ma'am, don't you hear the Death Tick? It has been going on this hour." My Mother, very provoked, went back to bed. The following Sunday, the 13th November, Lucy being better, my Father and I set off in our carriage at two in the afternoon, travelled all night, and arrived at Bath at half past seven the next morning. I had just time to run up to Lansdowne Crescent to see the Miss Fourniers and my school-fellows, and then we set off towards home, making a bed for Lucy in the carriage. We got as far as Tewkesbury that night. At the Inn my Mother asked for a strong porter to carry Lucy, as she was quite helpless. The Innkeeper told her he had a "Herkelus" of a porter, and soon after the Hercules appeared and carried her safely upstairs. The next day we got home; Lucy recovered slowly, but then had returns of rheumatism and never had strong health after, but was always cheerful and patient.

The following week, the 20th. November, my poor Mother, who had scarcely recovered from nursing my sister, received a crushing blow, a letter from Captain Maling telling us of the death of his wife last August, my Mother's last surviving sister, Harriot, at the age of thirty-five. Captain Maling wrote to my Father, telling him the country around Valparaiso was in such an unsettled state that he could not bury his wife out there with any comfort; he was sending her Remains home and requested him to manage her funeral at Breadsall. My Father and Mother went to my Grandmother at the Priory and found her overwhelmed with grief. *H.M.S. Shipley*, with my Aunt's Remains and her maid, arrived 23rd. December, but it was some days coming up to Sheerness, where the coffin was landed. On the 7th. January 1826 my Aunt was laid by her Father and Sister in the vault at Breadsall Church.

*

Another terrible anxiety at the end of 1825 was a general panic in the money market and consequent run on all the Banks in the Kingdom. It was said to have been begun by a cart having overturned opposite a bank, which caused a crowd, which was magnified into a run on the bank. In the excited state of the money market, this caused a run upon all the banks, and spread all over the country. It was a most anxious time; many banks stopped payment, which increased the distrust.

During the days it lasted, we used to drive around Birmingham, to see if any bank had shut up. Two small banks stopped. The difficulty was to get ready money, as all the banks wanted to borrow instead of to lend. My Uncle Hubert went to Barclay's, our London bank, to borrow, and found there ten partners of the various Gurney banks, come up for the same purpose. Fortunately, the run began in the middle of the week, so Sunday came as a breathing time, or many more banks must have stopped.

Much kindness was shown at the time; many wanting really to draw a cheque for current expenses would not do so, as it would increase the distrust. Mr. Alston collected a thousand sovereigns in a bag and threw it down on our bank counter, with a chink to be heard, asking the partners in a loud voice to take care of it for him, a most reasonable kindness.

A gentleman, seeing a crowd coming out of Lloyd's Bank, rejoicing that they had changed their notes into gold, said: "Why, have you not heard that the sovereign bank has stopped?" Back they all rushed to beg for notes instead of gold! The run lasted about a week, I think, and then calmed down, but the strain on my Father and the clerks was very great. Our bank weathered the storm very well, but of course it entailed great loss, as securities had to be sold at once at a disadvantage, and my Father (on whom lay all the responsibility, his brothers giving little help) determined from that time gradually to draw in and close the bank, which was finally done in 1831. Many customers returned, begging my Father to take their money back, and many gratifying circumstances occurred to show confidence in our Bank. One of the customers had gone out of his mind, and my Father asked another customer if it had not been unexpected. He replied that he had been quite prepared for it, for his friend, some weeks before, had asked him in confidence whether he thought Galton and James safe. "From that moment, Sir, I knew he was insane!"

Before the "run," the banks issued one-pound notes, but afterwards none under five pounds. Another consequence of the run was the setting up of Joint Stock Banks.

At Derby, where the banks suffered as much as elsewhere, Mr. Crompton, partner in Crompton and Evans's Bank, who was a very droll, genial man, heated a quantity of sovereigns so hot that you could not hold them, brought them on a shovel, and shoved them on the counter saying, "We are coining as fast as possible," which quite satisfied the lower classes to leave their money where it was.

Talking of Crompton's Bank puts me in mind of an anecdote of my Grandmother Darwin, who banked there. Her youngest son John at the time was a lad of seventeen or so, and went to the race course at Derby Races. While walking about he was accosted by a showily

Galtons Bank, Steelhouse Lane Yard, Birmingham

Birmingham, ________________ *182*

GALTONS and JAMES,

Pay ________________________________ *or Bearer,*

____

£ ______________

A Galtons and James Bank blank cheque

dressed man who made himself very agreeable, walked with him, telling him anecdotes about the horses, &c. The next day, John Darwin met him in the street. The stranger joined him, and as they came to Crompton's Bank said, "I must just go in here to cash a cheque; I wish you would introduce me to one of the partners." John Darwin unthinkingly did so. The cheque was cashed in consequence, found to be good for nothing, and the Bank came upon my Grandmother for the money. She was very angry, saying that they should have questioned so young a man about what he knew of the person, and in consequence she drew out all her money and placed it in another bank in Derby. Next morning, she came down to breakfast and said to her daughters, "My dear girls, I have not had a wink of sleep; I am sure that bank is not safe, and I have ordered the carriage and shall go to Derby and take my money out." Her daughters exclaimed, saying how odd it would be to take the money out so soon, no doubt it was safe, &c. "No, my dears, I shall go: there was a look in that clerk's eye when I gave him the money which has haunted me: he seemed so pleased to get it." My Grandmother drew out the money, which was reluctantly paid her, and within a week the bank stopped payment.

*

In March 1826, Lord Byron returned in *H.M.S. Condor* and did not go to sea again. He was appointed Lord-in-waiting to King William IV, and also to our present Queen Victoria, for many years. He was a capital mimic, and amused us relating and taking-off nervous ladies at a presentation at a Drawing Room.

On 17th May we left the Priory, and went on a delightful tour in Derbyshire. We breakfasted at Belper, and then drove to Matlock, where we stayed a night. The next day we breakfasted with my Uncle and Aunt Gisborne at Darley Dale, where they then lived, and I saw a wonderful old Yew tree in the Churchyard, supposed to be a thousand years old. We then went on to my Uncle Sir Francis Darwin at Sydnope, who sent a pair of horses to help ours up the steep hill to the house. It was a wild place, but a very amusing visit. The six children slept in hammocks and kept pet snakes. My Aunt was in bed, having just been confined of Violetta. We went in the afternoon to Edensor, and saw Chatsworth, Hardwick Hall, Castleton and on to Buxton. We then went through Dovedale to Ashbourne, to stay a night at the Miss Parkers, where my Mother had been to school.

Captain and Mrs. Griffiths came to Dudson on a visit. Captain Griffiths was in the Navy and wrote a great deal against the system of press-gangs, which he was very instrumental in abolishing. It was a cruel way of manning our ships; any sailor who had served at sea, even if he had only just returned home after many years, could be seized upon by a press-gang and made to serve on board a ship for many years again. Captain Griffiths was a kind-hearted man, but annoyed us young ones by playing us tricks, and pouncing upon us when we entered a room. Great was our delight when one day, standing behind the high screen to throw a pillow upon one of us who was expected downstairs, the pillow flew upon pompous Evans, the butler, who was bringing tea, but who never moved a muscle!

Captain and Mrs. Griffiths came on a visit to Dudson every year, after visiting Leamington, and he was most kind in helping my Father when Erasmus decided to go to sea.

This summer (1826) we made a large balloon, eight feet high, with my Aunt Sophia's help. It was made of strong silver paper, with string pasted in some of the seams. We had a party of young people to see it go off. A little grate with hot coals was suspended under it, to fill it with hot air, and it went up beautifully to a great height, when a current of wind blew it on one side; it caught fire and dropped somewhere far off. Soon after, we made another ten feet high, which went up as high as we could see and then vanished.

About this time, Sir George and Lady Throckmorton came on a visit to the Hubert Galtons, which they often did, and they brought their Priest, Dr. Fletcher, with them. They were all very agreeable and friendly. A younger brother of Sir George was one of those who were detained in France by Bonaparte for many years, after he broke the Peace of Amiens. This Throckmorton returned to his family after ten or twelve years' absence. Before he went to France, the butler was in the habit of bringing him a cup of tea and an egg in his bedroom every morning, as the family breakfast was late. The morning after his arrival, the old butler appeared with the tea and egg as before!

*

In September my Father, Mother, Lucy, and I went to Abberley, to visit the Bromleys. The house [replaced in 1837-1844 by the present Abberley Hall] was at the top of a very steep hill, in a lovely country, in Worcestershire; from the drive we could see thirteen counties. My cousins had just set up archery, and we practised all day. As soon as we returned home, we got bows and arrows, and practised every possible day during the winter. While we were at Abberley, Captain Winnington invited us to meet a few friends to shoot at Stanford Hall, his brother, Sir Thomas Winnington, being from home. He got a boy to pick up our arrows, which went in all directions but the right one. Just as we were beginning to shoot again, Captain Winnington asked the boy what he meant by standing just before the target. The boy innocently replied that he thought it was the safest place, as none of the arrows went in, a speech which disgusted us all greatly.

This Captain Henry Winnington, a very agreeable man, was travelling in Russia some years before, and arrived at a town where he expected to find letters of credit, but to his dismay they had not arrived. He had come quite to the end of his money and did not know what to do. He knew no one, and was walking slowly, thinking whether a bank would trust him with a small sum, when suddenly he was stopped by a very gentlemanly man, who said, "I beg your pardon, but is not your name Winnington?" "Yes," was the reply, "it is," "I was sure of it," said the gentleman, "you are the image of my old friend Sir Edward Winnington. Can I do anything for you?" Captain Winnington explained his penniless situation to his friend in need, who took him home with him, and made his stay there most agreeable until his letters came.

*

Soon after, we (my parents, Lucy, and I) went to Shrewsbury to visit my Uncle Dr. Robert Darwin, where we had a very pleasant visit with our six cousins. We went with them to the Races and to the Race Ball, at which my sister Lucy "came out," and much she enjoyed it, while I was very glad to have a sister to go out with.

My uncle, Dr. Robert Darwin, was a tall, over-large man, weighing more than twenty stone, but wonderfully active for his size and very fond of his garden. He was extremely cheerful and agreeable, full of amusing anecdotes and considered a very clever doctor. His son Charles* was a very pleasant, energetic lad. When about fifteen, he was staying with us and went out with my Father to practise shooting. On his return we asked if he had been successful. "Oh," said my Father, "the birds sat upon the tree and laughed at him." Some time after, my Father and brothers went to Shrewsbury; my Father had hardly sat down when Charles begged him to come out on the lawn, where he threw up a glove and hit it shooting, without missing, two or three times.

About this time we set up a little Sunday School, in a room at the back of our house. We had about eighteen little girls; Lucy, Adele, and I each took a class. It was a great interest to us; most of the girls worked in manufactories and were very anxious to be taught. We continued the school until we left the Larches; most of our little scholars turned out well.

In 1826 we went to Hadzor, to the christening of my three little cousins, Theodore (aged 6), Douglas** (aged 4), and Herman, the baby. My Uncle being born a Quaker and my Aunt a Unitarian, they had not had the children christened before, but my Aunt (influenced much by my Aunt Sophia) had thought much more of religion and joined the Church of England; she was very anxious that her children should be baptised, and my Uncle (who was not a bit of a Quaker) made no objection. Theodore understood the service and behaved very nicely.

*

Before I begin on 1827, I must mention some old customs of these

**This is of course a reference to the great naturalist, Charles Darwin (1809-82)*

***Afterwards Sir Douglas Galton, KCB, the distinguished engineer, who appears again in Chapter 13, p208.*

The Larches

A sampler sewn by Elizabeth Anne Galton, aged 18

times. First, in ladies' dresses: we wore stays with very stiff bones, which we had to lace behind, from top to bottom, every morning. Our stays and petticoats all had shoulder straps, so that it was an effort to raise our arms. It was a great relief when elastic bands were made of India rubber for shoulder straps, and a still greater relief when doctors decided that shoulder straps were bad for health and they were discarded, when I was thirty or so. India-rubber, and afterwards gutta percha, only came into use for wearing apparel after I was twenty-four or twenty-five. We used to have ribbon sandals to our shoes, which were always coming untied. Doctors are now thinking it unhealthy for women not to wear shoulder straps and want them worn again; I recommend my young friends not to give in to them.

Our dresses all buttoned behind, so that we could not fasten them ourselves. Another fashion which is quite obsolete, which I like, was that every woman, when she married, let her be ever so young, wore caps. It was very becoming and made them look matronly and mistresses of their houses.

In those days, wives did not address their husbands as "Charlie" or "Willie," but always by the full name, or by the surname. There was more respect than now.

Till lamps for the table were invented, we used tall mould (not sperm) candles, which had to be snuffed constantly. Rich people burnt wax candles, which were very expensive.

Game could not be sold; gentlemen gave their game to their friends, and as it was a rule that they should pay the carriage for it, it was an expensive present. I remember when we were at Boulogne in 1829, how we enjoyed the game we could there purchase. There were no "battues" in those days.

Postage was very dear, and the receiver of a letter had to pay it. We paid ninepence for a letter from London or Bath, fourpence from Kenilworth to Leamington, and sixpence (I think) from Derby. It was thought a wonderful thing when a coach could go from Birmingham to London in twelve hours. My Father remembered when the post woman, who carried the letters from Birmingham to Wolverhampton, gave it up because "the road was lonely." But in my young days there was a coach passing on that road nearly every five minutes.

My Father remembered the time when the roads were so bad that people always made their wills before going to London, and their teeth were quite loosened with the jolting. The ruts were so deep that to go one stage (about fourteen miles) a day was as much as could be done. Before you went, the custom was to ask whether there was good "quartering" on the road, which meant, could you drive easily on the edge of the ruts without falling into them. Besides this, in my Father's time, there was the probability of being robbed by highwaymen.

Bridges were never made flat as they are now, but steep up and down. There is a bridge over the canal on the lower Warwick Road from Leamington, which is exactly like what all bridges were. In many places there were no bridges, and we had to go through the river at the ford.

A curious custom, not so very long ago abolished, was a "deodand." When a cart ran over a person and killed him, a deodand of one shilling had to be paid on the wheel which caused his death. If a horse killed him, a deodand of one shilling had to be paid on the hoof which did it, and so on in all accidents.

Servants were paid their wages only once a year, or twice a year at most. The maids always wore short sleeves at their work, never long sleeves till they dressed after work.

Elections lasted many days and could be kept open a fortnight. The drunkenness and fighting the whole time was terrible, as ale houses were kept open by the candidates the whole time, and much ill will was the result. When it was hoped that Birmingham would have a member (years before it had) both Whigs and Tories asked my Father to stand, and promised their support. He was considered upright and moderate in his opinion, but he declined on account of the expense and his attacks of asthma, but it was very gratifying.

Funerals were very different to what they are now. It was thought a want of respect to bury a person till a week after his death, and some one always sat up the first night near the corpse, in case he was not dead. He was first put into a shell (a plain coffin), which was then enclosed in lead and soldered down, and lastly in a handsome outer coffin. Many relatives and friends were asked to the funeral. Early on the morning, two mutes (men dressed in black, holding long staves, with black cloth on them) stood on each side of the hall door till the coffin came out. A man put crèpe or silk bands round each gentleman's hat, and he pinned a scarf round his shoulder and under one arm. A number of black gloves were on the table, for each to take a pair, besides which there were parcels containing a pair of lady's gloves and a piece of funeral cake for each to take to his wife. The cake was something like sponge cake, but made expressly for funerals. Mourning coaches were provided for all the invited guests, which followed the hearse, and their empty carriages and the carriages of all their acquaintances came after them. A funeral was a very expensive affair in consequence.

Before 1832, bleeding in the arm and with leeches was constantly used. I have had twelve round my eye at once when it was inflamed, and Darwin had them constantly on his temples when ill. Calomel was also frequently given, but after the cholera in 1832 and the influenza in 1833, all was changed, and instead of bleeding and calomel, mutton chops and wine were given.

*

In my early youth, many men and old ladies took snuff, a nasty habit. Mr. Rojet, an emigrant who took snuff and was very fond of coffee, told the young ladies that he had sent to London for a pound of snuff and a pound of coffee. It arrived, and he told the young ladies what a misfortune had occurred: when he opened the outside parcel, he found that the inside ones had given way, and the coffee and snuff had got mixed. The young ladies were much grieved, knowing he was very poor, and began thinking whether they could subscribe for some more, but he begged them not to distress themselves and said, "I did mix it all together and did draw my finger down the middle, and I said, 'This side shall be my coffee, and this shall by my snoof!'"

My Uncle Hubert Galton was the first to set up a pony carriage in Birmingham, and it created great interest. Once he wanted to go some distance and wished to hire a post horse for the carriage, but no postillion could be prevailed upon to go – "he would be laughed at."

My Father knew a very old man who told him that he could remember Cherry Street (out of New Street in Birmingham) as a cherry orchard.

Among the celebrities we knew in our early youth was Zerah Colborne. He had marvellous powers of calculating and could extract the cube root of a difficult sum in a minute, and answer the most difficult sums in a moment. He and his father dined at the Larches, and my Father and Dr. Delys had prepared questions in arithmetic to ask him. They asked us one when he was playing with us; he went on playing, but answered the question at once. He could not explain how he did it. He was then about fifteen years old. His father was an American, and both he and his son had six fingers on one hand: one grew out of the little finger.

*

I have said how frequently in the early part of this century travellers were stopped by highwaymen, which puts me in mind of an anecdote my Mother used to tell, and which I have since seen corroborated. A lady was travelling in a stage coach to London. There were three gentlemen inside, who talked together, but she kept quite silent. When they got near Houndslow Heath, then famous for robbers, the gentleman opposite her said, "I trust we shall meet no robber here, for I have forty pounds in this pocket," touching his waistcoat pocket. The other gentlemen agreed with him, but the lady kept silent. In a few moments the coach was stopped, a pistol put in at the window, and "your money or your life" demanded. The two gentlemen gave up their purses, but the one opposite the lady assured the robber that he had nothing.

To his amazement, the lady spoke to the robber and said, "Sir, that gentleman is my husband; he never gives me a farthing, though he has now forty pounds in his right-hand waistcoat pocket." The gentleman was furious, but seeing the pistol pointed close to him, he was obliged to give up the money, and the robber left.

They continued the journey, when his wrath burst upon the lady. How dared she say that she was his wife – if there was not another woman in the world he would not marry an ugly old woman like her, and then to tell the highwayman he had money, &c., &c.

The lady said nothing, and he stormed away till the coach stopped at some hotel in London, where they all got out. The lady engaged a handsome sitting room and ordered a good dinner. She then sent her compliments to the gentleman who had sat opposite her and requested to speak to him. He came, very grumpy. She begged him to sit down, and said she wished to apologise for the liberty she had taken in saying he was her husband. Her reason was that she had her whole fortune of £25,000 in her pocket, and it struck her that, if she told the highwayman that he had forty pounds in his pocket and was her husband, she would not be questioned. She then presented him with forty pounds in place of what he had been robbed of, and hoped that he would forgive her, and dine with her.

The gentleman was quite overcome and did not know how to apologise for his rudeness, and they became quite good friends during the dinner, and what with the lady's agreeable conversation – and her fortune of £25,000 – he begged to be allowed to call upon her, and before long they were married.

*

We used to go at least once a week to Dudson to see my Grandfather and Aunts, and they used to come to us as often. My Aunts Sophia and Adele were very kind to us, and if they saw any faults they corrected us so nicely that we never forgot what they said. I remember one day, Lucy and I told my Aunt Sophia that we were going to give a pair of shoes to each of our schoolchildren, and we boasted that we had settled with Gibbon, a little shoemaker, to make them each sixpence cheaper than his usual charge. My Aunt said, "Then it is Gibbon that makes the present, not you only, if you make him give you sixpence out of each pair, which he ought to receive as his due." I have never forgotten that speech, and need not say that Gibbon received the full price for his work.

My Aunt had a day school for poor children. The governess lived in a cottage of my Grandfather's, with two women who distributed my Aunt's charities and assisted her in various ways. The surname of one of them was Pendril; she was descended from the Pendril who helped King Charles to hide in the oak.

My Sister Adele still lay down most of the day on account of her spine. Her great interest was teaching little Francis, who was very fond of her and would always come to his lessons when she called him. He was a wonderfully clever child, and she taught him so thoroughly and without tiring him that he knew more than children twice his age, and was fond of his lessons because he understood them well.

Adele was very patient and always cheerful, though she could not enter into the amusements we did. She was much beloved by all our young friends, over whom she exercised much influence for their good. She was always trying to do good to others. Emma was strong and very helpful. She was always the right hand of my Mother.

All my sisters were very good tempered, especially Lucy. She was always ready to do a kindness and full of fun, although not strong in health. She was loved wherever she went. She drew remarkably well in perspective and had very good abilities.

From his birth Darwin was a very beautiful boy, with very winning manners, and made himself so pleasant to his teachers that he often got excused for doing his lessons badly. My Mother cautioned the French master, M. Duchemin, on the point. He replied "You need not fear, he won't get over me." A short time after, she was present when M. Duchemin came, and she was amused at seeing Darwin rush at him, and hang his great coat to the fire to warm.

Erasmus was very straightforward, and from a very early age anxious to go to sea. He was constantly pushing himself about in a tub on one of the ponds. The boys both lived on their ponies and were capital riders.

Dudson, or Duddeston, where my Grandfather lived, was part of the Aston Hall Estate. My Great Uncle John Galton took a ninety-nine year lease of it from Sir Lister Holte; a lease which my Grandfather renewed some years after. At my Great Grandfather's death my Grandfather added two large handsome rooms in front, and two storeys of rooms above, which made it a large house three storeys high.

*

About this time (1827) a trial which made a great sensation took place, of Mr. Edward Gibbon Wakefield for decoying a young heiress from school, a Miss Turner of Cheshire, an only child of rich parents. Mr. Wakefield was son of Priscilla Wakefield, an excellent woman and author of several books; she was first cousin to Mrs. Fry. Miss Turner, a girl of fifteen or sixteen, was at school when Wakefield drove to the door and told the governess that Mr. Turner had been taken ill suddenly, that he had been with him at the time, and that Mr. Turner had begged him to fetch his daughter. He was so plausible in manner, and so gentlemanly, that he persuaded the governess to believe him, and she let the girl go. His brother and his brother's wife joined them directly after. When Wakefield got Miss Turner into the carriage, he told her that her father's illness was caused by the loss of all his fortune, and the only thing to save his life would be for her to marry him, as he was rich and could help her father. The poor girl was persuaded to consent. In the mean time, a letter to Miss Turner from her father at the school opened the governess's eyes to the fraud, and she set off at once to Mr. Turner. The girl was immediately followed and rescued before the marriage took place. The two Wakefields were tried, and Edward Gibbon was sentenced to some years in prison, most of which time he was in Australia (Botany Bay, I think). When he came out, he wrote a clever book upon prison life. His brother was sent to prison for a shorter time, so far as I recollect. Miss Turner married some years later.

[According to an old book Reminiscences of Manchester Fifty Years Ago, by J.T. Slugg, FRAS (Cornish, Manchester, 1881), Wakefield and his accomplices got as far as France before they were caught by the young lady's uncle. According to Mr Slugg "it was clearly proved at the trial that there had been no cohabitation", and the young lady married a member of a prominent Cheshire family. Mr Slugg also provides an ironical footnote to the whole business, however: "Her father was reputed to be immensely wealthy, but at his death this was proved to be an error".]

*

In September, 1827, my Aunt Adele married Dr. Booth. She was married from our house, my Mother and Uncle Howard attending her to Church. My Father was not well and could not go. It was a marriage not approved of by her family, and it did not turn out happily.

In January 1828 Lucy and I paid a visit at Hadzor, which was always a pleasant one, so many young people, and often a dance in the evening. Our old friend, Mrs. Charles Lloyd of Bingley, died this month, aged seventy-nine. She was a Miss Farmer, and her Aunt Mary Farmer married my Great Grandfather. She was first cousin to my Grandfather. She and her husband, strict Quakers, were excellent people and universally respected. One of Mr. Lloyd's daughters married Mr. Paul Moon James, the working partner in our bank. Another married a Mr. Wordsworth, and two married two Mr. Braithwaites.

We were very intimate with the Moilliet family, Mr. Moilliet was a Swiss and came to England, and by hard work and unremitting energy he made a good fortune. He set up a bank with Mr. Woolley, besides which he was connected with a Foreign Office [i.e. import/export business], sending goods abroad. He married Miss Keir, only child of Mr. Keir* of Hill Top, near Birmingham, a member of the Lunar Society and a great friend of my two grandfathers, In her youth she had often been to Dudson to visit my Aunts. My Father, when a boy, had just read "The Rape of the Lock," and the next time Miss Keir came he cut off a piece of her hair. He was much puzzled what to do with it. At last a bright idea struck him, and he corked it up in a glass bottle, to the amusement of the family. Her eldest surviving son, James, married my sister Lucy.

The eldest daughter, Emily, married in May of this year, a Mr. Knight, who died suddenly soon after. She was confined of a daughter, Philippa, some months later, who married Mr. Shirley and lives at Oxford. Mrs. Knight married secondly the Rev. Mr. Powys, and had

**James Keir, FRS (1735-1820), chemist, industrialist, and pamphleteer, who frequently presided over the meetings of the Lunar Society, and took the chair at the "Bastille Day Dinner" which touched off the infamous "Church and King" riots in Birmingham. He established the first process for making caustic soda by a completely synthetic route.*

two sons. She died in 1890 at a great age.

Theodore Moilliet married, for his second wife, Miss Townsend, daughter of the Reverend Charles Townsend, Rector of Castle Bromwich, who had a large family, all exceedingly tall. Mrs. Townsend was six feet four, and could not walk in Birmingham, she was so followed as a sight.

Mr. and Mrs. Ryland lived at the Five Ways in Birmingham. Mr. Ryland's father, whose house was burnt at the Riots, made a large fortune in business, which his son increased immensely. The Rylands had one daughter, Louisa, whom we knew. She was very strictly brought up, totally unselfish, and taught by her governess, Miss Randall that riches were a great responsibility, and that she would be only steward of her wealth and accountable to God how she spent it.

In the Spring of 1828, Mrs. Hurd came from Somersetshire to pay us a visit. She was wife to my Grandfather's principal tenant, a very active woman, but as she came to "visit ladies," she brought no work, but sat with her hands before her. At last she could not avoid expressing her astonishment at seeing our Mother and ourselves always employed. She said she thought ladies never did anything. Her husband came to Dudson a year or two before and was so delighted with the gas lamps in the town that he went into a shop to buy one for his "Missis", and of course only got laughed at.

This reminds me that, some years before, harvest was bad, and the farmers could not sell their produce, trade being also bad. One day, to my Grandfather and Grandmother's horror, a huge waggon came to Dudson, full of cheeses, the farmer not being able to pay his rent in any other way.

In April 1828 Admiral Maling and his nephew Irwin came to see us, and went on to Abberley, where the Admiral fell in love with Jemima, Colonel Bromley's second daughter, a very beautiful woman. He married her the following August. He had three children, Ann who married a German and died soon after, Tom who married and went to Australia or New Zealand and has a large family, and Jemima who married the Rev. Edmund Morgan and has no family.

I think I have mentioned that Irwin Maling was born in India, and was brought up by my Aunt Maling, to whom he was much attached.

His father, Major Maling, lived in India and had a large family. He was seized by a tiger and carried off. His friends feared to shoot the tiger for fear of shooting him, but seeing it was the only chance, one of them fired. Fortunately he killed the beast and saved Major Maling, who was severely bitten in the back and was always lame in consequence. He went afterwards by the name of "Tiger Maling".

*

In September 1828 Lucy and I were invited to Osmaston for the Derby Music Meeting, but when the time came, Lucy had one of her rheumatic attacks, and Emma went in her place. Caroline Darwin came to us from Shrewsbury, and we travelled together. Charles Darwin joined us at Osmaston, and we were a large, merry party of cousins. We went to some of the performances and heard the famous Angelica Catalani; her voice was wonderful, so powerful and so sweet. Her "Rule, Britannia" was a thing never to be forgotten, and I was rejoiced she sang it when we went to the evening concert. Our Mother told us that, when our fleet returned victorious from some battle and was stationed at Spithead, Catalani was shown all round the Flagship, and after seeing all the wounded sailors, she mounted the poop and, to the delight of all the ships, she sang "Rule, Britannia" in her powerful voice, which all could hear. She had a fine, commanding figure and looked like Britannia herself. The crews of all the ships cheered her and were charmed.

William Fox was making a collection of butterflies, and Charles Darwin immediately began to do the same, and this was the beginning of his interest in collecting. He and William Fox struck up a friendship, which continued all their lives.

I have never mentioned my old Great Aunt, Mrs. Darwin, mother to Mrs. Fox, who lived with them at Osmaston and had her own rooms there. She was widow of William Alvey Darwin, one of my Grandfather's Brothers, and as the two other brothers never married, William Alvey became the head of the family and owner of Elston, the family place. They had three children, William (at this time, 1828) head of the family, Mrs. Fox, and Eliza who died single.

Mrs. Darwin's son William offended her direfully by falling in love and marrying my cousin Fox's Governess, Miss St. Croix. She would not speak to her son for some time, and I think would never see his wife. They had a young family, most of whom died young of consumption. The only two who survived were Charlotte, who married Mr. Rhodes, who took the name of Darwin, and Sarah who married Mr. Noel. Both had families and are now dead. Their Brother Robert, just lived to be of an age, and able to leave the estate to his Sister Charlotte before he died, otherwise it would have gone to my Uncle Darwin of Shrewsbury. Mrs. Darwin died in 1835 aged upwards of ninety.

We then went to the Priory, where the rest of the family joined us. Irwin Maling was there and left to join *H.M.S. Southampton* going to the East Indies. While we were there, a Mr. MacConnell called on my Father. At this time a Mr. McAdam was making a great alteration to roads. Instead of mending a road with large stones and round pebbles, as was the custom, which were always wearing out and getting into horses' shoes, he would not allow one to be larger than a walnut, and all round ones were broken into small pieces. He made the roads a little higher in the middle for the wet to run off, instead of being flat or (from wear) rather lower in the centre. He sent his assistant, Mr. MacConnell, to Derby to improve the roads there, and my Father invited him to Birmingham and took a great interest in the matter. The consequence was that there were no more ruts, and it was trotting ground the whole way from London to Holyhead.

*

During this year (1828), my Father and Mother, seeing Erasmus so bent on going to sea, gave their consent to his wishes. Colonel Bromley and Lord Lyttleton kindly exerted their influence to get him a berth in a ship, and Lord Lyttleton had just secured him one in a small ship, when Captain Griffiths, who had been most kind, wrote word that his friend Sir Edward Owen, who had been appointed Admiral on the East India Station, would take Erasmus as his midshipman on board his Flagship *H.M.S. Southampton*, the very best appointment that he could have, and the same ship that his friend Irwin Maling had joined. In December, my Father took Erasmus to London to enter his name, and to change from the small vessel to the flagship.

CHAPTER 4

SOME LONDON CONNEXIONS (1829)

On the 4th. February, 1829, Emma and I went to stay with the Horners in Upper Gower Street, a very memorable visit. The Horners took us to see many sights. At their house we met many celebrated scientific men, including Mr. Hallam, who wrote "The Middle Ages", and Sydney Smith, who had just taken leave of a friend who was going out as Bishop to some Island of black people. His parting words were: "Good-bye, my dear fellow; I hope you will disagree with the cannibal who eats you."

I ought to mention that, in London and at school, we were always introduced as granddaughters of Dr. Erasmus Darwin, and made much of in consequence. Our schoolfellows were very jealous of us, because two of our ancestors, Barclay the Apologist and Dr. Darwin, were mentioned in Priestley's Biographical Chart, which hung up in the schoolroom. In London we were received in the kindest manner by all clever people, when they heard who we were, and they always noticed us whenever we met them.

While we were at the Horners', my Father and Erasmus came to town. My Father was first-rate at showing us sights, and took us all over London. He took Emma with him and Erasmus next day to Chatham, where Erasmus joined *H.M.S. Southampton*, Admiral Sir Edward Owen, Captain Fisher. We all felt parting with him, a boy of thirteen and the first break in the family, but it was his earnest wish, and he would be miserable not to go.

*

Emma returned to London a few days after. My Father told us that our Great-aunt, Mrs. Hudson Gurney*, was coming to call on us and invite us to St. James's Square, which alarmed us not a little, as we feared she would be too grand to care for us. She arrived soon after, and was so kind and affectionate that we lost some of our fears. She was half-sister to my Grandmother Galton and about my Father's age. On 4th. March Emma and I left the Horners with much regret. The Gurney carriage came for us, and we went to 9, St. James's Square, a very large, handsome house, six men-servants and everything rich and good. Mr. Gurney was immensely wealthy, and immensely generous with his wealth. He had of course no end of begging letters, and he employed two men to find out those that were deserving of help. He was, or had been, a remarkably handsome man and was very clever. He was in Parliament for Newtown, Isle of Wight, and used to say that all his constituents could go in a gig, viz. Two! When the Reform Bill passed, he gave up Parliament.

To our surprise, we were told that dinner was at eight o'clock, a thing unknown elsewhere, as six or half-past six were then thought late. There was no five o'clock tea, but we had a jar of Diss gingerbread in our rooms which was very good; Diss is a town in Norfolk.

My Aunt took us to all the sights, Panorama, Diarama, Theatres, Opera – everything she thought we would like. Mr. Gurney engaged Signor Rossetti**, famed for his work on Dante, to give us lessons in Italian. He was a very clever man, and at our last lesson he said that, if we would give him a subject, he would improvise upon it to us, which he did in rhyme, to a sort of singing chant. We were introduced to shoals of relations, who greeted us most affectionately as Tertius Galton's children: Gurneys, Barclays, Hoares, Buxtons, Trittons, Hanburys, Frys, &c., &c., all second cousins to my Father, and we were asked to dinner by most of them. We got so puzzled with so many new relations that, as soon as they were gone, we got Miss Morse to tell us how we were related, and I then drew up the long

**Born Margaret Barclay Allardice, daughter of Robert Barclay Allardice, MP, of Ury, she was the wife of Hudson Gurney, FRS (1775-1864), antiquary and verse writer. Various members of this gifted family, who are perhaps best known as bankers and philanthropists, appear in these pages.*

***The father of Dante Gabriel Rossetti (1828-1882).*

pedigree which I have.

Mrs. Fry* called one day. She was a very striking person, tall and dignified, and yet so kind and motherly that one felt one could open one's heart to her. We saw her several times, but regretted we never heard her preach.

*

On the 30th. April, George IV held a Drawing Room, which had not been done for some years. It was largely attended, and Mr. Gurney very good-naturedly took Emma and me for a walk, where we could see all the carriages going to Court. Mr. Gurney was a first-rate herald and told us the names of the ladies from the arms on their carriages. The coachmen wore cocked hats, two or three footmen hanging on behind, with staves in their hands, tipped with silver, and all wearing large bouquets of flowers. The fashion then was for ladies to wear three ostrich feathers standing upon the top of the head, so when they went to Court, they had the cushions of the carriage seats removed to give some height, and many had to sit with their heads bent across the carriage – and this for an hour or two – till they could get to St. James's Palace. One lady of high rank went in a sedan chair, with several powdered footmen walking on each side of her chair.

In the beginning of May, my sister Adele fell ill with scarlet fever, and my Aunt, who had taken a great fancy to us, especially to Emma, begged my Father to let us stay with her instead of going to the Priory, where we had been invited. This month we went to the Caledonian Ball with my Aunt and the Innes's. It was a splendid ball, all the Scotch in tartans, according to their clan, and the chiefs wearing eagles' feathers. My Aunt wore a dress of the Royal Scotch Tartan, which she had a right to do as an Allardice, whose ancestor was a son of King Robert II of Scotland. Emma and I were rather taken aback at all the gentlemen having bare knees, which amused the Innes's. The reels danced were very amusing. In the middle of one of the quadrilles, the Duke of Sussex, dressed in Royal Tartan, with a

**Elizabeth Fry (1780-1845) née Gurney, the great Quaker penal reformer.*

kilt and bare knees, arrived. Immediately the dance stopped, the band played a few bars of the National Anthem, and then the quadrille went on. Soon after, the Duke of Cumberland came, and the same form was repeated, so we saw two Royal Dukes. At twelve o'clock there was a pause in the dancing, and a piper came in playing the bagpipes, followed by all the children of the Caledonian Schools. They walked in procession all round that room and then retired, and the dancing recommenced. I think we enjoyed the ball more than anything else.

*

I have mentioned the Innes family, with whom we became very intimate. Mr. Innes of Raemoir lived near my Uncle Barclay of Ury; his Brother married Cameron Barclay, eldest sister of my Aunt Gurney. She had three daughters, and died when they were very young. Mrs. Hudson Gurney adopted Cameron and brought her up. She married Colonel Latour, and had one child, Cameron, who married Mr. Goff. Mrs. Latour was divorced from her husband. Mrs. Innes's second daughter Elizabeth married Mr. Abercrombie and died of consumption. She had one son Robert, afterwards Sir Robert Duff, and two daughters, whom my Aunt Gurney brought up after their Mother's death, viz. Mary, who married Herman Galton, and Maggie, who married Colonel Lyons. Robert went into the navy for some years, but at his Father's and Uncle's deaths he came into the Glassaugh and Fetteresso property and changed his name to Duff. He was made Governor of New South Wales and died there leaving a large family. Mr. Innes of Raemoir married Miss Brebner and had one daughter, Christina, and several sons. We met them first at Shrewsbury, where they went to consult my Uncle Darwin about their daughter, who they feared was in a decline, so many of the Brebners had died of that disease. Christina had no appetite and disliked all food. My Uncle asked her if there was anything she could fancy, and she said the only thing she could eat, and which she had a longing for, was cheese, but she knew it would be thought bad for her. My Uncle told her to eat as much cheese as she liked, and from that time she began to recover and, I believe, is living still in Aberdeen. She must now (1897) be ninety or more years of age; she married a Gordon.

We saw a great deal of Mrs. Opie, the portrait painter, a most agreeable person. She had been fond of gaiety but had become a Quaker, it was thought in the hope of marrying Joseph John Gurney, and certainly she had not much of the Quaker in her manner, though strict in her dress. She told us we should never talk of rhubarb tart, as it brought unpleasant ideas of medicine – we should call it "spring fruit".

At this time my Aunt took us to Tottenham to call on Mrs. Lizzie Forster, who was delighted to see another generation of Galtons. She was friend and housekeeper to my Great-grandfather Galton. Her sister Mrs. Bevan lived with her and was blind in one eye, owing to the cork of a soda water bottle flying out and striking it. We also called on Mrs. Pym, another old Quakeress, who had been friend and housekeeper to Mr. Hudson Gurney's father or grandfather. We did enjoy these visits – the lilac and laburnums were out, and the country looked so beautiful we felt like birds out of a cage.

*

I must digress here to say a few words of Mr. Hudson Gurney's grandfather, David Barclay of Youngsbury and Walthamstow, my Great-great-uncle. He was an excellent man, always doing good. Although immensely wealthy, he often had to wear a shabby coat: he had given so much away he could not afford a new one. Many young men owed their start in life to him, and one of them, walking with my Father in London, stopped and took off his hat as he passed a house, and said "Mr. David Barclay lived there, and I always take off my hat when passing the door. His kind and timely help set me up, or I should have been ruined." He became possessed of some slaves in the West Indies, in payment of a debt. He knew that, if he liberated them at once, they would die of starvation; so he sent them to New York, had them taught trades, and then set them up and liberated them. It cost him nearly £10,000. I have a pamphlet with the history of these slaves.

In May, 1829, we came home, Caroline and Susan Darwin travelling with us, very sorry at leaving my Aunt, but very glad to get home again.

Chapter 5

Birmingham (continued) and Some More Travels (1829 - 1832)

My sister Adele was terribly pulled down from the scarlet fever, and Mr. Hodgson made it such a point that she should go to the sea at once that on 30th. June my Mother, Lucy, Adele, and Francis went by easy stages to Ramsgate, where Adele rapidly recovered. Emma and I stayed with my Father, who was laid up with his usual attack of Asthma; when he got well on 16th. July, he, Emma, and I went to London, saw the Gurneys, and went next day by steamer down the Thames to Ramsgate, a delightful trip and a marvellous sight, with all the merchant shipping, men of war, ships, &c., giving one a wonderful idea of the riches of the country. The views from the river were interesting: Greenwich Hospital, Tilbury Port, &c. We passed the Isle of Dogs, on which were still to be seen three gibbets, on which three men had been executed a long time previously. One day, whilst at Ramsgate, we saw the Duke of Wellington arrive in the steam packet, and as he remained some days at Ramsgate, we saw him two or three times.

At the end of this month we heard of the death of my Uncle Edward Darwin, which was a great sorrow, especially to my Mother.

At the beginning of August my Father had to return to the Bank, and took Darwin and Francis to their schools. The following week we left Ramsgate, intending to stay at Dover, but when we got there we did not like the place, and we persuaded my Mother to go to Boulogne, Lucy and I promising to take all the trouble off her hands. The family of Captain Fisher of *H.M.S. Southampton* living there was a great inducement, as we hoped to hear of Erasmus from them, so the next day my Mother and we four sisters crossed the Channel.

A woman on board the packet came and sat by us, but we did not like her looks and went to another seat. She evidently wanted to appear one of our party. When we reached Boulogne, a Custom House Officer came on deck, seized her, and carried her off to be searched; a quantity of contraband goods were seized on her. They were very lenient to us, and we soon passed. Lucy and I sallied forth to find lodgings and got some very soon in the principal street, and we all sat at the window, much amused at everything so different to England.

There was a very mixed society: gamblers and men who could not show their faces in England, and a very pleasant society of families living there for cheap education for their children. We had a drawing master and a lady to talk French at one franc a lesson. My Aunt Gurney gave us some introductions, and we got acquainted with many pleasant people.

Soon after our arrival, my Mother and I walked up the steep hill to the High Town to call on Mrs. Fisher, who was delighted to have someone who could talk to her and sympathise with her about *H.M.S. Southampton,* where her husband and two sons were on board; she had four daughters and her two youngest boys living with her. We young ones fraternised at once; the Fishers walked out with us and taught us how to shop, and we met every day. We changed our lodgings to some in the High Town, which were better in every respect. There were ramparts all round, where we walked every day. There was a large boys' school at Boulogne, kept by Mr. Berry, chiefly English boys, but French masters, and my Father heard the school so well spoken of that he determined to send Francis there when he was old enough.

My Father joined us in September. Emma and two of the Miss Fishers were confirmed by an English Bishop, and we had the pleasure of hearing good news of *H.M.S. Southampton* from Mrs. Fisher. I had a severe cold and swelling in my face, and Dr. Campbell was sent for, and his fee was five francs. At the end of October we left Boulogne, spent a day at Chatham to see Dr. and Mrs. Davies, old

Tenby friends, a day in London sight-seeing, and then home.

Miss Anderton, whom we knew, was at Boulogne when we were there and left soon after we did. She told us she had bought several silk dresses and had run them up to wear as petticoats when she crossed, so as to escape paying duty. She put them all on the day she left; the sea was very rough, and she was so ill that, on getting out of the ship into the boat, she slipped and fell up to her neck in the sea, and all the silk dresses were spoilt. In those days everything was contraband: gloves, silk, tea, steel, and all had to pay duty. A woman brought some beautifully worked collars to tempt us and saw my Mother's cutting-out scissors on the table and offered her any one of the collars if she would let her have the scissors, but my Mother did not consent.

There was no pier at Dover, and passengers had to get into a boat from the ship and, when as near shore as the boat could go, to be carried by men or get wet feet.

*

In the autumn of 1829 the young Queen of Portugal came to England. She was only four years old, and her uncle Dom Miguel was trying to dethrone her and seize the Kingdom of Portugal for himself; so she was sent to England to be out of his way, and to enlist our Government on her behalf. The sea was so rough she was landed at Falmouth, where our relations Mr. and Mrs. Fox took the child into their house till arrangements could be made for her to go to London. She was introduced to George IV, but he was so infirm and unwieldy he could not bend down to kiss her, and she had to be lifted up to him.

*

In March, 1830, my Father went to Worcester to hear the trial of the Oddingley murderers. In the previous autumn, my Uncle Howard Galton had desired a barn in one of the fields should be rebuilt. Some objection was made, but it was done. The man employed on removing the floor found a skeleton, which he was sure was his brother-in-law Hemming, who had been missing many years. Hemming had been employed by three most influential farmers and a Captain Evans, a magistrate, to shoot the Rev. Mr. Parker, whom they disliked because he was particular in getting his tythes paid. He was shot in the evening, in a field, while driving his cows home. No one endeavoured to find the murderer, who had been promised fifty pounds for the job. The farmers, however, finding the magistrates were taking it up, and fearing Hemming might get them into trouble, hid him in the barn belonging to Clewes, went at night to the barn, knocked him on the head, and buried him in the barn, telling his wife and everyone that he was gone to America. Captain Evans the magistrate, Barnet, and Clewes were tried, but Hemming being away, they were discharged. At the trial this month they got off on a point of law. The trial caused a great sensation, the discovery of Hemming being thirty years after his murder.

*

We often heard from Erasmus, who was perfectly happy, and we heard from Admiral Griffith that he gave satisfaction to his Admiral and Captain. His letters were four months coming to us – wonderfully quick, it was considered, as a short time previously it took six months to bring a letter. What a difference now.

We always went two or three times a week to Dudson, and they came to us, generally to tea, which in those days was early, about six or half past.

In June, 1830, Miss Ann Wozencroft came to visit us from Carmarthen. I have not mentioned them before: Miss Wozencroft had an uncle in business in Birmingham, who adopted her, put her to school, and it was thought he had made money and would provide well for her. My Mother took an interest in her and often had her to stay with us when she had a holiday. When she was sixteen, her uncle died, and instead of leaving her anything, was in debt. She returned to her family and soon after her father died, and at sixteen she was left with six sisters younger than herself and scarcely any money. She immediately set up a school for the tradespeople's daughters, educated them and her sisters, and managed to support them all. As her sisters grew up, they helped her, and they got on very well.

My sisters and I used to learn all the fancy work we could, and when Miss Wozencroft visited us we taught her, which she said was most useful, the parents thinking more of fancy work than of any other accomplishments. She and her sisters often visited us. Some years after, when her sisters grew up, she married a Mr. Mortimer, a chemist in Carmarthen, a marriage that promised well, but he failed, her one child died, and after many troubles she died.

*

This year in June George IV died, and Miss Ann Wozencroft and I went to Birmingham and heard King William proclaimed.

We went to Handsworth Church to see an excellent monument to Mr. Watt by Chantrey, a full sized figure sitting and a good likeness.

In August, the Duchess of Kent and the Princess Victoria, aged eleven, came to Birmingham for a few days. They went to see Boulton's Manufactory and Sir Edward Thomason's. At each place the little Princess struck a medal purposely prepared for her. All who saw her were surprised at her remarkable intelligence and simple, childlike manner. They were staying at the Royal Hotel, in Temple Row, and the Duchess and Princess came out on the balcony to show themselves to the crowd below, who cheered. They then retired, but while the Duchess was arranging some matters with a gentleman, the little Princess came out on the balcony again, made a low curtsey, clapped her hands, and said "Now cheer again," which the crowd heartily did.

In September my Father took Francis to Mr. Bury's School at Boulogne. He was eight years old and it was a great trial to us parting with him.

My Father went in September to Sir Robert Peel at Drayton to see the Duke of Wellington on some business. He met them again at a grand public dinner given to the Duke at Birmingham by the High Sheriff, Mr. Chance, and my Father had the honour of sitting by the Duke. (*See opposite.*)

BILL OF FARE.

FOR 160—THREE TABLES TO CORRESPOND.

WILLIAM CHANCE, ESQ. HIGH BAILIFF.

First Course.

Twelve Treens of Turtle.
Remove with
Turbots, Severn Salmon, Crimped Cod, &c.
Remove with
Six Haunches and Six Necks of Venison.
Braized Beef with Spanish Onions.
Boiled Chickens, with White Sauce.
Turkeys with Cellery Sauce.
Venison Pasties.
Raised Pies.

Westphalia Hams and Tongues.
Mutton Kebobbed.
Shoulders of Lamb Braized.
Mutton Cutlets.
Chickens and Puree of Almonds.
Legs of Fowl, a la Francaise.
Stewed Partridges and Cabbage.
Fricandeaus, Veal, and Sorrell.
Larded Fillets, Curries.
Fowls and Tomato Sauce.
Souttee of Lamb and Cucumbers.
Voluvents, Veal Olives.
Veal Fillets with Stewed Peas, &c.

BARON OF BEEF.

Second Course.

Roast Black Game.
Grouse.—Part ridges and Leverets.
Noye au Creams.
Grapes in Jelly.—Chantilly Baskets.
Italian Salads.—Apricot Tourts.

Citron Souflies.
Fried Oysters —Apricot Tartlets.
Stewed Mushrooms.
Fondieus
Ratifia Puddings, &c.

DESSERTS.

Pines.—Gra pes.—Melons.
Pea ches.
Nectarines.—Egg Plumbs.
Green Gages.
Plums.—P ears.—Apples.
Filberts .—Walnuts.
Preserve d Apricots.

WINES.

Hock.—Champagne.
Sparkling Burgundy.—Moselle.
Sauterne.
Sherry—White Hermitage.
Ea st India Madeira.—Old Port.
Claret.—Red Burgundy.
Constantia, &c.

LIQUEURS.

Birmingham, Temple Row, September 23, 1830.

Menu from dinner given for the Duke of Wellington

There was a large Political Union meeting in Birmingham, three thousand seven hundred people. King William was recommended not to go to the Lord Mayor's dinner, as was the usual custom, in the first year of his accession. Popular feeling was so strong, wanting reform, &c., and the dinner was given up.

In October, Mr. Brunel of Thames Tunnel celebrity dined with us, and told us many anecdotes, and what a fright was caused by the roof giving way in one place and the river rushing in. I think he said his son, in escaping, broke his leg and was only just carried in time to the water mark.

At the end of December we went to Derby to stay with the Miss Bents for the Christmas Ball, at which their niece, Elizabeth Bent, came out – her son married Sophie Moilliet.

*

In February, 1831, my Father took Emma and me to stay with my Aunt Gurney in London. In March the Reform Bill came on again. We went one evening to the Ventilator in the House of Commons to hear the members speak. It was not a pleasant place, being just over the large chandelier, a sort of chimney to it, but it was the only place where ladies could go in the old House of Commons.

The Daniel Gurneys and William and Joseph Fry dined with us one day and sang to us. I never heard more beautiful voices than all the young Frys: their ballad singing was most touching. Mrs. Fry, as a Quaker, objected to singing, but her children picked up the tunes from the barrel organs and got the words elsewhere. They all sang and drew remarkably well; Catherine and Hannah Fry stayed a few days in St. James's Square with us, and while we dressed we used to listen to Catherine in the next room, singing while she did her hair.

The House of Lords threw out the Reform Bill, which created such disturbances that King William went at a moment's notice and dissolved Parliament. We heard the guns firing but unfortunately were too far off to see the King go by. On the twenty-seventh there were illuminations all over the town for the passing of the Reform Bill. The Tories would not illuminate. Mr. Gurney had two or three flambeaux held up, if the mob came, to save his windows. We saw the mob come into the Square and begin to break the windows of the Junior Conservative Club. Two or three young men rushed out of the Club, seized two or three of the rioters, and the whole mob rushed away like a flock of sheep. It was an amusing sight.

*

Mr. Robert Barclay of Leyton took Emma, Margaret Barclay, and me, with four or five young cousins, to see the London East India Docks, which were very interesting, and would have been more so if we had not been expected to taste different wines stocked up in the docks, a wonderful sight. We went on board an East Indiaman, and finished up with a whitebait dinner. At the end of the dinner, a basin of rose water was handed round, which puzzled us much to know what to do. As I was the oldest, all the cousins' eyes were towards me to set an example. Luckily it struck me to put a corner of my dinner napkin in, which was right – the others gave a sigh of relief and did the same.

On going into a shop one day we met our old schoolfellow Miss Crawshaw, whom we were very glad to see. She was the eldest daughter of the great ironmaster and immensely rich. He was an odd man. He dressed his children according to the fortune their mother brought him. Our schoolfellow's mother had little or none, and she was the worst dressed in the school: her clothes too short and very few of them. The second wife had a good fortune, and her children were well dressed. His wife one day complained of the smallness of the house, with their increasing family, when he struck the table and vowed that that day six weeks she should enter a larger house which he would build in that time, and desired her to send out cards for a house-warming we would give that day six weeks. He went out that night with a party of workmen to measure out the plan of the foundations, set his army of workmen to work, and just as the Company began to arrive they were fastening the knocker on the door and the house was finished. When we told our Father of this, he thought it a schoolgirl's exaggeration or mistake, but we heard it so often confirmed by people in the neighbourhood that we found it was a fact.

In April my Aunt Gurney gave a grand ball, to which all our relations in Town were asked: Poles, Byrons, Bromleys, Horners &c. In May we spent a very pleasant day at Mrs. Fry's and saw nearly all her family, also the Samuel Gurneys, who lived close by in a large house.

Mrs. Fry was a most lovable, motherly woman; she gave each one of us one of her little text books, in her kind manner. I do not know whether I have mentioned an anecdote of her, showing how she knew how to gain and draw anyone to her. She came to Dudson, where a large party were asked to meet her. She told my Mother she would like to meet Francis, then a year and a half old, as her youngest child was about the same age. My Mother said she would fetch him, but that he was so shy she feared he would not make friends with her. Mrs. Fry said, "Oh never mind, I think he will." My Mother brought him in the room when, seeing so many people, he hid his face on his mother's shoulder and would not look up. She sat down by Mrs. Fry, who took no notice of him; soon after, she took a little box full of comfits out of her pocket and held it out towards the child, but looking the other way and talking to the Company. My Mother whispered, "Look, Francis," and the child, seeing no one observed him, sat on my Mother's knee looking at the comfits. Bye and bye he slid down, seized a comfit, and ran back. Mrs. Fry took no notice, and he soon stood by her, helping himself. She then gently lifted him up on her knee, taking no notice, and he soon began talking to her!

Another of the Earlham family we knew was Joseph John Gurney*, an excellent man and very clever. We often heard him preach at Quakers' meetings, and one could never forget his sermons or help being the better for them. The Earlham Gurneys were second cousins to my Father.

*

On 9th. of May, we left London by the night mail and travelled back with Mr. Hodgson, our medical friend. Soon after, Lucy and I

**Joseph John Gurney (1788-1847), Quaker Minister, writer, prison reformer, and a prominent helper in the cause of negro emancipation.*

spent some days at Hamstead, near Birmingham, with the Moilliets, when James became attached to Lucy.

On 31st. May, the Bank was closed. My Father had been quietly bringing it to an end ever since the run in 1825.

After a short visit to the Priory, we went to Worthing, where we found the Hubert Galtons, Robert and Ford Barclay, and their families. In August my Father, Emma, Francis, and I went in a steamer to Portsmouth, passing through Sir Edward Codrington's splendid fleet at Spithead. Next day, after seeing the fortifications, we steamed round the Isle of Wight and saw Norris Castle, where the Duchess of Kent and Princess Victoria were staying, and back to Portsmouth. The following day we went over the dockyard and there met Mr. David Chapman, who introduced us to Mrs. Hilliard, wife of Captain Hilliard of *H.M.S. Revenge*. She very kindly took us in her barge on board the Flagship, where we saw the Captains and the Admiral sitting at a Court Martial. She then took us over *H.M.S. Regent*, and then to dine with her on board the *Revenge*, a day we thoroughly enjoyed. Of course we also went on board Nelson's ship, the *Victory*, and saw the spot where he fell. We left Portsmouth and went to Southampton, stopping to see Netley Abbey, and then returned by coach to Worthing.

This year (1831) had been one of constant excitement: first the Reform Bill, and riots every time it was thrown out, either in Lords or Commons, and secondly, the dread of the *cholera morbus*, which was slowly but steadily spreading over the Continent, and every day we dreaded to hear it had arrived on our shores. Every precaution was taken: all foreign letters were perforated and fumigated at the Post Office. At last, on the 5th. October, the news arrived that a man had died of it on arriving at Sunderland from Hamburgh. I cannot describe the terror it occasioned everywhere. Little was known of the disease except that, though well in the morning, you might be dead in the evening; nothing seemed to arrest its progress. At first it was suggested to draw a cordon around an infected town, and to allow no one to pass in or out, and to write "infected" on every house where one was ill; in short, to act as was done in the time of the Plague described by Defoe. However, on consideration it was seen that all these arrangements would only increase people's fears, and make them predisposed to take it. There were several cases and deaths, but as winter came on they decreased, and we hoped we should have no more of it.

Early in October we left Worthing and went to Leamington in lodgings, opposite Copp's Hotel in High Street. When our bank closed, my Father and Mother decided upon leaving Birmingham and living in Leamington. Some good houses were being built in Lansdowne Place, and we went to Leamington to see if one would suit us, which it did, and was finished according to my Father's orders. We then returned home.

At the end of November, news came that the cholera had reached Newcastle.

*

My Father was made a Deputy Lieutenant in 1832.

Towards the end of January, my dear Grandmother Darwin became ill, and on 5th. February, just as it was hoped she was getting better, she died, to our great sorrow. She was eighty-four, and had had twelve children*, forty-one grandchildren, and twenty-eight great-grandchildren; some had died in her lifetime, but she had sixty descendants living at the time of her death.

James Moilliet, who had called often the last month, proposed to my sister Lucy in February and was accepted, an engagement that gave great pleasure to my Father and Mother, the two families having been intimate for three generations. Mrs. Moilliet's Father, Mr. Keir, was an old friend of both our Grandfathers and a member of the Lunar Society. James was then Mr. Moilliet's eldest son, John, who was older, having died in India.

In the beginning of March, Mr. and Mrs. Joseph John Gurney came to Birmingham. They were strict Quakers, but most kind and cheerful. We went several times to hear him preach at the Quakers' Meeting House, and in chapels that were lent to him and which were crowded. Mrs. Gurney was an American and very lovable. They

**This includes six children by her first marriage, to Colonel Chandos-Pole, as well as her children by Dr Erasmus Darwin.*

dined with us to meet a family party, and after dinner Mr. Gurney read the eleventh chapter of Hebrews to us and preached upon it, after which he prayed for us all and for our young brother at sea, It was a most interesting evening, which we could never forget. We met them at all the relations' houses and were very sorry when they left.

On the 29th. March, 1832, my dear sister Lucy was married. Being so near after my Grandmother's death, it was a very quiet wedding, only the Moilliet family and my Aunt Sophia present. They were married at Aston Church.

*

In April Lord Cranstoun came to Birmingham, with an introduction to my Father, who asked him to dinner. He was a very pleasant young man, but had come on purpose to make love to Miss Ryland, then about sixteen years old and known to be a great heiress. Lord Cranstoun asked my Father to get him permission to have the Canal Company's boat, as he wished to invite a large party to go and see the Dudley Caves, and asked us to go. My Father got him the boat, but declined the invitation for us and, hearing why Lord Cranstoun had come, he gave Mr. Ryland a hint, who refused to go also, and took his family to London. Lord Cranstoun followed them and, watching Mr. and Mrs. Ryland out, knocked at the door and asked to see Miss Ryland. Being told she was not at home, he pushed by the servant, saying he had seen her at the window. He rushed upstairs, found a young lady in the drawing room, and began to propose to her, when she stopped him, saying in broken English that she was the French governess.

James and Lucy came to see us after their honeymoon in Wales, and then settled in their house at Smethwick Grove, about a mile from Birmingham. In May my mother, Emma, and some of the maids went to Leamington to unpack and get the house in Lansdowne Place ready for us.

In May there was great excitement and monster radical meetings about the Reform Bill, which at last was passed by the House of Lords, and received the King's assent early in June.

Chapter 6

Leamington (1832 - 1838)

On 26th. May, 1832, my Father and I left the Larches for Leamington. Our terrier, when he saw us get into the pony carriage, seemed to know we should not return and jumped in, which he had never done before; he was in the habit of barking at everyone up the Drive and down the Drive. When he got to Leamington, he was quite silent for a day or two, and then seemed to know what belonged to us and began barking at everyone going up and down the area.

Leamington was then a smaller place, no houses before or behind us. The principal families lived on the Parade. The Society was very good: many of the best Scotch, Irish, and English families came for the winter, for hunting, and to be under Dr. Jephson, who was then in full practice, having a world-wide reputation. He had often twenty patients at a time at the Regent Hotel. His manners were abrupt, but he was a most kind and liberal man. If a poor clergyman consulted him, and the Doctor saw rest and change would do him good, he would pay for a curate and send him to the sea, and the same with over-worked governesses; he would never take a fee from them, but attended them as long as they required it. He was the making of Leamington, and building went on in every direction, to be filled with patients as soon as finished.

When we first came to Leamington, there were only two butchers, two fish shops, and three mercers.

Lady Katherine Howard (the Earl of Wicklow's sister), Lady Eastnor, and Lady Farnham were Queens of Leamington. No one could get on in Society unless visited by at least one of these ladies, and as they were very particular to visit no questionable person, the

Society was very good and pleasant – many evening parties, ending in a dance, nothing extravagant, but sociable.

We knew the Swinfin family, who introduced us to all the best families, and this summer Mr. and Mrs. Wood came to live at Leamington, with their niece Charlotte Wood, who had just left school. Mrs. Wood was a Miss Ryle, sister to my Aunt Lady Darwin, so we became very intimate. Charlotte used to walk with us and go with us to parties, and was like another sister.

Early in June my Grandfather Galton, who had been failing for some time, became much worse, and on the 10th he took to his bed. On the 13th. my Father took me to Dudson, as I had promised my Aunt I would come to her then. My Father stayed two nights but was then obliged to go home, as the asthma might come on at any moment, which it did a day or two later. I saw my Grandfather, who took leave of me, and on the 10th. June, the day after his seventy-ninth birthday, he died calmly in the evening. My Aunt took me to see him after his death, the first time I had seen a dead person who was grown up. He was buried in the Quakers' burial ground on the 26th., my Uncle Hubert the only son present, as my Father was laid up, and my Uncle Howard was abroad. Mr. Moilliet and his son James, Mr. James, James Lloyd, and Mr. Cadbury attended the funeral, which was quite plain, being Quaker, no plumes or hatbands. Many carriages followed: Dr. John Johnstone's, Mrs. Watt's, and others.

At my Grandfather's death, my Father came into a good deal of property entailed on him by his grandfather, besides what his father left him, which with what he had before was about £120,000. My two uncles were also well provided for by their father. Of course this addition of more than double made a great difference to us; my Father increased our allowances and we had more servants.

I stayed with my Aunt about three weeks and then returned home, and found Francis home from Boulogne.

*

We were invited to a small evening party to be introduced to Lady Katherine Howard, who received us politely but with great dignity. In the course of the evening she asked us if we were any relation to Mr. Darwin Galton, who was with a tutor at Geneva. On hearing he was our brother, all form vanished, she shook our hands and hoped to call and see more of us, who had such a delightful brother! Lady Katherine was terribly deformed; Mrs. Minchin and three Miss Budgens lived with her. Darwin, who was always kind to old or "unprotected" people, had paid great attention to Lady Katherine, handing her to her carriage, getting the old ladies negus and cakes at Geneva parties, so that they were quite fond of him and were delighted he was coming to us in a short time.

Two other old ladies called upon us, hearing Darwin was our brother, to whom they said they were under the greatest obligations. It turned out they were at Geneva, and Darwin took one of them in a car (now called a toboggan) down the Russian Mountain. On arriving at the bottom, the lady was missing, having fallen out. Darwin picked her up and (as she was hurt and could not walk) carried her to the Hotel and up three pairs of stairs to her room, so no wonder they were grateful!

*

In the middle of August my Father took Emma and me in our pony carriage to Bath, where we stayed two days to see the Miss Fourniers, and then on to Glastonbury, as my Father and Uncle Hubert (who joined us there) wished to see the farms now belonging to them. We saw the Tor and the beautiful Abbey, while the gentlemen went over some property at Meare. We greatly enjoyed visiting the farmers, who gave us apricot tart and clotted cream in abundance. Our amusement was to see our Uncle's horror at our venturing to eat fruit, for fear of cholera; he carried brandy with him for fear of an attack. From Edymead we went to Loxton (Somerset), the bells ringing us in there and at High Ham. At Loxton we visited the Cheddar Cliffs and Caves. Then to Clevedon for a night, a pretty little place, but so deserted we could hardly get anything to eat. From there to Yatton, Bristol, and Chepstow, where we saw the castle, Tintern Abbey, Ross, and from thence to Cheltenham and home – a most enjoyable trip indeed.

*

Amongst many with whom we got acquainted was Sir Arthur de Capel Brooke; we had met him at the Gurneys, and we renewed our acquaintance when he came to Leamington. He had travelled a good deal and had written a book of his travels in Norway. He was a rather silent and reserved man: he had lost his right arm by a gun accident when shooting game, but wrote and ate so well with his left hand one scarcely observed it. When he came to Leamington, there was a rush to get his book of travels from the Library, but the old ladies were much shocked at a suggestion in the book that, as there were so many more women than men, he thought a man should be allowed two wives. He was a kind man and did much good among the poor.

This spring (1832) the cholera broke out all over the country and numbers died from it. It would attack every house on one side of a street and none on the other. The poor and dirty suffered most; Leamington escaped, and we were told that some other towns with salt springs were free from it. In the Black Country it was terrible: cartloads of coffins were continually going from Birmingham to Walsall and Wednesbury for the dead, and at Bilston there were so many orphans left that an Orphan Establishment was set up to receive them. When winter came on, the cholera gradually declined and left the country. As it was very bad in Worcester, the Worcester Yeomanry came to Warwick for their week's training, and it was a very pretty sight on the race ground: the scarlet uniforms of the Worcesters and the light blue of the Warwickshire Yeomanry who kept the ground. We knew many of them, and my Mother invited them to a little dance at our house.

*

On the 12th October, *H.M.S. Southampton* arrived at Portsmouth from the East Indies. Erasmus wrote that the ship was ordered off to the Schelde [presumably to take part in the Anglo-French operations against Holland during the establishment of Belgian independence?] so that he could not get leave to come to us. My Father and Mother at once decided to go to the Isle of Wight to see him, and on the 18th. we went to Ryde. As we drove through Portsmouth on our way to the packet, the carriage was stopped by a smart young officer, very sun-browned, who said he was Erasmus. He was so altered, from having been very fair and stooping to being so upright and tanned, it was some minutes before we could feel it was himself, and very pleased we were to see him. He got leave to stay a day or two with us.

Our cousins the Foxes were in the Isle of Wight, and we made many expeditions to the dockyard, *H.M.S. Victory*, and went round the Isle of Wight, which then took three days to do, seeing all the sights on the way. (I wonder if they still have a donkey at Carisbrooke Castle to trot inside a large wheel to bring up the water out of a well? The donkey always knew the moment he was to stop and get out.) What was most interesting was to see our fine fleet of men of war-ships, collecting to go up the Schelde, and to hear each ship, as she came to Spithead, salute the Fort at Portsmouth. A few days after, a large fleet of French men-of-war arrived which, after saluting, took their station near ours – the first time the two fleets had met as friends. Every politeness was shown them. We could not but be amused at the differences of the two nations. A French boat landed at Ryde – two of the sailors began waltzing, and there was none of the smartness and precision in their operations on deck.

Erasmus was with us on leave and was taking a long walk with us on 1st. November when, looking towards the sea, he saw the Blue Peter flag on the *Southampton*, showing she was going off, and before he could get back, he saw the English and French fleet sail off to the Downs. It was a grand sight! Erasmus wished us good-bye and hurried off by coach to join his ship at the Downs. He had not been on board long before a flash of lightning struck the *Southampton* and set her on fire. There was only one flash, but it fired off two cannons, and one ball was fused in so curious a manner it was sent to the British Museum. A lieutenant on board had been much laughed at for having a bell put in his cabin, which he could ring for one of the sailors, and that bell saved the ship. The mast which was struck went straight into the powder room, but this bell wire drew the lightning off to the cabin, part of which was much injured. Two men were blinded for a time. Both French and English ships sent boats to help, and the flames were soon put out, but it was a providential escape. After Erasmus went, we left Ryde and returned to Leamington.

*

All the best families called upon us. Old Mr. and Mrs. Gladstone came next door to us for the winter. Their son was Mr. W. Gladstone, afterwards Prime Minister; he was a young man then, but was thought very clever. We knew the old people well; they were quiet, unpretending, clear-headed people, proud of their son's talents. Mr. W. Gladstone came to see them for a short time and dined at our house.

Mrs. Kemble, widow of John Kemble*, lived on the upper parade; she was an old person, but did most beautiful work. She knew all the great people in London, and what was going on in Parliament and elsewhere, and was very agreeable, though her language was sometimes too forcible for a lady. Her man-servant, who had been with her for many years, was pronounced by all the ladies the best maker of negus.

Among others who called upon us in 1833-34 were Dr. and Mrs. Jephson. His was a remarkable career. He was a poor boy, employed in sweeping out a chemist's shop and running errands. He was very observant, and he and one of the apprentices amused themselves on the sly, trying chemical experiments, in one of which Dr. Jephson blew two of his fingers off. When he had been some time there, picking up all he could, his master was sent for to an invalid, but being out of the way, Jephson went instead, cured the patient, and his career began. He became partner to a chemist, I think in Leamington. He was in the height of his fame when we came to live at Leamington. He had an abrupt manner, and insisted on obedience from his patients. His success lay in dieting: no sweets, vegetables, or made dishes, just mutton chops and boiled rice, and plenty of exercise. I have amusing lines on the subject, written by a patient. He used to take patients a drive with him and then, to their dismay, set them

**John Kemble (1757-1823), actor and manager, and brother of Mrs Siddons. Mrs Kemble's death is referred to on p. 155.*

down a mile away to walk home!

He was a kind and liberal man, though coarse in his appearance, and rough in his manner. Every morning early, he saw the poor gratis, and gave the same attention to them as he did to a Duchess. One morning a butler with a watch-chain dangling at his waistcoat appeared. The Doctor prescribed and then put out his hand for a fee. The butler said he thought there was nothing to pay if he came at that time. The Doctor replied, "If you can afford a gold watch-chain, you can afford to pay your doctor."

Many amusing tales were told of Dr. Jephson which I have not room for. I remember one day when we were dining at Colonel Steward's with a large party, when a lady, newly arrived in the town, observed: "I have resolved on two things that I will not do while I am here – I will not drink the waters, and I will not consult that Quack." Here Colonel Steward, with great presence of mind, called out, "Dr. Jephson, may I have the pleasure of taking wine with you?" to the relief of all present. Dr. Jephson had not had a regular medical education, so at first was called a quack by those who did not know him. He quite made Leamington, gave most liberally to the Hospital and to set up the College, and to everything useful in the place. If he were walking with a Duke or a Duchess, and met a poor man whom he knew in former days, he would stop and speak to him. He married Miss Geldart and had one child, who died at six months old, and we were told that the child had presents to last him till he grew up. Some years before he died he became quite blind, which must have been a severe trial. He went with some other gentlemen to London to present a petition to the Queen, and returned with her permission that the town should be called "Royal Leamington Spa."

Mr. and Mrs. Wood and their niece Charlotte Wood came at this time to live in Leamington. Charlotte's eldest brother John Ryle Wood was tutor to Prince George of Cambridge, and when Mr. John Wood came to visit his Uncle at Leamington, the young Prince sent his Latin exercise every day to him. When John Wood left the Prince, he became Chaplain to King William and Queen Adelaide for some years and then Canon of Worcester. He married first Miss Winnington Ingram who died at her confinement. He married secondly Miss

Child. His son is married and lives in Worcestershire.

Mr. and Mrs. Ryland and their daughter came to Leamington this winter. Miss Ryland was an amiable, generous, unselfish girl of seventeen, highly accomplished, having had the best masters. When she came out, she was persecuted by fortune hunters and penniless elder sons. Three noblemen proposed to her in one fortnight, to our knowledge; one had the impudence to send his man of business to say that he wanted a fortune, and she could get a title by marrying him. One regiment stationed at Coventry proposed to her, from the Colonel to the Cornet. The poor girl used to beg us to let her sit behind us at a ball, to escape being asked to dance, and often wished she had a brother and was not an heiress. When Miss Ryland came into her fortune, she was most liberal and did immense good in an unostentatious manner, often giving large sums to a charity and having her name put down as "A Friend". She gave two parks in Birmingham for the recreation of all classes – they were prettily laid out, and much enjoyed.

*

On 23rd. February, 1834, my brothers were anxious to have a barrel of oysters; so it was agreed we should have an early dinner, with the oysters at seven o'clock in the dining room. The next morning, Sunday, I observed the marks of men's shoes in my bedroom, and my yellow case tampered with, but nothing taken. It then appeared that footsteps were seen on the stairs, and drawers injured by chisel marks, but as nothing was missing we went to Church. On our return, my Mother went to her room, where there had been no marks, looked in the drawer where she kept her diamonds, and found they were gone. The robbery must have been done between seven and eight o'clock, while we were downstairs, and the thieves must have known that we were out of the way at that time, and on that day. In those days there were only constables – no police – and the constable knew little of his business. The servants were examined, but were offended and gave little help. We remarked afterwards that, when we were downstairs, the footman waited and the butler did not appear till my

Mother asked where he was. It was evident to us from things that transpired afterwards that the butler had been bribed by the thieves, who had got in through the next house, which was empty, through the attic windows, and the butler had stood on the staircase to give warning in case we came upstairs. Of course we heard nothing of the diamonds. As we knew that the thieves must have had help from one or other of the servants, though we could not fix it on anyone, we felt very uncomfortable with them. We did not like to injure them by discharging them all at once; so we kept them on and after some weeks parted gradually with them all.

*

In March my Aunt Sophia, to our surprise, married Mr. Charles Brewin – a marriage totally beneath her in every way, and greatly disliked by the family. He was my Grandfather's steward for many years. He made her a good husband, and she always expressed herself as most happy with him.

I went to stay with my sister Lucy at Smethwick Grove [Birmingham], and on the third of May she was confined of Amy (afterwards Mrs. Biggs). I was very proud of my little niece.

About the middle of May, my Father and Emma took me in our pony carriage on a delightful tour to Manchester, where we saw a cotton manufactory, then to Liverpool by the railway – then the only one in the country*, where we saw the docks, then to Chester, where we walked round the ramparts, saw Eaton Hall, then to Conway and to Bangor to see the chain bridge, then the great wonder of the world. We spent two days at Capel Curig Inn and were delighted with a blind harper who gave me some Welsh tunes. We went up Snowdon – a lovely warm day and the view perfectly clear from the top, which it seldom is – it took us six hours. From there we went to Beddgelert, where of course we visited Gellert's grave. We visited Carnarvon Castle, Dolgelly, and then on ponies to the top of Cader Idris – a lovely clear day. While on the top of the mountains we distinctly heard the

**Elizabeth Anne does not mention the older Stockton and Darlington Railway, probably because it was not built to carry passengers.*

Church bells of Dolgelly, six miles off, I think. The guide said he had never heard them before from that place, and that no one would believe he had heard them. We also saw the house where Owen Glendower accepted the crown of Wales in 1422. From thence we went to Aberystwith, where we found my Mother and Adele at Coburg house. Adele and I began to learn the Welsh language from a Mr. Edwards, a curate to Mr. Hughes of Llanbadarn; the Welsh were highly flattered at hearing we were learning their language.

While we were at Aberystwith, a new Church was opened, and we went to the opening, It was a fine day, with a bright sun, and as no blinds had been put up, the heat came straight down upon our heads – when, with one consent, at the same moment, up went everybody's parasol. It was a curious sight in a Church, but it saved us from sun-stroke. We remained at Aberystwith till my Father had recovered from the asthma, which we thought he suffered less from at the sea-side, and on the 29th July we returned to Leamington, stopping to see Worcester Cathedral and the china manufactory on the way.

*

In April I went to my sister Lucy at Smethwick, and she was confined on the ninth of Adele (later Mrs. Cameron Galton).

I do not think I have mentioned that in 1833, when the cholera ceased, influenza began and carried off more people than the cholera had done. It was an extraordinary visitation, whole families down at once. A gentleman calling on a nobleman in London was surprised at the said nobleman opening the door. He explained, "twenty-nine are in bed, and the thirtieth is waiting upon them, so I have to attend the door."

*

My sister Mrs. Moilliet had a bad illness after her third confinement, and it was settled that she and her children should join us at Weymouth, where we were going. My Father, Emma, and I went in our little pony carriage, and my Mother and Adele posted in our closed carriage. We took our riding horses, which made it very pleasant. It was interesting how well even then King George III and his family were remembered and spoken of with affection. Many lodging houses boasted of a chair or table that had been in the King's house. There was a figure of the King on horseback, cut out in chalk, on the side of the hill near Weymouth, which they used to point at and say, "The King is going from Weymouth," and so it was, for the King never returned after. There were several pretty villages in the neighbourhood, and one day we rode to a hamlet called Galton, from where our family originally came.

One day my Father and Emma rode to Dorchester and passed the barracks where the soldiers were at drill. In a moment, Emma's horse dashed into the barracks and took his place in the line, to Emma's horror. One of the officers came to her assistance and at once recognised the horse as having belonged to Captain Vivian, who had been quartered some time in Dorsetshire.

The bathing was very good, and we could get out some way in the sea without being too deep; so Emma and I determined to learn to swim, and we promised the bathing women a pound of tea each if they would hold us up till we could go loose, and we soon managed to swim tolerably well.

*

About this time we heard of a terrible accident that had befallen Erasmus in Malta, where his ship, *H.M.S. Favourite*, Captain Rodney Mundy, was stationed. Erasmus and Mr. King (one of the lieutenants) were asked to carry a bag of money to some place near, and set off on horseback. They met a sailor, who offered to carry the bag for Erasmus. Soon after, they came to a narrow road between two low walls, when out jumped three men and caught hold of the horses. One man hit Erasmus so violent a blow on the head, it was thought he was killed. Mr. King was a powerful man and kept the men from doing him much harm, and fortunately some people came by and the thieves were taken up and punished. Erasmus was unconscious for many hours, and was a long time in the hospital before he could rejoin his ship, and felt the consequences for a long time after.

*

In September, 1834, my Father allowed us to have a little school for poor children, chiefly for Adele's pleasure, as she could enter into so few amusements. He built a room for it next door to our stables, and we took forty little girls. The children of the poor were shamefully neglected; the only Church of England school was the National School, so badly managed no one liked to send their girls to it.

My sister Adele had a wonderful power of teaching and influencing those about her. She taught them to act on principle, and it was wonderful how well they managed themselves and how well they turned out. The girls were taught reading, writing, arithmetic, sewing, marking, and cutting out. We also taught them to plait straw and make their own bonnets. When they were old enough to go into service, our Mother allowed us to have the girls in the house for a fortnight, to learn under our maids, who took great pride in their pupils and turned them out tidy little servants. My Mother made it a condition that there was to be no noise; the children came and went quietly and were not to speak till out of Guy's Street, so no one could complain of them.

Two or three years after, we persuaded Mrs. Lawton of Cheshire, Mrs. Young, and two or three of our friends to set up a similar school, and as at that time many of our girls were ready to leave, Adele determined to fill their places with boys, who were quite neglected in the town. It was marvellous, the power Adele had over them: they would do anything for "Miss Adele." She told them she had a weak spine and was obliged to lie down and therefore must trust them to be good. Many clergymen begged to see the school and marvelled how she kept them in such good discipline. I remember once they had done something very wrong (I think they had spoken in Guy's Street); Adele spoke to them in much sorrow and told them to fix on their own punishment. I forget what it was exactly – it was to stand or lie down a certain time in a most uncomfortable position – and my sister told me she was in agony the whole time for fear anyone would call to see the school then, for they would look upon her as a slave-driver. She never missed being in school every day and had a very good governess, Miss Betts, who was a model of propriety, to help her. Everyone took a kind interest in the school; Mr. Pritchard our surgeon vaccinated them all when small-pox was about; the chemist offered us medicines for them, and Mr. Lincoln Galton who was curate at the Episcopal Chapel, allowed the children to sit on the steps to the Communion Table, and said they were an example to the congregation, they were so quiet and attentive.

On May Day, the whole school dressed up and went round the town together singing – quite a pretty sight – and then had a good tea, bought with what they had got.

My sister Emma had a class of boys every Sunday evening. Many of the principal shopkeepers had been among Adele's and Emma's pupils. More than once in after years, when Adele has gone into a shop at the sea-side, and once in Paris, the Master after looking at her has said, "Are you not Miss Adele?" and has been so pleased to see her, telling her how well he had got on, all owing to her teaching.

When the boys were ready for service, if they wished to go into a stable they were put under our groom for a fortnight, or if as a page they were put under our footman, and it was wonderful how much they learnt in so short a time. We kept a little savings bank in the school, and every Monday they brought us what they liked, and I made little savings bank books for them to keep. It taught them all to save, and when they wanted money out for shoes or anything, they could draw it out without any trouble. When we had girls in the school they did a great deal of work, and every six months we had a sale of it to the mothers only at the price the material cost – no charge for making. It was much liked, and everything was bought up.

It was curious in those days, and especially when we lived at the Larches, the objection there was to teaching girls to write. It was constantly said to us: "What is the use of them learning to write? They will only be writing love letters, &c., &c." Many clergy set their faces against it.

*

About this time my Uncle Howard Galton (of Hadzor), who had been in Italy, invited a clever young man, Signor Roos, a painter and decorator, to come to England to get employment. Uncle Howard asked our Father to let Signor Roos paint our ceilings, as so many would see them, and it would be an introduction to those with large houses who visited Leamington. He painted them in beautiful designs and got many orders.

*

[Here follows a long list of people, mostly very "agreeable," who visited Leamington in 1834-1835. Perhaps the only family worth mentioning are the Whelers of Leamington Hastings, for reasons which will become apparent later.]

In January 1835 old Mrs. Darwin of Osmaston died at a great age, eighty-nine. She was the widow of William Alvey Darwin, Brother of my Grandfather Dr. Erasmus Darwin. She was Mother to Mrs. Fox, and soon after her death Mr. and Mrs. Fox left Osmaston, and at length settled in London, where they died some years after. Before going to London they were for a short time at a house they took at Elstree, Hertfordshire, where I visited them, before and after my marriage.

At this time my Brother Francis, now thirteen years old, went to King Edward's School at Birmingham, to be under Dr. Jeune, who had recently been appointed Head Master. He was the son of Jersey parents of no family, but very clever and made his way, took high honours at College, became Head Master of the School in Birmingham, and eventually Bishop of Peterborough. Soon after Francis went, Scarlet Fever broke out in the School, and little Johnny Booth, Dr. Booth's only son by his first wife, died of it, to the great sorrow of his Father and my Aunt, who was a kind Mother to him.

In February Mr. Alfred Arkwright, son of Peter Arkwright, came to visit us. He had been at Geneva in the same Pension as Darwin, where they went to learn French. He and Darwin were great friends, and Darwin went some time after to visit the Arkwrights near Matlock, where he became acquainted with Fanny, his second wife.

In April, 1835, Mrs. Young invited us to meet Sir John and Lady

Franklin* who were staying with her, and we little thought how soon he and his crew would be lost. He was a very pleasant, sailor-like man.

In August, we heard that two of the Miss Amphlets, who lived near Hadzor, were come to Miss Walker's school, and we invited them to spend an afternoon with us. They were so reserved we could not get on, till Darwin luckily called and took them in hand. He got out of them, that they had had a grand ball on Miss Walker's birthday, when all former pupils in the neighbourhood were invited; it was a fancy dress ball to surprise Miss Walker. Darwin asked, "And what were the fancy dresses?" "Oh, officers," laconically answered the young ladies. It appeared the young ladies had borrowed from brothers and cousins, and were very pleased with their appearance in regimentals. The ball went merrily on for some time, when the conservatory door opened slowly, and in walked a ghost, waving his arms as he walked through the frightened guests, through the passage, and out at the other door. The consternation was dreadful – the Lancers fainted, the Guards screamed, and the Hussars ran behind the window curtains. The mistresses did all they could to recover them, and had just succeeded in persuading them to resume dancing, when again the ghost appeared. Mrs. Torre (the dancing mistress) tried to seize him, but in vain. Again the effect was terrible, and neither officers nor ladies had the nerve to go on. The ball was stopped, and Miss Stubbs had to sit up all night, they were too frightened to be left alone. The next day Mrs. Torre went to all the fly men and insisted on knowing who had driven a ghost to Miss Walker's. At last a man confessed that he had taken Mr. Middleton, the surgeon's brother, a lad of sixteen whose sisters were gone to the ball, and that he was the ghost. She then called upon Mr. Middleton and desired that his brother might go at once to the school, and while there show himself as a ghost, and then in their presence show himself shorn of his ghostly disguises.

In September my Father and I rode to Berkswell to see the railway which was being built from Birmingham to London. My Father was much interested watching its progress. In those days most

**Sir John Franklin (1786-1847), discoverer of the Northwest Passage, lost with all his men in the polar ice in HMS Erebus and Terror.*

landowners set their faces against railways and objected to their going through their property. People were set to watch night and day, to warn off anyone who came to measure out the grounds – but in vain, the railways were carried through in spite of the owners of the land, who were however paid considerably more than the land was worth. Many towns objected to railways, and Worcester, Gloucester, and others gained their point, much to their sorrow some years after, when they found the inconvenience so great that they went to the expense of making a line from their city to the branch line. The owners of property, too, in time discovered that railway companies gave such liberal compensation, and the convenience of having a station near was so great, they were much pleased when it went through their ground.

About this time our clergyman made himself very disagreeable to us. He set his face against our school, as he did against anything for good done in the Parish, refused to give the children seats in the Church, and was so angry he cut us and would not speak to us. We were much amused some time after: Adele, who had had the quarrel with him, went with my Father to dine at Mr. Russell's. When dinner was announced, Mr. Russell, who did not know anything about it, to Adele's dismay asked the clergyman to take her down to dinner. He did so, and she wondered what would happen: however, he talked to her all dinner just as if nothing had occurred. The next day he happened to meet her, and cut her as before!

In December we heard that Mrs. Schimmelpenninck (cf. p.5) had arrived in Leamington to consult Dr. Jephson. As all intercourse had ceased between her and her family for twenty-five years, owing to her unfortunate habit of mischief-making and the misery she consequently caused, my Father did not wish to renew it, and we were therefore glad when, some weeks after, she left.

*

In February, 1836, after paying my sister Lucy and my Aunt Booth visits, I went to stay with my Aunt Mrs. Gurney in London, where I met my Uncle, Captain Barclay Allardice (cf. p.5), the famous pedestrian. I rose much in his estimation, because I remembered which horse had won in the steeplechase the day before in Leamington. He was thorough Scotch and very good-natured to us. He introduced me to Mr. Apperley, who wrote "Nimrod," and tried to impress upon me that I should be very proud of the acquaintance. Margaret Barclay was his only child, and was chiefly brought up by my Aunt Gurney.

In April, Mr. Samuel Gurney's second daughter, Catherine, was married to her cousin, Edward North Buxton. As Samuel Gurney could not countenance the marriage of his daughter to a husband of the Church of England, she and her brother and sister came early to St. James's Square, and my Aunt Mrs. Gurney took her to Church and acted mother. As there are two Mary-le-Bone Churches, the bride went to the wrong one and the bridegroom to the other, and the mistake was only found out just in time for the marriage to take place. They then all returned to Ham House, where her father and mother received them.

My Aunt took me to see the British and Foreign School for the poor, as I was commissioned to choose a Governess for my Aunt Howard's school at Oddingley, a heathen village near Hadzor. I was to be sure to choose a very plain one for the post, and the matron sent me one to see, the very plainest woman I think I ever saw. She answered admirably and was many years at Oddingley. There were two black African girls in the British and Foreign School, for whom my Aunt paid. The school was very well taught.

In May, Erasmus returned to England from the Mediterranean. My Father and Emma came to London and took me with them to Deptford and over Greenwich Hospital, where we saw one thousand nine hundred men at dinner.

On 27th. July, 1836, my sister Mrs. Moilliet was confined of twin boys*, and I went off at once to her. They were so exactly alike we never could tell one from the other, and when anyone looked at them, they would say "I'm James," or "I'm Lewis." Even then, their mother

**The twins were James Keir Moilliet (1836-1906), general manager of John Lewis Moilliet and Sons, Bankers, at the time of their amalgamation with Lloyds Bank in 1865, and John Lewis Moilliet (III), Rector of Abberley from 1865-1904, who died in 1909.*

sometimes mistook them. I stayed with my sister till she recovered, and on 15th. August my Father, Adele, Emma, and I set off to London.

*

On 19th. August we embarked on board a steamer at nine in the evening and slept in the cabin. The ship sailed at two in the morning, and we got to Ostend at 4 p.m. The next day, Sunday, we went to the English Church and walked about on the sands. King Leopold arrived the day before, and we met him and the Queen walking quietly about like anyone else. He was a fine looking man.

The next day we went by canal boat, drawn by four horses, to Bruges, where we saw all the sights in the town, and the following day on to Ghent, by canal. One of the passengers was a nun, who soon made friends with Adele. She amused us much at dinner. Every dish that was offered to her, she helped herself to liberally, and the passengers amused themselves by handing dish after dish to her, and she never refused and never seemed at all overdone with eating. She was going to the Convent at Ghent. We went to see her Convent the next day, and to the Cathedral, and all that was to be seen.

From Ghent we went by steamboat to Antwerp. Here we saw all that was interesting – and much there was: Cathedral, paintings, the Palace at Laeken, and then on to Brussels, where we stayed a few days.

On Monday, 29th. August, my Father, Emma, and I set off early to Waterloo and Mont St. Jean. We got a Belgian guide, the English one unfortunately being engaged. We saw Hougoumont, orchard and wall, and were deeply interested in every part. We saw where the English stood and where the French, La Haye Sainte, &c., &c., and then to the house at Waterloo where the Duke of Wellington wrote his despatch. The ground was much altered, so much having been used to make a mound for the Prince of Orange's Monument, which was a pity. Of course I picked up relics. The next day we spent seeing the palaces and sights in Brussels.

We went again on 1st. September to the field of Waterloo, as we wished to go over it again with the English guide, Sergeant-Major Cotton, who gave us an excellent account of the whole battle. He mentioned how much the Duke cheered the men when he was among them, making such observations as "Well, my good fellows, this is hard pounding, but we'll see who can pound longest." My Father bought a good plan of the battle, which I still have, and an interesting account of it, which he and I used to read every 18th. June, and which I continue. We returned to Brussels and drove about to see all the sights. We wanted to go to some place – I forget where – and my Father told the postillion to take us. He demurred and observed, "It is a *diable* of a road." My Father replied, "And how much more would make it an angel of a road?" The man laughed and mentioned a franc or two more, and took us. We stayed a few days in Brussels; there was so much to see: sculpture, lace-making, paintings, &c. On 3rd. September, having spent our money, we left Brussels by railroad to Antwerp, where we again stayed a few days sightseeing, and spending what money we had left upon collars and cuffs, beautifully embroidered. On 7th. September we left Antwerp in a steam packet at eleven in the morning, and on the 8th. landed at Gravesend, passed our luggage at the Custom House, and then went by another steamer to Margate, a pouring wet day. [After visits to Ramsgate, Walmer and Chatham, they returned home.]

*

The winter of 1836-1837 was a very pleasant one. [Here follow more lists of "agreeable," if insignificant people who wintered in Leamington]. After Erasmus passed his examination at Woolwich, he told my Father he wished to leave the Navy, which we were very sorry for, but he had been much injured by the attack of thieves at Malta, and would not have been able to go to any hot climate, so it was settled he should go to Scotland and learn farming, and then settle down at Loxton. He went for a year to Mr. Robson, who had a large farm in the South of Scotland.

We saw much this winter and spring of the Skenes and Camerons. Miss Cameron was a very superior person, devoted to everything of her clan. She took great pains to find out their proper tartan. After the Culloden battle, the Scotch were forbidden to wear tartan, and many were difficult to find. She found theirs, and we bought shawls of the Cameron Tartan*, which is a very pretty one. I collected all she could tell me of the Cameron family, and I drew out a genealogy which pleased her so much I copied one for her, and I was much amused to find some years after that it had been photographed and copies given to all the members of the Clan. They were all very agreeable, friendly, and cousinly people.

In May of 1837 there were great rejoicings when the Princess Victoria came of age, eighteen. A good dinner was given in the Jephson Gardens to two thousand people, and tea and cakes to one thousand children. Our little school marched into the Gardens with a large flag and had a table to themselves. It was a pretty sight, and we all went to see it; it began and ended with the National Anthem.

A grand ball was given in London to the Princess, at which the King and Queen were to have been present, but King William was beginning then to suffer from his last illness and could not go. All felt that the young Princess would shortly be called to the throne.

*

On 29th. May we all went to London to an hotel for two or three days, to see our friends the Gurneys and Horners and many others in Town, and on 2nd. June we arrived at Worthing, where we found our old friend Admiral Griffiths. We took our horses with us, and Emma and I rode in turns with my Father to all the interesting places in the neighbourhood.

On 20th. June, King William died, and our young Princess became Queen. It was said that the last sign of consciousness King William made was when the Union Jack, which the Duke of Wellington sent every 18th. June, was laid on his bed He touched it and said, "It was a glorious victory." There was a prophecy said to be written in an old

**Elizabeth Anne and her family were entitled to wear this tartan by virtue of their descent from Une, the daughter of Sir Ewan Cameron of Lochiel. At least three of the male Galtons had "Cameron" as a Christian name.*

Almanac of 1730 which ran:

"By the power to search the great ways of Heaven
In one thousand eight-hundred and thirty-seven
Will the year pass by without any spring,
And on England's throne shall not sit a King."

Of course the interest in the young Queen was very great, and there was a great rush for the newspapers to read what she was doing, and how she managed, and all spoke in the highest terms of her propriety of manner, her self-possession, and her good feeling. As we were from home, we saw none of the rejoicings at her accession.

At Worthing the vegetation grows down to the sea, the sands were good, and as the sea went down a long way, at low tide the jog down in the very crazy bathing machines was terrible! We dare not undress till we came to the sea, expecting the machine to break down every minute. The spring tides brought up quantities of seaweed, which were left and smelled very badly; after some time it was carted away and used as manure on the fields, but the smell made it very disagreeable when we rode out.

On 4th. July, 1837, the Birmingham and Liverpool Railway was opened. This became afterwards the London and North Western Railway of today.

*

Erasmus joined us, so we were a large party. (*See silhouette, p113.*)

*

In August this year Caroline Darwin of Shrewsbury married her cousin Josiah Wedgwood.

Early in September, Ferdinand Arkwright came to Leamington for the Races, and he and Erasmus went to them. A few days later, Erasmus became very ill, and three days afterwards he broke out with smallpox. He remembered that, at the Races, a woman begged of him and showed him her child covered with a rash. He had the smallpox very badly, and all the servants were vaccinated at once. My Mother and I, with the help of one manservant, nursed him, and everything was done to prevent infection. I had been re-vaccinated four years before and so was tolerably safe. When the crisis passed, Erasmus got well rapidly, but was much marked for a long time.

Emma and I went to pay a visit to Hadzor. We went to see the Oddingley School, which was doing well under the mistress I had chosen in London. We left Hadzor the 3rd. November after a very pleasant visit. We were much attached to my Aunt, who was only ten years older than myself. All her family were Unitarians, but after her marriage she became influenced by my Aunt Sophia Galton, and joined the Church. Some years after, she met some excellent members of the Plymouth Brethren, and joined their plain and simple worship. She was a most devoted, earnest Christian, and bore her many trials with true patience and submission. [The last of the Hadzor Galtons were Roman Catholics, and Hadzor Hall was for some years a Roman Catholic school, St Richard's College.]

*

Early in 1838, my Mother gave a large ball, and it was a very pleasant winter. Darwin went to visit his friend Alfred Arkwright near Matlock and fell in love with the third daughter, but as he was in no profession, Mr. Arkwright was not satisfied with his prospects. Fanny, however, became his second wife and was much beloved by us all.

In February my Aunt Mrs. Booth came to visit us. Her marriage was not a happy one, but she resolutely did her duty and bore her troubles with submission; her visits to us did her good. She and I walked out every morning before breakfast, and one morning we walked to Guy's Cliffe and back before nine o'clock. Dr. Booth considered early morning walks good for the health, and he and my Aunt used, summer and winter, to start off at five o'clock in the morning on foot for a couple of hours. He was a clever man, but very peculiar and absent, generally beginning with "Oh, de-ar, 'pon my word, Ha," and then answering your question.

*

In March, 1838, my Great-uncle Captain Barclay Allardice took lodgings in Leamington for the hunting. He dined nearly every day with us, and was very pleasant and kind to us young ones. He took great interest in Claverdon, and instructed my Father how to turn Paul's Piece into good grass land, which was done exactly as he recommended.* He was thoroughly Scotch in manner and speech, and always ready to talk of his exploits if we wished it, but not unless. One day he told us that, when in the Army, he had volunteered to be tied to the sails of a windmill and to whirl around, I think three times, adding "I nearly lost my senses the last round." My Father, in his droll, quiet way, answered, "I think you must have lost your senses before you went up." This delighted my Uncle so much, he repeated it to everyone.

We had a large dinner party one day to meet him, and he was drawn out to tell of his wonderful exploits. I remember how badly the servants waited that day, all too intent upon listening to think of their duties. He told us when he undertook to walk a thousand miles in a thousand hours, he thought it would be so easily done that he did it without previous training, The last few days he suffered much, his legs swollen, and he finished with difficulty. When it was over, he made a good meal and slept fourteen or sixteen hours, and got up quite well and walked about for some hours. A day or two after, he went off on the Walcheren expedition, and though he took no precautions was one of the few who escaped fever. He said he was so thin from the walk, there was nothing to take the fever. He remained till the end of the month and then left.

**Although Claverdon, Warwickshire, was Samuel Tertius Galton's main property, he seems to have spent very little of his life there. He could not have found a better agricultural advisor than Barclay Allardice, whose greatest accomplishments were in improving agricultural methods in Scotland, even though he is chiefly remembered for his spectacular feats of strength. The most famous was his 1000-mile walk at Newmarket from June 1st to July 12th, 1809, which he accomplished in 1000 hours, including all rests. According to The Times, over £100,000 was wagered on the outcome, and the walk was witnessed by many of the nobility and gentry, and a very large crowd of the lower orders,*

A family reunion in 1837: reading from left to right, Samuel Tertius Galton, Adele Galton, Erasmus Galton, Emma Galton and Elizabeth Anne Galton.

Claverdon, pictured in 1910

*

An interesting couple this winter was General Sabloukoff and his wife. He was a Russian, and I think she was also, but I am not sure. She was young looking, but her hair was snow white, which her husband was very proud of, and he often related how it happened. He was in the Army, fighting, and news was sent to his wife that he was killed. The account affected her so deeply that, when she got up next day, she found her hair quite white. Though her husband returned home safe, the hair never regained its natural colour.

Lady Maynard Hazelrigge had invited me to come and pay her a visit, which I accepted in the forlorn hope that, being in London, I might possibly be fortunate enough to get a ticket for the coronation. I went to her in April. The next day I called on my Aunt Gurney at St. James's Square, and she asked me to come to her when I left Lady Hazelrigge's. Miss Calcraft was staying with my Aunt, a very fashionable lady. Her brother Mr. Calcraft was Member of Parliament and had married one of the Duke of Manchester's daughters, with whom my Aunt was very intimate, I was told that Mr. Calcraft had been a thoughtless young man on religious subjects, and very worldly. He was staying in a country house with a large party of young people and was going with them to a picnic party, when just before they started he sprained his ankle severely and was obliged to remain at home on a sofa, unable to move. Just as the rest were hurrying off, he called to one of them and asked her to give him the novel which was on the table. In her haste she seized the book and tossed it to him. To his dismay, instead of an entertaining novel she had given him Wilberforce on Christianity; however, there was no help for it, he could not move, so he opened the book, soon became deeply interested, and from that time became a religious man.

I heard at this time that Emily Knight, who was Emily Moilliet, had married the Reverend Mr. Powys. She lived to a great age and had, I believe, three sons. [Among her numerous grandchildren were the writers John Cowper Powys, Theodore Francis Powys and Llewellyn Powys].

*

On 23rd April, Darwin came to Town for a few days. Lady Palgrave and Lady Isabella Wemyss came to stay a few days to go with my Aunt to the young Queen's Drawing Room. Lady Isabella, a charming woman, was sister to Lady Harriet Gurney and Lady-in-Waiting to the Dowager Queen Adelaide, and went therefore in deep mourning for King William. My Aunt was to present Lady Palgrave, who was very nervous about it. Sir Francis Palgrave* came to luncheon to go with them, and I was much amused to see his awkwardness with his sword, which he could not manage but stumbled over every minute. However, everything went off well, and he did not injure the Queen, as I feared.

Early in May Mr. Wharton Duff and his two daughters came to Town for the season. Their mother, Lady Ann Duff, had been a particular friend of my Aunt's, and she wished to do all she could for the girls, as the Duchess of Richmond (who would have chaperoned them) was too near her confinement to go out. They amused us much; they had never been away from home, where they were grand people, and were totally ignorant of the customs of Society. They thought they would be considered grand people in London and were quite offended one day, when they went shopping, that they were not allowed to carry away what they had bought without paying! They were amiable girls, and Miss Wodehouse and I did our best to instruct them in the ways of the world. They were to be presented at court and were dreadfully alarmed about it, the eldest saying, "I know I will faint" – and so she did, just as she entered the Throne Room. The Queen kindly sent word that she might consider herself presented.

Mr. Gurney gave a dinner to several clever men: Lord Aberdeen, Lord Braybrooke, Sir Gore Ouseley, Mr. Wynn (he and his brother were Members of Parliament; one had rather a blustering voice and the other a sharp voice, and they went by the names of Bubble and Squeak), Sir Thomas Phillips, Sir Francis Palgrave, Mr. Hallam, and sereral others – all celebrated men and members of the Antiquarian Society. Sir Thomas Phillips lived near Pershore in Worcestershire

**The historian, father of F.T. Palgrave of Golden Treasury fame.*

and had a wonderful collection of old manuscripts and missals – he lent me an old missal to copy. Mr. Pettigrew was an agreeable man and told us many anecdotes. He had been surgeon to the Duke of Kent and had vaccinated the young Queen. At this time he was Librarian to the Duke of Sussex, who gave him a large sum (I think two thousand a year) to buy valuable additions to his library. He said he often went down back streets to look at second-hand book stalls, and one day he saw an old Prayer Book, which he bought for two or three shillings, seeing to his delight that it had belonged to Charles I. He showed it to us, pointing out the King's marks and observations as to which parts were to be used in Scotland. Mr. Pettigrew took us to see a mummy unwrapped – not a pleasant sight, but one in which he was much interested. He gave me some wheat taken out of a mummy's coffin to sow, but it did not grow. [This disclaimer does much to confirm one's faith in Elizabeth Anne as an honest reporter!]

London now began to be very full, people from all quarters flocking in, and much gaiety going on.

The young Queen's birthday was kept on 17th. May, and we went to see the Guards on parade and hear their band. Mr. Wharton Duff took me with his daughters to walk in the Park, and we saw the Queen returning from the Drawing Room. In those days the Drawing Rooms were held in St. James's Palace, and much official business had to be done there, but this was done away with some years after, it was so inconvenient.

Another interesting sight we saw on this day was the last procession of Mail Coaches. The horses were decked with ribbons, the coachmen and guards were in their new crimson livery, and the coaches were full of their wives and friends, smartly dressed. All the Mail Coaches in London passed in order, one after another before the house of the Postmaster General, who at this time was Lord Lichfield. He lived a few doors from the Gurneys in St. James's Square, so we saw it all. His Lordship came out on the balcony, full dress, cocked hat, &c., and returned the salute as each Mail Coach went by. Railroads from London were now springing up, and mail coaches were not required. In the evening we drove out to see the illuminations. The next day my Aunt Gurney gave a grand ball, to which our friends who were in London were invited.

On 25th. May I left the Gurneys and went to stay with the Hubert Galtons in Portman Square, where my Uncle Howard arrived the next day. My Cousin Diana Galton was in very delicate health and unable to ride, and she lent me her horse. I had many delightful rides with my Uncle Howard in the Park, where we seemed to meet everyone we knew, all the world coming up for the Coronation, but alas! no hope of a ticket for me. The first time I rode in the Park, the horse went oddly after some time, and my Uncle said "Jump off at once," which I did. The horse was just going to faint; something in the saddle hurt it. Fortunately, my Aunt was driving and met us, and took me home in the carriage, and the horse was led back.

On 5th. June, to my sorrow, I left London with my Father and came home, all hopes for the Coronation being over, and Emma went in my place to stay with the Hubert Galtons. My Father and I went by the new railway as far as Denbigh Hall, then got out and went by coach to Rugby, the Kilby tunnel not being finished. We then went by railroad to Coventry, and by omnibus from Coventry to Leamington. We set off at half past nine and got home at seven o'clock.

On 19th. June, to my great joy, Emma wrote to tell me that the Hubert Galtons, hearing from her how eager I was to see the Coronation, asked me to return to them to see the Procession, for which they had tickets. Of course I accepted with delight. Adele and I settled about a proper banner for her schoolchildren, and their feast on that occasion, and I set off to London by coach with Miss Ryle. On 22nd. June, my Aunt Hubert gave a ball, and as I knew everyone, I enjoyed it much. My Aunt Gurney came to it, and I remember Emma sending her word not to come in her handsome yellow satin gown, because the chairs and sofas were covered with yellow.

Darwin came to London and took lodgings. We drove or rode every day in the park, Emma and I taking it in turns to ride Di's horse, and much we enjoyed it, meeting every day fresh friends just arrived. We also met the splendid equipages brought by the Ambassadors who were to take part in the Procession. That of the French Ambassador was most magnificent.

We also constantly met the young Queen and the Duchess of Kent driving and Queen Adelaide.

On 26th. June Francis came to London to stay with Darwin at his lodgings and spent most of the day with us in Portman Square. It was his first stay in London and we took him out every day sight-seeing. In the evening Uncle Howard and Darwin went to the Caledonian Ball dressed in the Yeomanry Uniform of their own county.

Chapter 7

The Coronation of Queen Victoria (1838)

[Miss Elizabeth Anne Galton to her parents, Mr and Mrs Samuel Tertius Galton, of Lansdowne Place, Leamington]

Portman Square, June 26th 1838

My dear Mama,

Our time is so fully occupied and we are in such a whirl of excitement that I really have not had a moment to write, and now I hardly know where to begin, and can only exclaim like Dr. Booth "Oh dear – 'pon my word." There certainly never was anything like a Coronation for variety and amusement, and my two Uncles and Aunts are so kind, we see everything.

And now to begin where I left off, which I believe is the best plan. After seeing the Queen's Crown on Saturday, we drove in the Park and I saw the Queen and the Duchess of Kent three times, beautifully, and each time they bowed to me – flattering, very. On Monday, Emma and I set off shopping, Uncle Hubert kindly lending us his man whenever we like, William* not being considered sufficient protection for us, though he does wonderfully well in London, talks of Piccadilly <u>Street</u>, Pall Mall <u>Street</u>, and looks quite knowing. Emma and I have Di's horse between us and have most amusing rides. We have not seen Marshall [sic] Soult, or the Duke of de Nemours [sic]

**William was Darwin Galton's newly acquired "man," aged ten. A respectable young lady like Elizabeth Anne would not go about in London unprotected.*

yet, and they are the two I most want to see. I have seen some of the others – poor Count – I forget his name, the Neapolitan Ambassador, has not been provided with sufficient money from his Government to keep up his dignity like the others, and can make no show at all. Another Ambassador, Prince de Ligne, brought no servants over with him, but plenty of liveries, when he arrived he got servants to fit the liveries, they come every morning and put them on, and at night take them off and are turned loose till the next day to save lodging. What a foreign trick! The Ambassadors give themselves airs, and are very cross that they are to make part of the procession to show off to the English people. I should have thought the Duke of Wellington had thrashed the conceit out of them.

The equipages are splendid. They have already placed barriers in all the streets to prevent more than one carriage passing at a time, and the scaffolding outside the Clubs and houses, preparing for spectators, and covered with calicos, laurels, &c., and the illumination at the top is really beautiful. We have got tickets for The Reform Club, which is close to Whitehall, and we shall see splendidly, and they treat us to breakfast, luncheon and Strauss band – all free gratis for nothing. The streets will be lined with military (London is "stodged" with them), and no tune to be played but "God Save the Queen", which is most grateful to my feelings. It really will be a most glorious sight. I am now reconciled to not being in the Abbey; I see there are so few seats that will see anything of the ceremony. We are just come from the rehearsal, which was splendid, and the Abbey beautifully decorated; galleries all round, and every seat covered with crimson cloth; the Queen's chair covered with gold, and a gold cloth for her to walk upon. We saw where every bit of the ceremony is to be.

My satin gown came this morning and is most beautiful; it created quite a sensation in the Abbey, particularly when surmounted with a new white bonnet and pink roses I bought yesterday! Many thanks for it. Edward and Uncle Hubert are gone to see a person in a state of clairvoyance at Baron du Potes. They are just come back but only saw the same sort of thing Papa did, and are faithless.

*

Tuesday evening

Francis is just come. Thursday will be the Coronation and we will see he gets a place somewhere. The most fashionable is a pair of stirrups across the top of a lamp post, where you sit in style! I am quite sorry to hear that dear Papa is so poorly and on thinking the matter over have fixed the following plan, viz. that Francis and I will take our places tomorrow for Saturday night by the W. Mail, by which means I shall be home two days sooner. On Sunday, then, at cock-crow we shall arrive, full of news. I feel very much obliged to you and Papa for letting me come at this time; it certainly has answered all my expectations and will add materially to my happiness for ever. Miss R. tells me she fears she cannot get a seat at the Reform Club, which I am sorry for. [Presumably this is a reference to Miss Ryland, cf. p97]. The fact is, I suppose, they wish for once to have it full of Tories, and therefore bribe them with Strauss's band. The procession does not begin till between ten and eleven o'clock Thursday, and we are all to start at six o'clock for the Club. I do long for the day, and if it is fine shall have nothing to wish for. We are obliged to have a glass coach for the rehearsal and for Thursday, but we mean to keep it hard at work the whole night, seeing the illuminations, to make it pay.

Give my love to Emma Wheler and tell her I depend upon her seeing that a candle or lamp is put in my bedroom tomorrow night for an illumination, as she values my friendship. I wish I could give you an idea of the preparations making for spectators, illuminations, they are most splendid. Fancy every house with three tiers of seats in front, covered with every coloured cloth, and most splendid illuminations above. Two of the Ambassadors at Mivarts are to illuminate in a manner unique. We have seen some of the equipages and they are indescribably splendid, and the Fair in Hyde Park will be "de qui." Cannons fired five or six times during the day, twenty-one each time and forty-two when the crown is put on, and we shall be in full hearing; I sadly fear my head will be quite turned, it is going fast.

Believe me,
Your affectionate daughter,
E. A. Galton

*

Portman Square, 28th June 1838

"God save the Queen"
"Rule Britannia"

My dear Papa and Mama,

You will be surprised to hear from me when you expect Francis and me so soon, but instead of having taken a place at Leamington, you will be grieved to hear they have secured a place for me in a Lunatic Asylum, and I believe St. Luke's is the one fixed upon, the reason why I will now tell you.

The Gurneys dined here yesterday, and we talked of the Coronation, and my wish to see it. They went home, and Emma and I were in a deep sleep, dreaming of the Reform Club (where we were going next morning), cream coloured horses, procession, &c. when at twelve o'clock we were roused by a knock at the door, and Uncle Galton's voice, begging us to open it a crack, while he read a note from Mr. Hudson Gurney, saying that a ticket had been sent them <u>for the Abbey</u> and I was welcome to it! I believe I screamed for joy. Uncle Hubert, in the kindest manner, though it was then past twelve and I was to set off at <u>four</u> in the morning to St. James's Square, insisted that I should accept it, and he would see I was called in time, ordered his carriage to be in readiness to take me, and breakfast to be ready at half past three o'clock. My state of mind was grievous to behold. I jumped up, put by my morning satin and new bonnet, pulled out my pink satin (which I had put in my trunk the last thing as a forlorn hope), and then tried to forget the Abbey and go to sleep.

At half past two I was up, and my Uncle came to call me, and my Aunt would get up to see I was comfortable, and off I set to St. James's Square, where Mr. and Mrs. Gurney were waiting for me, ready dressed at half past four, with breakfast, and Burgess ready to dress me up, and my Aunt sent me ornaments to cut a figure in.

I had many misgivings after I accepted the ticket, thinking it would probably be a Peer's ticket and I should see nothing, and would be better off seeing the procession. Judge then my delight when I found it was one of the Earl Marshall's [sic], from whence I could see everything, and close by the Orchestra, and the Procession would pass close before my seat. Can you wonder at my being fit only for a Lunatic Asylum? I was provided with the Coronation Service, thanks to Mary, who has taught me "to be prepared for either state," and at half past five Miss Woodhouse [Wodehouse] and I set off with her Father. We found our seats were far apart, but he placed us safe in each, and then left us to join the House of Commons. We were three quarters of an hour getting from St. James's Square to the Abbey, and many people had set off at three o'clock.

Nothing could be better than all the arrangements at the Abbey, refreshment tables and civil police in all directions. At first I felt rather forlorn alone among strangers, and being in the third row I thought I should see nothing, but as I could not remain silent, I began to make friends with a very gentlemanly young officer, about twenty-eight or thirty, who sat next me in full uniform and moustaches. He told me everything – the names of everybody, the uniforms and every particular, and made me stand where he was, and by degrees by helping others to see who were behind me. We all became such friends that by taking it in turn we all saw everything to our heart's content, and they (seeing I suppose my enthusiasm for the thing) made me see all the interesting parts. I stayed in the Abbey from half past six in the morning till about five in the afternoon, and I do not think I sat altogether one hour, never felt hungry, thirsty or tired, and such was the continual interest that, though it was four and a half hours before the Procession entered, I was sorry when it began and had not at half the scene before me. It is impossible to describe it. The Abbey is in the shape of a Cross. At the East is the Altar, the West, close to where I sat, the Orchestra, under which the Procession entered – North the Peeresses, and South the Peers sit – Two tiers of galleries for spectators and the House of Commons, and under my tier sat Judges, &c., opposite lower tier all the Ambassadors' suites, and further on the Royal Family.

It was most interesting, seeing the Peers and Peeresses come with their crimson robes and ermine capes and long trains, varying according to their rank, and followed by such pretty little pages in crimson, carrying the coronets. Lord Ward looked very well. The Duke of Nemours came in privately, and I saw him thoroughly. When the Peers, Bishops, House of Commons, Judges, &c., had all come in, the guns fired, announcing that Her Majesty had set off from the Palace, and about half past ten the Procession began of the Ambassadors, and I saw Marshall Soult, Esterhazy, and all of them, and had the pleasure of seeing that no uniforms were equal to the British. My friend the Brigade Major told me all their names. Then came the Royal Dukes, Duchesses and pages, and then the Queen.

It was quite an affecting sight. She walked slowly, with the greatest dignity, as pale as marble, slightly bowing, dressed in white, with a beautiful tiara of diamonds on her forehead, and her splendid train of velvet, nine yards long I think, borne by eight young ladies, dressed in beautiful white and silver gowns, and wreaths of roses in their hair, then her Maids of Honour and Ladies in Waiting. She looked so young and yet so Queen-like and so pale, we thought she must have fainted, particularly as on her entrance the Coronation Anthem was played, which is beautiful and quite overcoming. It was a splendid sight. She walked with the greatest composure to her chair, however, and knelt down, and then rose and went through every part beautifully.

The morning was cloudy, and early it rained a little, but as soon as she entered a gleam of sunshine burst through the Abbey. She was then presented to her Subjects by the Archbishop in his splendid blue and gold robe, and all shouted "God save Queen Victoria," and then the National Anthem was solemnly and beautifully played. After the Litany and Communion, a beautiful Sermon by the Bishop of London was preached. She took off her robes and appeared with a gold mantle and no train, and nothing on her head, and took her place at the Altar, when her Oath was administered, and she was anointed and made the offerings, &c., after which the Archbishop crowned her, and all the Peers and Peeresses put on their coronets and the shouting began inside and outside the Abbey – the guns fired a double salute, and a most inspiring anthem was played. At this moment the sun again burst forth gloriously, straight upon her crown, and as she moved her head about slightly, you cannot conceive the effect of the sun upon the brilliants, and with her Crown and the gold mantle, and her youth and dignity, I never saw anything so interesting, and the Peers looked like what British Peers should look, with their coronets, and just for that one moment I could not help wishing I were a Peeress, to have had the pleasure of putting on my coronet. It was a beautiful effect, and no one can imagine it without seeing it. She was then enthroned on a chair covered with gold, placed upon steps covered with a magnificent blue and gold carpet, and first the Royal Dukes saluted her, and then all the Bishops and Peers in turn walked to her, taking off their coronets and paying their Homage. One of the Peers tumbled down flat before her, and she jumped up to help him to rise.

During this ceremony, the medals were thrown about and scrambled for in a most undignified manner, the Peers falling over each other to get them. I forgot to say all her Maids of Honour, dressed in white with wreaths and veils, and the Ladies in Waiting in blue, were in a box by themselves and looked beautiful, many looking at their Queen with great anxiety at first, to see how she bore it.

She then took the Sacrament with the Bishops, and the Procession left the Abbey, as it came, only the Queen first, wearing her Crown, and all her ladies, then the Ambassadors, and old Soult was cheered, and the dear Duke of Wellington doubly cheered, but my pleasure was much damped by seeing how old he has become.

The Peers and Peeresses went home in their coronets, and much, much as I had raised my expectations, the reality has far, far exceeded them, and now I feel I am a happy woman for life. The music was splendid, and not for one moment did the interest flag. The Queen was cheered the whole way through the Abbey. The foreign ladies' diamonds were splendid, and many of our Peeresses', and with their coronets they looked lovely. I saw all our Heroes, Marquis of Anglesea [sic], &c., pointed out to me. We stayed nearly two hours in the Abbey before Mr. Woodhouse came to us, and then I went to St. James's Square and my Aunt drove me back here.

The illuminations are splendid and fireworks are in sight of my window, and so ends the happiest day of my life – "God save the

Queen."

The only thing is, it will be rather expensive to me, as of course I never can think of wearing my pink satin gown, shoes or gloves again, after the honour they have had of being at the Coronation, and therefore I shall pin them up and write "Coronation gown &c." on them and keep them as heirlooms. Uncle Howard and Emma went to the Reform Club, Francis to a capital situation in Pall Mall, Darwin to Mr. Collins' to see the Procession, and they all returned equally pleased and delighted with the Procession and all they saw, but they must describe their day, for my mind is full of the Abbey.

I cannot tell you how much I enjoyed it.

The Review will be splendid on Saturday, but I fear we shall not see it. Good night, I have only had two hours sleep during the past forty hours, and do not feel a bit sleepy.

Friday morning. I thought of Adele and the schoolchildren several times yesterday.

I am ready to go through it all again.

I have much more to tell you, but it must wait now till we meet. The illuminations were splendid last night and the Ambassadors have done themselves and their nations credit by their part, for their houses were a blaze of light.

Believe me,
Your affectionate daughter,
E. A. Galton

CHAPTER 8

ROYAL LEAMINGTON SPA (1838-1839)

In July, 1838, to the great delight of the Leamington shopkeepers, the Queen made the town "Royal Leamington Spa." On the 24th., Dr. Jephson arrived from London with the "Joyful News," with laurels on his post chaise; bells rang, and Leamington was delighted.

In August, a pleasant family, Mr. and Mrs. Sympson and daughters, came to York Terrace. Much of their property was in the West Indies. Soon after, all West India property became of much less value, and the Sympsons among others were ruined. The whole family behaved wonderfully. Mr. and Mrs. Sympson were elderly people, but there was no murmur. Their old servants, who had been with them for years, had to be dismissed. The two eldest daughters arranged everything to be sold, the married daughter to live with the parents in a very small house, and the two eldest to go as companions to families. When I last heard of them, one of the daughters had a private boarding house in Switzerland.

We saw a great deal of the Whelers this autumn.

This autumn several pleasant families came for the winter. Mr. and Mrs. Hay Mackenzie, a man of very large property in Scotland, reaching from one coast to another. He told my Father (I think I am correct) that if he could get twopence an acre rent, he should be a rich man, so much was barren moor. Their only daughter, a little child, afterwards married the Duke of Sutherland. A curious custom of these Scotch families, when they left home, was to send their servants to attend school during their absence, that they might be learning instead of wasting their time.

*

November 11th, 1838: we went to a musical party at Mr. Russell's, where we met for the first time Louis Napoleon (afterwards Emperor), Count Persigny, and Dr. Conneau. They came for the winter to hunt, and took 6, Clarendon Square. The Prince was not tall, Persigny shorter, and Conneau very short, They always walked together down the Parade, and made themselves agreeable to everyone, went to balls and dinners every evening, hunting all day, and everyone observed how completely he seemed to have given up all thoughts of the Throne and had no idea beyond hunting and dancing, little knowing that the three were plotting all the time and making their arrangements. We met them at a dance at Lady Hodson's, when the Prince asked to be introduced to my sister Emma and danced with her; and from that time he and Count Persigny danced with her at every party they met. Prince Napoleon, when he became Emperor of the French, never forgot anyone who had shown him attention at Leamington. If he saw anyone at Paris whom he knew, he would recognise them and desire one of his officers to attend them sight-seeing. He stayed in Leamington the whole winter, and then made the foolish attack at Boulogne. Reginald Darwin was at Boulogne at the time and was bathing when he saw something going on, got out of the sea and dressed, but all was over before he arrived.

*

Lady Mulgrave and her three daughters, the Ladies Phipps, came for the winter; Lady Mulgrave was sister to Admiral Maling [see p.12] who married my Aunt. She was too ill to see anyone, but the Ladies Phipps often came to see us and were much attached to Adele. Mrs. Welsh, another sister of Admiral Maling, and her son and daughter arrived, and we saw much of them. When the late Lord Mulgrave was in power, the Welshes had a sinecure place and were very rich, but when Mr. Welsh died and sinecures were given up, they became wretchedly poor. Miss Welsh, some years after, was glad to undertake the care of the little black Princess, for the sake of the salary the

Queen gave her. She was a very excellent and agreeable woman.

The black Princess was an African. Her whole family were murdered, and the Captain of one of our ships begged the child's life, and the murderers gave her to him. He brought her to England, the Queen took charge of her, and she was much at the Palace with the Royal children. She was christened Victoria Forbes Bonetta, after the Captain and the ship who had brought her home. When she grew up, the Queen placed her with Miss Welsh. She married a black missionary, went with him to Sierra Leone, had one child, and soon after, she and her husband died.

(February 1899. My children urge me to go on relating the events of my life. I am now ninety-one years of age, so must be excused if I repeat anything I have written before.)

*

There are a few old customs which I do not think I have mentioned before. In my youth it was usual in country Churches to see loaves of bread on a shelf, one of which was given to each poor person who took the Sacrament. The Royal Arms were always over the entrance inside a Church, to show that the Sovereign was the head. St. Philip's Church, Birmingham, was generally called the "new Church."

In stage coaches there was no carpet for the feet, only straw, and in cold weather it was usual to petition for more straw, and even sometimes there was only straw in hackney carriages, and I remember when we went to a party with the Horners, I was cautioned to see I had no straw sticking to me when I got out!

All thread and silk, and often cotton, were sold in skeins, not wound, and to save time they were cut through and paper wrapped round them, and these thread papers were tied three or four together, with the threads of different thicknesses. At bazaars you often bought a set, prettily painted.

When a lady married, it was a custom to give all her clothes to her maid, and to have nothing but what was new to take with her.

Long necklaces and chains almost always had a Cross hanging on them as an ornament, but when the Oxford High Church movement began, they were left off, as they were considered a sign of Ritualism.

False teeth were real teeth, and I have often heard it remarked how shocking it was after a battle, men going round to draw the teeth of the killed.

Beds were formerly raised very high, so much so that "bed steps", viz. three steps, were on each side of the bed to enable one to mount, and curtains were drawn, all round the bed by many people.

*

At this time (1838) my sister Lucy's Work Book came out. She had for many months been arranging the book, teaching how to cut out linen &c. to the greatest advantage and no waste, knitting receipts &c. It was very well done, and the plates were nicely executed. It was much liked, but too expensive for many to buy, and many cheap little books have since been published in imitation, but hers was the first of its kind.

The Granvilles were a large, pleasant family from Derbyshire. Mrs. Granville was a good, kind woman; everyone liked her. She was a Roman Catholic, but all her children were Protestants. She was a Ferrers of Baddesley Clinton, and told us how she had eloped from there with Mr. Granville. He came in a boat with a rope ladder, and she got out of her window but slipped from the ladder into the moat and got a good ducking.

In January, 1839, we went to a ball, where we met Sir Walter Scott, eldest son of the Sir Walter. I forget whether I have mentioned an anecdote which he told my Father: that when he and his sister Anne were children playing by themselves in their father's study, they quarrelled about a roll of paper, both wanted it, and when he tried to snatch it from her, she threw it in the fire. Sir Walter luckily came in and rescued it – it was the manuscript of "Waverley"!

We were much shocked at hearing of the sudden death of Miss Manners Sutton, of angina pectoris, a disease that all five sisters died of eventually. They were most kind, pleasant women, and we were very intimate with them. They always dressed to a pin alike, and all five walked out together, two and three. They gave very pleasant balls in the Assembly Rooms, and invited the whole of every family to them. At all Public Balls there was one country dance for the Miss Manners Suttons, and their partners made a point of rushing with them down the middle from the top of the room into the entrance and back again. They always treated their youngest sister, who was past forty, as a young girl, calling her "Baby". They were the daughters of the Archbishop, and sisters to the Speaker of the House of Commons.

*

Edward Wheler and his sisters were constantly in Leamington during 1839, choosing furniture, and always came to us for breakfast or lunch, and we often went to see them now that they lived so much nearer. The consequence was that Edward Wheler became attached to me. His sister Emma Wheler, who was staying with us, first told me of her brother's feelings, that he talked to her about it and felt that, as he had not money to marry, he ought not to accept invitations to our house, and wished us to know the reason. I told him that, as we had not money enough to marry, we must try to forget it, that there must be no sort of engagement, but that both should feel able to marry elsewhere, and that we should meet as friends always. From that time we did so, and the subject was never alluded to by his sisters, at my request. It was of course a severe trial, as I had unconsciously become much attached to him.

*

A new Church, St. Mary's, was just finished building by Simeon's trustees, and it was offered to Dr. Marsh, who left Birmingham and came with all his family, and we became most intimate with his daughters, Matilda and Catherine, and frequently went to St. Mary's to hear Dr. Marsh preach. The Church was consecrated on 27th. July: we all went with the Whelers to the service. Dr. Marsh had four daughters and one son. The son, whom we called "the Beau" because he was rather spoilt by his sisters, was Curate to the father. Dr.

Marsh's sermons were excellent, and many went to hear him, though it was a long walk to his Church. Catherine told us that on a Sunday morning many ladies called at their house to ask the maid who would preach that morning, and if the answer was that Mr. Marsh would, they heard the lady exclaim "Then I shan't go," which was not complimentary to her brother, whose sermons were not thought worth the expense of a sedan chair.

A few years after, Matilda made a romantic marriage. A great friend of hers married and went to India. She and Matilda constantly corresponded, and a few years later, her friend died, leaving two little boys. Her husband, Mr. Chalmers, had been so pleased with Matilda's letters that after a year's mourning, though he had never seen her, he wrote to ask her to be his wife. She however refused him. He would not despair, but threw up his appointment and appeared in person at Dr. Marsh's with his two boys. The end was that Matilda married him; he went into the Church and was Curate to his father-in-law. We often spent the evening at Dr. Marsh's house and, after prayers, always finished with singing "From Greenland's Icy Mountains."

One of Mr. Craig's [another clergyman in Leamington] curates, who did duty at the Episcopal Chapel, was Mr. Lincoln Galton, an excellent hard-working clergyman. He was no relation to us, but his wife was distantly so; she was a Miss Bevan, and we liked them both much. He had no assistance, but besides morning and afternoon service, he had one at five o'clock on Sunday morning for cabmen, which was well attended. His sons turned out clever men.

Chapter 9

A Scottish Pilgrimage (1839)

On 2nd. September, 1839, my Father, Francis, and I set off for a tour in Scotland, a country I had longed to visit. We went by rail to Liverpool and embarked on a steamer for Greenock in the afternoon, slept on board, and after a very pleasant voyage landed at Dumbarton and saw the Castle and Wallace's sword, which is kept there. Next day we drove to Loch Lomond, and in a steam packet sailed up Loch Lomond to Tarbet, where we slept. The view was lovely all the way, and the mountains covered with heather. A party of ladies and gentlemen arrived at the Inn, who on enquiry proved to be the Queen of Beauty and her friends, come from the Eglinton tournament.*

In the evening, one of the gentlemen kindly came to our room to tell us there was a fine display of Aurora Borealis, and it was splendid, the white rays dashing about all over the heavens. The next day was pouring wet till the evening, when we saw a curious sight: a beautiful rainbow lying on the side of the mountain.

From there we crossed the Lake to Inversnaid, and mounted ponies to take us over the hills to Loch Katrine, where we took a boat and saw Ellen's Island, the boatman repeating Scott's lines and showing us all the places mentioned in the poem. We were struck by how intelligent the lower class were in Scotland compared to what they were in England. We saw Roderick Dhu's and the McGregor's country, and

**This famous affair was a last attempt to hold a tournament of chivalry in this country. It was unfortunately spoiled by a torrential downpour of rain – which may have given the coup de grace to the institution which Sir Walter Scott and others had tried so hard to revive!*

landed at the Trossachs, a lovely glen by the river. It was pouring with rain, and as we had to walk some way to the Inn, I was wet through, and had to borrow a dress while mine dried.

*

The Scotch Inns were very primitive and small, the chamber-maids bare-legged, and their hair looked as if it had never been brushed, but they were civil and nice mannered. As the Inns were small, on the arrival of a steamer there was a rush to secure room, as there was seldom room enough for all. Francis soon found this out and, as we neared a place, he quietly edged nearer to where we got out, then jumped out and outran the others and got us taken in. At one Inn, there was only one window to two bedrooms, the division being in the middle of the window. We were detained a day by the pouring rain, but returned the day after on ponies to Tarbet, dined, and went in a steamer down Loch Long to Greenock, where we spent a Sunday and went to the Scotch Kirk. Monday we steamed up Loch Goil, and then in a curious car of three or four benches, and very jogging, to Inveraray.

We got a car to drive us over to the Duke of Argyll's grounds and were amused at seeing the Judge arrive, four men walking before him blowing trumpets. The next day we saw the Judge set off on foot, dressed in scarlet, with his hat on the top of his wig, two councillors in wigs behind him, and two trumpeters before him, to the Town Hall.

From Inveraray we went to Oban, passing Dunstaffnage where the Scotch Kings were formerly crowned on the Stone of Scone, which is now in Westminster Abbey. Oban is a nice town on the sea coast; Miss Cameron had given us a letter of introduction to McDougall of Lorne, which we took with us to his castle, but unluckily he was not in, so we did not see Bruce's brooch, which his ancestor seized from Bruce. We wrote our names in the visitors' book with an eagle's quill.

Next morning at five o'clock we started in a steamer and sailed round the Isle of Mull to Iona and Staffa. In Iona Cathedral are the tombs of the Norwegian Kings in one row, then the Scotch Kings and Warriors. While there we saw five or six eagles on a rock, and flying about most majestically. We then sailed to Staffa, and into Fingal's cave – most interesting. From Oban we went to Ballachulish, where the Cameron's country begins. The scenery was most lovely. We got into a car and went through the Pass of Glencoe, and saw the hill where the poor inhabitants were buried after the massacre – the scenery lovely beyond description. At Ballahulish the inn-keeper and his men were dressed in Highland tartan. The huts were miserable places, like what we read of the Irish, smoke dried. The women were making a bit of hay, throwing it about with their hands.

We then went to Fort William, got on ponies, and went up part of Ben Nevis, a very high mountain. From Fort William we went to Benavie, a miserable dirty Inn, but close to the Caledonian Canal. This was the most interesting part of our journey, the country of our Forefathers. We drove to Mr. Cameron's house, Achnacarry, with a note to his factor telling him to show us everything, which he did. We saw the remains of the old house, which the Duke of Cumberland burnt. The fine trees with fissures in them, which the soldiers made by boiling their kettles in them. We then were shown the cave where Prince Charles lay hid for some time. It poured with rain, but we did not mind.

Next day we drove to Glenfinnan, the most lovely romantic spot, where Prince Charles summoned the Clans to join him. There is a statue of him looking anxiously down the glen to see if the Camerons were coming to join him. We passed Fassifern, and saw the monument to the son of Cameron of Fassifern, who was killed at Quatre Bras. We were grieved to leave this romantic country. We went by the Caledonian Canal to Inverness, passing beautiful country and waterfalls. We drove from Inverness about six miles to see the plains of Culloden, where Prince Charles was beaten by the wicked Duke of Cumberland.

We left Inverness about six o'clock in the morning – passed Forres where the witches met Macbeth – arrived at Aberdeen at seven o'clock, drank tea at the Inn, and then came on to Stonehaven, where we slept. After breakfast we drove to Ury, which had belonged to the Barclays for some centuries. Margaret Barclay showed us over the curious old house (now blown up, and a modern house built by the

Bairds). She showed us the old Meeting House of the Quakers, close to the house, which all Quakers, when travelling in Scotland, come to see – a tiny closet, out of the large sitting room, is where my Great-great-great-grandfather Barclay wrote his famous "Apology for the Quakers." We went up a small hill at the back of the House to the Chapel, where all the Barclays are buried. Then into the garden where my Great-grandfather pushed a bull over the wall, sixty feet down. We went over the farm with my Uncle Barclay, and walked through a wheatfield, the stalks higher than our heads. In the sitting room we saw a movable panel, behind which was a secret chamber to hide in.

Margaret Barclay showed me a lock of Prince Charles' hair, and after much urgent entreaty, I got her to give me the one hair I have. She also showed me a miniature of Queen Anne set with diamonds, which Queen Anne gave to my Ancestor. She gave presents to many of the Jacobite families, it was supposed with the hope they would espouse her brother's claims to the throne after her death.

[In December, 1922, Hesketh Pearson, the writer and biographer, who was Elizabeth Anne's great-great-nephew, made his pilgrimage to Ury, on which he sent the following report to his mother. It was copied into Elizabeth Anne's reminiscences by her daughter, Mrs Lucy Studdy:

"Aberdeen was gorgeous: we enjoyed every minute of it, and we went a pilgrimage to Ury and spent nearly an hour in the Mausoleum of the Barclays. It was really quite wonderful – a marvellous walk through the Ury estate, which is now owned by Sir John Baird. The Bairds bought it from the executors of the sixth and last Barclay of Ury in 1834. The present house was built by the present Baird's grandfather. The Mausoleum, which the Scotch call "The Hous," is marvellously situated on the crest of the highest hill on the estate. It is in the form of a chapel. A little clump of firs and other trees surround it, the whole enclosed by a stone wall. The rest of the hill is quite bare to its base, and all around the moors and fields extend, with a lovely glimpse of the sea and Stonehaven, two or three miles off. Within the chapel are the graves of the six Barclays of Ury, beginning with David, the first to own that estate, immortalised by Whittier. Robert, the great Quaker Apologist, was the second; then a third and a fourth, both in direct succession. Then the fifth, still remembered by tradition and hearsay in these quarters as the famous – the most famous – athlete of his day. Then the sixth and last, who presumably died heirless. Several wives and daughters of the foregoing also lie there in the inner half of the chapel. (I forgot to say the chapel is divided into two parts; the inner part is sacred to the Barclays. The part into which one first enters is being used by the Bairds as a burial ground.)

"One has to obtain keys from the carpenter, and the gardener who took us to the carpenter's house was most interested to hear that I was in direct descent "o' the historical folk up at the Hous." The news spread among the people working on the estate – many hats were touched and greetings given.

"Altogether it was a most memorable pilgrimage, and I shall not easily forget it."]

*

My Uncle Howard Galton arrived while we were at Ury. We very much enjoyed our visit to my Uncle Barclay, and after two days there set off in the stage coach for Edinburgh. We stopped to breakfast at Laurencekirk, and bought some prettily turned wood articles, then passed Glamis Castle, Birnam Wood, Dunsinane to Perth, where we dined, then to Kinross where we saw Loch Leven and the Castle on the Island, from where Queen Mary escaped and threw the keys of the Castle into the lake. (A few years ago – I am writing this in 1899 – these keys were fished up, and are now in the possession of the Leslie Melvilles.)

We arrived in Edinburgh at half past seven – a twelve hour journey from Aberdeen! While in Edinburgh we went up Calton Hill, all over Holyrood Palace, saw the large room in which Prince Charles held a large assembly.

The woman who showed us round was a strong Jacobite, and was pleased at my buying the little portrait of Prince Charles.

We then went over the Castle and saw the Regalia which had been lost for so many years, till Sir Walter Scott discovered it in an old chest. I had several commissions to buy Tartan shawls, and Romaine [sic] and Patterson, where I bought them, gave me all the specimens of the Clan Tartans named. We stayed two days in Edinburgh, and on the 25th. September we set off at seven in the morning by coach for Carlisle, where we arrived at half past four, passing Abbotsford on our way. The boundary between the two Kingdoms was two turnpike gates close together, six miles from Langholm. The next day we left Carlisle at half past eight and arrived at Preston at six o'clock, and the next day from Preston to Leamington, after a most enjoyable journey.

I had longed all my life to see Scotland, and especially Achnacarry and Ury. The scenery on the Western Coast is beautiful and grand beyond description; so different to anything I had ever seen before. We arrived at home on the 28th. September. Our first calls were on Mrs. and Miss Cameron and Miss Maclean, to tell them how useful their introductions had been, and how much we had enjoyed our tour.

Chapter 10

Royal Leamington Spa (continued) (1839 - 1845)

On 5th December, 1839, the fourpenny postage began, and was to be tried for a while to see if penny postage would answer. All letters to any part of England, Scotland, and Ireland paid fourpence only – a great change. Letters from London to Leamington had cost ninepence. It was the same to Bath, and I think we paid fourpence to Kenilworth and Rugby, so we used to make our letters there into a parcel and send them by Carrier for a penny. On the following 10th January, the penny postage began; we could prepay our letters or not, as we liked. Stamps were not yet issued.

*

On 15th January, Mr. Innes called and told my Mother that Margaret Barclay* (the daughter of Captain Barclay Allardice) had eloped with a Private Soldier! She was a strange person, eaten up with pride and her own family, and determined to have an heir to the Airth and Menteith titles, which her father was laying claim to. The man she married was a respectable Scotchman, and my Uncle Barclay and Mr. Gurney thought the best thing to be done was to settle them in America. My Uncle Barclay came to us for two days and then went with them to Montreal. After her marriage, my Uncle gave up trying for the title, as it involved great expense, and his daughter would not have money to keep up the title.

Soon after, we heard what a narrow escape Francis had had from

** Margaret Barclay-Allardice retained that surname after her marriage to Samuel Ritchie.*

drowning. He was in a steamer on the Thames, which struck against one of the piers, and was much injured. The paddle box was wrenched off and Francis dashed into the river. He tried to rise, for he was an excellent swimmer, but found he was under the paddle box, which kept him down. With great difficulty he at last extricated himself and was picked up, covered with blood, by a boat. When he recovered, he found himself in bed in some small Inn, and a doctor looking after him. He soon got well, but it was a frightful accident.

*

On 28th April, 1840, I left home and slept at my Aunt's, Mrs. Booth's, in Temple Row, Birmingham, and the next day James Moilliet, Lucy, and their four children called at six o'clock in the morning for me, and we set off for Tenby. The first night we arrived at Brecon, and arrived next day at Tenby. I enjoyed going over our old haunts again and found many who remembered us when I was only twelve years old [c.f. p24]. I went to see my little sister Violet's grave in the Church, and Noot, the same sexton who had buried her in 1817, showed it to me.

At this time we had the pleasure of hearing that Francis had gained a prize at King's College for Anatomy and Chemistry. He was studying to become a medical man.

Another event was the issue of penny postage stamps and postage reduced to a penny, and those curious envelopes with elephants, etc. upon them. But they did not take, and caricature envelopes were made and they were soon given up. It was now made compulsory to prepay letters, a thing which was hitherto considered an insult to your correspondent to do, as if they could not afford the postage.

In May the Hubert Galtons came to Leamington to consult Dr. Jephson about Diana, their second daughter. He told them there was no hope, which was a terrible shock to my Uncle. My Aunt was more prepared for it, having long foreseen what was coming, but had not dared to tell my Uncle. Diana died on 9th. June She was a very amiable, bright girl, and had been much influenced by my Aunt Sophia to think of religion. She died very happy, trusting in her Saviour.

On 14th July, we went with much sorrow to take leave of all our pleasant acquaintances in Tenby, and on the 15th. the maids and I left in the steam packet for Bristol, the Moilliets going by land. From Bristol I went by coach to Birmingham, slept one night at Dr. Booth's house and home the next day.

On 24th. July, we heard that my brother Darwin was engaged to Mary Phillips of Edstone; she was just eighteen. We all went immediately to call.

*

My Mother and Adele went to Loxton (Somerset) to stay with Erasmus, and it was fixed that Adele should come and live with him. Dr. Marsh and his daughters took over Adele's school and established it in the Holly Walk. They also kept on Miss Betts the Governess, who was an excellent one, very precise and formal in manner. Her mother had been a lady's maid to a lady who was in Brussels at the time of the Battle of Waterloo. Adele therefore went away without anxiety about her scholars. While with Erasmus she did much good at Loxton. The farmers and people were very ignorant, and she had meetings for them and taught them various things, which interested them very much.

She was much amused at the curious names of some of the children: two little girls were called "Castor" and "Pollux." On enquiry, she found that a young man had stayed a few weeks in the neighbourhood for a change of air, being very out of health. For want of amusement, he attended all the christenings, and gave the parents half a crown if he might name the child.

*

On 20th September, Darwin was married at Wootten Wawen to Mary Elizabeth Phillips. It was arranged that Darwin and his wife were to live at Edstone with Mrs. Phillips and her daughter Emma.

Colonel Pocklington (who came for the winter) was told by his medical man that he must eat less at his dinner. As this was impossible, he told us that once a week he took a long walk and missed his dinner entirely, and then thought he might enjoy himself for the rest of the week. Mrs. Pocklington came to my Mother to enquire the character of a cook who had left us. She wished to know if the cook knew three hundred and sixty-five different soups, as the Colonel expected a change every day!

In January, 1841, we had our usual ball, one hundred and thirty people. The Horners stayed some days with us.

My Mother invited two little boys who were at Mr. Atwood's school at Kenilworth to spend the day, Master Grant of Monymusk and Master Bontine. The boys were playing in the room when company came in and one asked my Mother how my Uncle Captain Barclay Allardice was succeeding in proving his claim to the Earldom of Airth and Menteith. My Mother answered that his claim was likely to be proved, when up started little Bontine, who exclaimed, "No it won't, my Father claims the titles." We were much amused, and found that Bontine's father was a claimant, but could not prove it.

On 17th. January, very high floods, the water all across the bridge, near the Pump Room. It was on a Sunday and rose so rapidly that a boat had to take the people across when they came out of Church. Mr. and Mrs. Boulton were taken out of their house through a window in a boat; the house was close to the river and was full of water. The Bishop of Chester tried to go through the water and fell into the river, and was with difficulty rescued.

*

Mr. Batt paid our friend Charlotte Wood a great deal of attention, and had done so ever since he came, and we joked her about him. Charlotte was invited to go to Cheltenham to her schoolfellow Miss Godson. Mr. Batt, hearing this, told my Mother he was going to Cheltenham by the coach and would see to Miss Wood's comfort. He dined with us and met Charlotte's brother, John Wood, who was tutor to Prince George of Cambridge. Darwin called next day and, hearing of this arrangement, said "Why, Charlotte, of course he will take all the places in the coach and propose to you!" Poor Charlotte got very nervous, and it proved Darwin was right. He had taken all the places and did propose, and was eventually accepted. She remained a short time with the Godsons and then returned to us.

My father was taken ill with gout and frequently had attacks of it. He was a most abstemious man but the gout had something to do with the asthma. The asthma was not so severe but the attacks of gout seemed to come more frequently.

On 18th. March, Charlotte Wood married Mr. Batt. On 3rd. April, I joined Miss Anastasia Leveson Gower, and we went by rail road to London. We set off at an quarter past eleven, and arrived at half past five, thinking how wonderfully short a time! How different now in 1899, when we go in two hours! I went to the Gurneys in St. James's Square.

A week or so before her marriage, Charlotte Wood went to London for a few days, and Queen Adelaide [the Queen Mother, widow of William IV] desired John Wood, who was her chaplain, to bring his sister to see her. She was most kind to Charlotte, asked her if she felt happy in her prospects, and presented her with a hundred pounds, part of which she spent in a handsome gold chain as a remembrance of the Queen. Queen Adelaide also insisted on John Wood's making a point with Mr. Batt that Charlotte should have a hundred a year in pin money – a delicate thing to do, as Charlotte had no money of her own; however, it had to be done, as the Queen had desired it. Mr. Batt agreed at once.

John and Charlotte Wood lost their parents when they were very young. They had ten thousand pounds each from their parents, which their guardian unfortunately put in to his business, and failed, and the young people had nothing. John worked hard at College, and was strongly recommended as Tutor to Prince George of Cambridge. When he was no longer required as a Tutor, King William IV made him Chaplain to himself and the Queen. He was much liked and respected by all the Royal family. Besides having no patrimony, he had been induced, when too inexperienced to know what he was doing, to sign a paper which, after his Uncle's failure, made him answerable for one thousand pounds to Mr. Nathaniel Phillips, who could call it in at any moment. Charlotte told my Mother of this when she was staying with us, and said it was this load on his mind that made him out of sprits. One day Mr. Phillips called and, my Mother being alone, talked of Mr. Wood. Mr. Phillips observed that he looked ill, and my Mother told him the cause: that this debt preyed on his mind. Mr. Phillips agreed it was a hard case, and that he should not have been asked to sign it. The next day, he tore up the Bond and sent it to Mr. Wood, who never forgot what my Mother had done for him. He had a living given to him in Worcester and was made Canon of the Cathedral.

*

On 9th. April, my Uncle Captain Barclay Allardice came to St. James's Square, on his way to America to settle his daughter and her husband there. To please him, Mr. Gurney invited Mr. Jackson, the celebrated pugilist, to dinner. He arrived and was in figure very like my Uncle, only a size larger and very powerful looking. Captain Barclay could not bear tight-fitting clothes, and when he wanted a new coat got Mr. Jackson to have it fitted on him, which ensured its being loose and comfortable.

I had been very out of health for some time, and my Aunt Gurney was anxious I should consult Dr. Holland, which I did. He was a most agreeable man, quite a Courtier in manner, full of anecdotes, &c., and a very clever man. He was related to my cousins, the Darwins of Shrewsbury, and called me his cousin. I saw him several times, and if he wished me to continue the same medicine, he would give me a useful prescription for a cough or something else in return for the fee.

*

[After Elizabeth Anne's return home, she paid a visit to Erasmus and Adele at Loxton, and the family made an extensive tour of the North: Scarborough, Whitby, the Yorkshire Dales, and the Lake District. Her father was taken ill on this tour and was with difficulty brought home towards the end of September.]

My dear Father went to bed at once and Mr. Pritchard came to see him. Mr. Hodgson, who had returned, came to him and called in Dr. Jephson, and my three brothers arrived and took it in turn to be with him night and day – and had the three doctors been his sons they could not have been more attentive. It was a time of agony for us all. We were three days running called in and told he was dying, when a rally took place. In all the Churches and Chapels he was prayed for, without our asking – he was so beloved. My sisters Lucy and Adele arrived; Mr. Hodgson came nearly every day. On 8th. October a change took place for the better, and from that time he slowly recovered. One thing I learnt in his illness: during the time he was apparently unconscious he remembered every word that was spoken by my brothers and the doctors, though he could not speak himself. I am therefore careful never to say in a sick room what a patient should not hear.

[Two clippings from a local newspaper which Elizabeth Anne preserved:]

"ILLNESS OF S.T. GALTON, ESQ – It is with no ordinary concern, that we announce the dangerous illness of Mr. Galton, who has been for some years past one of the most active members of our resident Bench of Magistrates: a gentleman no less distinguished for his private worth, than for the exemplary manner in which he has uniformly discharged his public duties."

"MR. GALTON – The friends of this highly esteemed gentleman, and, indeed, the public generally in this neighbourhood, will rejoice to hear that he is approaching a state of convalescence."]

*

Somewhere about this time a railway was begun from Rugby to Leamington, and from Leamington to Coventry. Before, we had to drive to Coventry if we wanted to go by rail. It was a great amusement to my Father to watch its progress, as long as he was able to ride. Emma or I used to ride with him to watch its progress. It was not opened till the end of 1844 after my dear Father's death.

An amusing incident occurred about this time; I will not mention names. A Mrs. B. and her sister Miss C. came to Leamington, fashionable, agreeable people. Mrs. B. determined to marry off her sister and chose a young curate of good family. They professed themselves very interested in one of his sermons, and asked him many questions about it. The Curate, somewhat of a dandy, was flattered by their interest in his sermon, and said he would call next day with a volume of "The Fathers," which would elucidate the point. He called, and the young lady and he talked some time on the subject, but as the knotty point was not yet quite clear to her, he said he would call again with another volume of "The Fathers" which would explain it. He appeared next day with a large book under his arm, was shown upstairs, and found Mrs. B. alone; she shook hands with him, saying, "My dear Mr. D., are you serious in these visits to my sister?" The curate, much mystified, replied "Oh, certainly, I came to show....." Mrs. B. threw open the folding doors to the next room, where her sister was, and interrupting the curate said, "My dear Sister, Mr. D. assures me he is quite serious in his attentions to you; I congratulate you both," and vanished. The poor curate, quite taken aback, did not know what he said, but got away as soon as he could, and begged his father to go and explain that he had no intentions at all. The next day it was reported in Leamington that the curate had developed symptoms of a clergyman's sore throat and had gone to the sea to recover, where he stayed till Mrs. B. and her sister left Leamington. The curate's sisters came to tell us of his adventure which, knowing all the parties, amused us immensely.

*

On 17th. June, 1843, I sat – or, rather, stood – for my picture. [See frontispiece.] Mr. Easton was a good portrait painter, but thought much more of making a picture than of getting a likeness. He took my Father and Adele, but we did not think them good enough for him to take Emma, which I now regret, as we have no good likeness of her.

I observed to Mr. Easton, he had taken my sister Adele seated in a grand room, whereas he ought to have put her in a schoolroom, teaching the poor. "Oh," said he, "I will put a view of a Church in the distance, which will make it quite all right," and so he did.

Captain and Mrs. Lake came to Leamington for a short time; he was an old friend of my Father's. The Lakes were a Liverpool family who, when my Father was there learning business, were very kind to him. They had several daughters and sons of my Father's age. They invited him and some other young men to a dance, and the next day these young ladies, about sixteen years of age, amused themselves by writing an account of the ball in poetry, which they thought so fine, they sent it to be put in the next day's newspaper. Mr. Lake was very angry and sent for them, and he finished with this cruel remark: "I should not have cared so much had it not been such execrable poetry." Captain Lake's son was at Rugby and was Dr. Arnold's favourite pupil. He became Dean of Durham and died about a year ago (1899).

Miss Lydia Maling took lodgings in Leamington; she was Admiral Maling's youngest sister. Miss Lydia never married. She was engaged to Colonel Phipps, Lord Mulgrave's brother, but he, finding her one evening at a ball, waltzing, broke off the engagement, saying he would never marry a woman who waltzed.

In August, little Adele Moilliet, who had not been well, came to us for about three weeks for a change of air. Whilst she was with us my sister, who was near her confinement, had a fright. Little Amy had been put to bed safely when, soon after the family were gone to bed, the Governess smelt fire and found the fire was in Amy's room. They had just time to snatch the child up and carry her away to safety, but there would not have been time to rescue Adele if she had been at home. James Moilliet soon put the fire out, but the bed was burnt, and it was a mystery what had caused the fire. Another shock the Moilliets had this autumn. Their manservant was missing one morning and was found hanging in the larder. He was a very respectable young man and was engaged to a lady's maid in Leamington. He was unfortunately tempted to bet at the races, lost all his savings, and hanged himself.

On the 5th. September [my sister] Lucy was confined of Tertius

Moilliet, and I went to nurse her.

On 10th. October, 1843, we heard that Mr. Hudson Gurney was taken very seriously ill. He was a delicate man, could never eat meat, and always dined on fish, and rarely on poultry. He and my Aunt had been visiting at a nobleman's house. It was the custom for the men servants to take what they called a stirrup cup on leaving; the Gurney's footman had taken too much and, on arriving, fell down the cellar steps and was killed. Mr. Gurney was a kind-hearted man and felt the death, and the cause of it, greatly, and it hastened on his severe illness. I wrote to my Aunt Gurney to say that, if I could be of any use or comfort to her, I would gladly come, and she wrote immediately accepting my offer, and I went on 20th. December and stayed some weeks with her. My Aunt was very glad to have me, as I could write for her to the numerous relations and could persuade her to go out occasionally for a short time. Mr. Gurney was seriously ill, and for many weeks his death was hourly expected. My Aunt seldom left his room; and she was very kind letting me have the carriage every day to see my friends and drive wherever I wished. Sir Henry Holland came at least once every day and Mr. Young the surgeon slept every night in the house, and I was amused at finding the house-maid changed his room every few days "to keep the beds aired." On 4th. January Adele came to stay a few days with me by my Aunt's invitation; she had never seen any of the London sights. She stayed till the 13th., and I took her to see Panoramas, Miss Linwood's work, Soho Bazaar, St. Paul's, &c. She made an observation after seeing St. Paul's which struck me; "How strange to have gods and goddesses in a Christian Church," alluding to the goddess of fame over Nelson's tomb and others. I took her to see all our numerous Gurney and Barclay relations and to see the Sam Gurneys at Upton. I returned home on 3rd. February, and Emma took my place in St. James's Square.

*

Early in March (1844) my Father became very ill and had a violent attack of nosebleeding, which lasted some time before it could be stopped and pulled down his strength greatly. He was extremely anxious I should learn double entry so that at his death I should understand his accounts. I was quite willing to learn and from that time made them up every month and learnt how to make a trial balance at the end of the year. It was a great comfort to me, after his death, that I was able to go on with his account books just as he would have wished, till all was divided and the accounts closed; I think it was this that made me like accounts, it always seemed to bring me nearer to him. He taught me arithmetic when I was a child, and I can never be sufficiently thankful for his teaching.

My dear Father from this time became more of an invalid and almost, if not quite, gave up riding with us.

In March we heard that my Cousins the Miss Bromleys had sold Abberley to Mr. Moilliet (Lucy's father-in-law), who began immediately to pull down part of the house and erect a large mansion there.

Miss Blair, a very agreeable person, came to Leamington with her Aunt. She was highly connected in Scotland, and she and Adele became great friends. Miss Blair knew Lady Olivia Sparrow, who was well known in the religious world – I think she had been an Irvingite.* Miss Blair was invited to pay her a visit, and she asked Adele to go with her, as she was sure she would like Lady Olivia. Adele went and was much interested in all she saw and heard; the conversation was chiefly on religious topics and frequent prayer meetings. Some time before, Adele had been acquainted with a lady in (I believe) Somersetshire. She and her daughter were extremely poor, but denied themselves in every way, that her only son might go to College and take orders. A living was ready for him, and they would live with him. He succeeded, but the first time be preached, as he came down the pulpit stairs, he suddenly became blind with gutta serena, and a cure was hopeless. Adele mentioned this to Miss Blair, who told Lady Olivia Sparrow, who immediately very kindly took him as her resident chaplain. My sister said how well he managed. He knew the Church Service off by heart. The butler read the Psalms of the day to him, and he could then repeat them in Church from memory.

**The "Irvingites," or Catholic and Apostolic Church, a religious body in the "Catholic" tradition, formed in 1835 by the followers of the Rev. Edward Irving.*

*

In April we all went to Claverdon and, finding that the Vicar had turned the school of girls adrift and did not intend to set one up again, I settled with Mrs. Gumbley, who had hitherto taught them and had a large room, that I would hire the room and have the school there. I got a very nice young governess Adele had taught, and very soon forty girls came. Adele undertook the boys at Mrs. Heritage's, and it was sad to see how ignorant all were of the very rudiments of religion. On asking the children if they ever said prayers, some of them said they did, the prayer:

"There are four corners to my bed;
There are four angels guard my head;
Matthew, Mark, Luke, and John.
God bless the bed that I lie on."

They were very willing to be taught and improved fast and were a great interest to Adele and me.

In April Emma returned from the Gurneys, Mr. Gurney still very ill, and Adele returned from Lady Olivia's.

On the 20th. I went to stay with the Moilliets at Selly Hall, near Birmingham, and dined one day at Hamstead Hall at old Mr. and Mrs. Moilliets', where we met Miss Edgeworth, her sister Mrs. Wilson, and her brother Pakenham Edgeworth. Miss Edgeworth was a little old woman, an incessant talker, clever and amusing, and liked a good listener. [This is of course a reference to the novelist Maria Edgeworth (1767-1849), who was a lifelong friend of Mrs. Amelia Moilliet, née Keir.]

On 26th. April I set off to London to stay with my Aunt Gurney, who much wanted one of us to write and help her in many ways. Mr. Gurney, who was very slowly recovering, was for the first time moved into the drawing room for a short time every day, and from this time gradually recovered and lived twenty years longer, dying at the age of ninety-one.

One day we went to see the Queen, the Emperor of Russia, and the

King of Saxony come from Windsor to London. The Emperor was very fine looking, and looked every inch an Emperor. When he arrived and was shown into the State bedroom, he desired to have some fresh straw, which was put in a bag on which he slept, in preference to a bed! It was a relief to all when he left, there was so much fear he might be shot by some Pole. In those days there were many Poles of high rank in England, who had been driven from their country, and all of course bitter against Russia. One lived several years in Leamington and was always seen sitting in Bettison's verandah on the Parade, talking to gentlemen who joined him.

On 28th. June I returned home and came from Coventry by coach with Mrs. Ford Barclay, Mrs. Sam Gurney, and Mrs. Foster Reynolds (Mrs. Fry's daughter). I found my dear Father very feeble. He had not strength to throw off his usual asthma this summer, and suffered in other ways in consequence. Mr. Hodgson came several times to see and advise my Father.

In July Mr. Hallam, the historian, his son and daughter, whom Emma and Francis had travelled so much with in Germany, came to Leamington and dined with us and were most pleasant. Darwin and Mary came to meet them and to help my Father to entertain them.

On 9th. September my dear Father, Emma, and Francis set off for London, where they left Emma to go to the Gurneys, and went on to St. Leonards-on-Sea, hoping the change would do my Father good, and on the 11th. my Mother and we all went to Claverdon.

Our little schools at Claverdon were a great interest to Adele and myself. Few of the people had Bibles, so we kept a stock at Mrs. Gumbley's, which we sold greatly under their price. Many were bought and, as they cost something, were prized. Adele had a little donkey chair in which she always went, not being able to walk much, and one day, in coming from her school, something frightened the donkey, who galloped off and upset the carriage against a hedge. Adele was much cut about her face and was obliged to be plastered on her cheek and forehead.

*

My Father seemed to get better at the seaside, and he wrote to us to say he was so much recovered that he should return, and desired the carriage should be sent to Coventry to meet him, but on the 29th. I (who was staying at Edstone) heard from my Mother that Francis had written to beg her to come; my Father was suddenly worse. He wrote also to Emma in London, who went down to him at once. On 1st. October my Mother and I drove to Coventry and by train to London, and on by road to St. Leonards, where we arrived that evening. We found my Father at the Hotel, very ill. He was anxious we should go out and see the neighbourhood, but we never left him. The Winthrops and Lincoln Galtons were at St. Leonards, very kind and helpful. My Mother got lodgings, as there was little hope of his being able to go home, and we moved there. On the 8th. my Father had another relapse and from that time gradually sank. On the 14th Adele came, and Erasmus came a few days after. Darwin and Mary took lodgings near us, and my brothers took it in turn to be with my Father night and day. He had rallied before, that we clung to hope as long as we could. On the 20th he became unconscious, and on the 23rd October the end came at 1 o'clock in the day.

To describe our grief I cannot. Never was a Father more beloved by every one of his children; he was their friend, their companion, their everything. My Mother felt it deeply. She had been very out of health for some years, but she bore up bravely and arranged that Darwin, Mary, and I should go to Leamington next day to prepare for all coming home and for the funeral. We had a wretched journey, all so depressed, and arrived late at night. The next day, Darwin and Mary went to settle things at Claverdon, and I was left alone. I could hardly bear the loneliness and was thankful that Elizabeth Wheler called to enquire after us. She stayed some time with me and was very kind, till her brother called for her.

On the 28th. my Father's remains came with Francis and our butler, and the next day the whole family returned home. My dear Father was buried at Claverdon on the 31st. My three brothers, James Moilliet, my Uncle Hubert Galton, and Theodore Moilliet attended. We asked Dr. Marsh to perform the Service. Darwin, James Moilliet, and I were left executors of my Father's will, and it was a comfort to me that I had so much to do, and to do it as he would wish. My sister Lucy was very near her confinement and could not come to us. She felt very acutely her Father's death, so I went to her for a few days to tell her all particulars.

*

I must now go back a little. I mentioned that Adele had been upset in her donkey carriage and her face cut and plastered up. The day after my Mother and I went to St. Leonards and Adele was left alone, Mr. Robert Bunbury called to see her. He had been curate to Mr. Craig at the Parish Church for some time and knew Adele, seeing her at the school and at Dr. Marsh's. He left Leamington and soon after got a living in Lancashire, and immediately came to Leamington to propose to her, saying that he had long been attached to her, but had not means to marry her till then. Adele, with her patched face, told him that she must think about it and talk it over with her family before she could give him an answer. When she joined us, she told me what had happened, and we both agreed nothing could be said or done while my Father was so ill. Adele wrote to tell him she could not think about it under the circumstances. He however was very persevering and, soon after we returned home, he told my Mother and came to Leamington and was soon after accepted. He was an excellent clergyman, much liked and respected wherever he had been. His Mother was a Shirley, his Uncle and Aunt a good old couple in Derbyshire, respected and liked by everyone.

On 9th. December the railway was opened from Leamington to Coventry and Rugby, a great convenience.

On 11th. December I went to Selly Hall to stay with my dear sister Lucy for her confinement, which took place on 29th. December at a quarter to three in the morning, of a little girl, Sophie. A day or two after, her husband had a letter from his Mother telling him that his Father was very ill and in great danger. James set off at once to Abberley, merely telling my sister that his father was not well and wished to see him; no mention of danger was made to her, it was so essential she should be quiet. James wrote to me every day, the accounts of his father getting worse, and on 6th. January, 1845, Mr. Moilliet died, having lived a few months at Abberley. He was seventy-five years of age and a Swiss by birth. [The diary which was kept later by the Sophia whose birth is recorded here, says that the old gentleman died of a chill, which he contracted by rushing home from Church on Christmas Day to admire the magnificent view from Abberley Hall, which he had just had built.]

On 24th. January I returned home, Mr. Bunbury came to Leamington and called every day, and was finally accepted by my sister. His cousin became bishop of St. Asaph, and a curious thing happened. Mr. Shirley, to escape legacy duty, made over all his money to his son the Bishop, who however died before his father, so that he had to pay all the expenses to get his own money back!

*

Edward Wheler, who was still attached to me, and I had many talks as to whether it would be prudent in us to marry upon between five and six hundred a year. I so feared it would not be enough to be independent, and I could not bear the idea of being a burden on my family, but after much thought, and consultations with my Mother and sister, we agreed to wait till all my fortune was paid to me by the end of the year, and then to marry.

My Mother made up her mind to live at Claverdon; my sisters and I therefore determined to let our house in Lansdowne Place. All the furniture, plate, pictures, &c., with the exception of what my Mother had, was left to my two sisters and myself, and we divided them amongst us. We were all very anxious to have my dear Father's picture, so drew lots for it and it fell to Emma, who most kindly sent it to the artist who took it, and ordered him to make a copy for Adele and me. The furniture was very useful to Adele and me, as we were going to marry, and what we did not want, Emma sold. We had a very quiet spring; Mrs. Chandos Pole, my Aunt, came to Leamington to drink the waters and used to go down to the Pump Room every morning on a donkey. She was a very fashionable old lady, and one we were all afraid of, but very courteous and condescending.

In April, 1845, we heard of the death of Irwin Maling. He was sent to the Sierra Leone station, caught the fever, was invalided home, and died just as the ship was in sight of England. We felt his death having known him from our childhood. He and Erasmus had twice served in the same ship and he often came to stay with us.

On 13th. May, my sister Adele was married to Robert Bunbury at St. Mary's Church. As we were all in deep mourning, the wedding was perfectly quiet: Darwin, Mary, James and Lucy, Erasmus, Francis, Mr. Thomas Bunbury, Emma and I went to Church. Darwin gave her away, and Archdeacon Shirley (afterwards Bishop of St. Asaph) married them. Dr. Marsh and Mrs. Chandos Pole came to breakfast with us and, soon after, Adele and her husband set off to the Isle of Man. We were delighted with Archdeacon Shirley, so truly religious a man, without any cant. Religion seemed to pervade everything he said, and we were sorry when he went.

*

In this May, Mrs. John Kemble [see p.95] died. She was the widow of John Kemble the actor, a very clever woman, She knew everybody and had a large correspondence with Ministers and people in power. My Mother told us her history. John Kemble was engaged by Lord North to teach his daughters, one of whom fell in love with him. When Kemble became aware of this, he very honourably told Lord North he wished to resign his situation. On being pressed for the reason, he told what he had discovered, and felt that it would be wrong in him to stay. Lord North was much pleased with his conduct and said to him: "If you will get married in three weeks, I will portion your bride, and that will settle the matter to my daughter." Kemble, after thinking whom he could marry in so short a time, fixed upon one of the actresses, a woman of excellent character, and married her. I forget her name.

*

Edward Wheler and his Sisters often came to see us, and I had very kind letters from all his family upon our engagement which was now announced. On the 4th. June I went to stay a few days with the Whelers at Kenilworth, and stayed there till the 9th. when I returned home.

On 16th. June, Emma went to London to the Gurneys, and a few days after, I left our home for good and went to stay at The Spring with the Whelers, and on the 24th. I went to stay with my Mother at Claverdon, to make it my home till I married, which could not be till the end of the year. My share of the furniture was housed at an Upholsterer. We felt much giving up our home in Leamington, where we had so many friends, and all reminded us of our dear Father. My little school was of great interest to me at Claverdon. Edward Wheler rode over frequently to see me, and I went to The Spring often.

In July I went to visit the Hubert Galtons in Portman Square. On the 30th. I went to the Hudson Gurneys in St. James's Square. My Aunt had felt my dear Father's death very much, and talked much to me about him. On 6th. August I left the Gurneys and joined Edward and Elizabeth Wheler at the station and went with them to Brighton, I to stay with the Moilliets and they to stay with their relations Margaret Sitwell and Miss Charlotte Wheler. We had a very pleasant time at Brighton. On 24th. September I left Brighton and paid a visit of some days to Mr. and Mrs. Fox at Elstree. Mr. Fox talked much of a strange disease this autumn among the potatoes, and how important it was to be careful in saving plenty to plant next year, and all small ones were put by for that purpose, many of which turned out, of course, good for nothing. This was the beginning of the potato famine.

On 4th. October, Emma, Edward Wheler, and I went to Hadzor, joined at Birmingham by Uncle Hubert – Edward's first introduction to my Uncles and Aunts. On arriving, it appeared that Edward's portmanteau had not arrived with the luggage, and there was a large party coming to dinner, and he was obliged to appear in his morning dress! However, the portmanteau appeared, and he was able to dress after dinner. We met many friends there and left on the 11th, Emma to the Moilliets at Selly Hall, Edward to Kenilworth, and I to stay a few days with my cousins the Miss Bromleys, who had taken a pretty, small cottage at Bewdley, which looked on one side into the Park.

Their old servant Titterington, who had nursed some of them, lived with them till her death some years later. My cousins, who had a very small income, spent their lives in doing good by denying themselves. As they dropped off, one by one, they were taken to Abberley, and all lie together in the old Churchyard, where my dear sister Lucy is buried.

(February 19th., 1900. This day I complete my ninety-second year, therefore any mistakes or repetitions will, I hope, be excused.)

I think it was on my return from Bewdley to Selly Hall that at the stations I found numbers of women and girls who had been hop-picking and had finished, waiting for the trains to go home. They looked healthy and well from their stay in the country and all had ropes of apples round their necks, and wild flowers and hops on their bonnets, being allowed to take as many as they could carry. It was a very gay and pretty sight.

About this time Robert Bunbury had the living of Swansea given to him, the value about £860 a year, and he and my sister were glad to leave St. Helens and remove there. Swansea was a large place, and many of the inhabitants were Unitarians, but Robert gradually made friends with them by conciliating manners, and was much liked by all the Protestants. He preached excellent practical sermons, and he and my sister did much good during the short time they were there.

I spent my time between Selly Hall, Edstone, and Claverdon, and was busy preparing for my marriage. [Our readers will appreciate that a round of visits was customary when a young lady was about to be married.] I spent some days with Mr. and Mrs. Wood, who invited me to stay with them to finish my shopping and take leave of all my Leamington friends. I had many useful presents: Mrs. Brewin gave me some plate and house linen; My Uncle Howard Galton, silver forks; Uncle Hubert Galton, a breakfast set; Aunt Booth, a chair; my Mother, brothers, and sisters, cheques – besides presents from very intimate friends.

*

On Christmas Day, 1845, the large new house at Abberley, which was just finished building, took fire, no one knew how, and was burnt to the ground. Queen Adelaide was then living at Witley Court, Lord Foley's place, at the bottom of the hill on which Abberley Hall stands. As soon as the fire was observed, one or two Princes and several men rushed up the hill to give assistance, and most useful they were. They tore down doors and chimney pieces and saved much that would otherwise have been destroyed. Queen Adelaide sent off to offer clothing, bedding, &c., and offered to take Mrs. Moilliet in; nothing could be kinder than she was, but Mrs. Moilliet stayed at the Rectory till she could find a house. There was no time lost in rebuilding the house, still larger then the last, and much money was spent upon a place too large for any of the family to live in after Mrs. Moilliet's death. [One detects a note of disapproval here – justified in the event! This account does need correcting in some respects: Lucy's mother-in-law in fact decided to stay at the Hundred House Inn, and later took Laughern House for a while, rather than accepting the Dowager Queen's kind invitation – in order to avoid making her neighbours jealous! The fire was a nine-days' wonder, and according to Aris's Birmingham Gazette the population for miles around repaired to the scene, "and deep indeed are the expressions of sorrow uttered by the peasantry that such a misfortune should have happened to a family who had so distinguished themselves by kindness to the neighbouring poor." Abberley Hall is now a well-known boys' preparatory school].

*

On 30th. December, Lucy with her two little girls, Amy and Adele, arrived, and on the 31st. Edward Wheler and I were married very quietly at Claverdon Church. Darwin gave me away, Emma and Elizabeth and the two little girls were my bridesmaids, Frederick Wheler married us, and Mr. Hume was Edward's best man. At 12 o'clock, after breakfast, Darwin lent us his carriage and coachman Yeeles, to drive us to Bromsgrove, where we got into the train for Clifton – a pouring wet drive. Mr. Hume had given me a large wedding nosegay of artificial flowers, which I carried with me. At some small station a gentleman with two little boys got into our compartment. He did not see me, being occupied with the boys' luggage, but I knew him at once as the Reverend Mr. Atwood, formerly of Kenilworth, at whose school Francis had been. I felt it would be very awkward to recognise him. I had not seen him since my Father's death, and he could know nothing of my marriage, so I whispered to Edward to take no notice of me, and I kept my nosegay up to my face and he never found out. Some months after, my sister met him, and told him what I had done. He remembered a lady in the train who seemed very fond of smelling her nosegay, but had no idea it was me!

Chapter 11

Early Years of Married Life (1846-1857)

We slept at Clifton, and the next day (January 1st., 1846) went to Exeter and posted on to Budleigh Salterton, where we took lodgings, a very quiet place. Sir Trevor and Lady Wheler were staying at Bicton with Lady Rolle, and a few days after our arrival Sir Trevor called upon us and invited us to pay them a visit at Cross, near Torrington. We stayed a fortnight at Budleigh, and on 19th. January we went to Sidmouth, a nice quiet little place, and the country around prettier than at Budleigh. We saw the house where the Duke of Kent died and took many pleasant walks. On 22nd. February we left Sidmouth and went to stay at Sir Trevor Wheler's at Cross. We had a very pleasant visit; Lady Wheler took me drives to show me the country. One day we went to Stevenstone, which Lord Rolle, who had recently died, had left to Lord Clinton's second son, a young boy at school, and there was much discussion whether he should be told or not.

This winter was a remarkably mild one, and the peaches out of doors were in full blossom and all vegetables unusually forward.

*

My sister Adele Bunbury was getting near her confinement and, as I was so near, it was settled we should go to Swansea that I might be with her. We therefore left Cross, after a pleasant visit, went by post to Ilfracombe, and the next day went in a small sailing packet across the Bristol Channel, being assured we should soon get across. All went well till we were half way, when the wind fell and there was a dead calm, and not an inch could we move. The cabin was a small place one could not move in, and no room to lie down in, and we began to think we should be all night. The sailors whistled for a wind, and after not moving for an hour or so, one exclaimed "She's coming," and soon after, a breeze came on and we landed at six o'clock at The Mumbles, not far from Swansea. A large omnibus, capable of carrying sixteen people inside, was just starting, and we went in it to Swansea. There was no one but ourselves in the vehicle, and we were consequently jolted all the way. We were received very kindly by Adele and her husband in their comfortable house, and we found her pretty well. The next day we took a lodging near her, which was fortunate, for I was laid up for some days and not able to leave the house.

I had good accounts of my Mother, who had long ago got tired of having a companion who was not a relative, and lived alone at Claverdon, Darwin and Mary often coming over to see her. Emma spent the winter in Italy with the Howard Galtons, which did her good.

I have said before that many of the principal families and others in Swansea were Unitarians, and soon after Mr. Bunbury came, they challenged him to prove they were wrong in their belief. Mr. Bunbury wished to decline controversy, but they insisted. In consequence, he preached a sermon, a copy of which I have, which created a great sensation in Swansea. It was delivered, a Sunday or two before we arrived, and everyone was talking about it and praising it. The Church was crammed to hear it – many Unitarians present. A young officer, Mr. Wills, told me the interest was so great, you might have heard a pin drop, as the saying is; though the service lasted three hours, everyone was sorry when it was over.

As soon as I was well, I spent most of the day with my sister, who was confined on 13th. March of a little girl, Millicent. She made a good recovery, and we stayed in Swansea till 26th. March. It was a large town and not well kept. The pipes which carried the water down from the tops of the houses did not go down into a drain, but stopped about a foot from the ground, and consequently the water ran upon the footpath after rain. Many lobsters were caught in curious baskets; the bay was covered with these baskets.

*

On 26th. March we left Adele well and happy with her child and went by steam across the channel to Clifton, to spend a few days with Mrs. Molony of Kiltanon, who was staying there with her daughter. Mr. Molony was in Ireland, which was in a very disturbed state. On 30th. March we went to Bath to spend a few days with Mr. and Mrs. Frank Mills. He was formerly Rector of Barford, and she was a Mordaunt, good and excellent people. Their second son, Arthur Mills, was with them, in very low spirits. Some weeks before, he had been shooting with Sir John Mordaunt, and somehow, in getting over a stile or through a hedge, his gun went off and hit Sir John in the leg. Mr. Hodgson was sent for, and for a few days the wound seemed to be doing well, but then erysipelas came on and he died, and Mr. Arthur Mills could not get over his distress for a long time.

Emma Wheler was staying with Mr. and Mrs. Mills. We met many friends in Bath, and I was introduced to a host of Wheler relations, and being determined to understand the family connections, I set down the names and relationship of each family we visited, and so began my Wheler genealogy. Lady Wheler helped me at Cross, then Mrs. Molony and Mrs. Mills.

On 4th. April we went to stay with my Aunt and Dr. Booth in Great Pulteney Street. The doctor had got tired of Birmingham a short time before and had come to live in Bath. I always enjoyed being with her. While there I went to see the Miss Fourniers, where I had been to school, and also Eliza Sitwell. One day we dined with Sir Edward and Lady Thomason. Sir Edward was quite a character. After the Battle of Waterloo, when the Marquis of Anglesea returned to England, the first person he saw was Sir Edward, with a wonderful false leg to present to him. Formerly a plain wooden leg was used, but this was made with a spring and looked like a real leg – probably like what is now common. Sir Edward amused us much, telling us of all the compliments he received, and how he went to Court to present some medals to George IV, and on entering "Fell upon his knees and, as it were, went up the room upon them."

On 13th. April we spent the day at Berkeley, near Frome, with the Henry Whelers. We found them in a very excited state. They thought we should come by rail and had sent a trap to meet and bring us. About a quarter of an hour before we arrived, the empty trap rushed by the house and no one in it, and they fancied, we must have been overturned &c., and were greatly relieved when we drove up in a carriage from Bath. We spent a pleasant day with them and the next day went to stay at The Spring, Kenilworth, and began to look for our future home.

On 5th. May we went to stay at Claverdon and saw a letter come from Adele, saying that Robert Bunbury was dangerously ill of gastric fever, which was just then very prevalent in Swansea; nearly every house suffered more or less. At one time the account of Robert was better, and we quite hoped he would recover.

At this time Captain Hibbert, hearing we had not met with a house to suit us, very kindly offered us a temporary home in a house at Dunchurch which, in consequence of his brother's death, was now vacant. It was a good sized house, and we were to have as many rooms as we wanted and a kitchen to ourselves. The groom and his wife had a room at the top and "did" for the Roman Catholic Priest, who had two rooms to himself. We went on 18th. May for one night to arrange everything for our coming to stay.

In the meantime, Adele was in constant anxiety about her husband and sent her baby and its nurse to my Mother, for fear it should take the fever, and she and Robert would follow as soon as he was well enough, but on 25th. May he had a relapse and became worse every day till the 28th., on which day he died. My poor sister had gone through much trouble, the two doctors disagreeing about his treatment and quarreling by his bedside! Robert Bunbury was only forty-two years old.

It was agreed among us that Edward and I should go at once to Adele, and we set off on the 30th., as far as Bristol, where we slept, and the next day we went on in the Swansea mail, a long day's journey. Being Sunday, there were scarcely any passengers but ourselves.

An intensely hot day, and the dust covering everything, I was alone inside, and very glad when Edward recommended me to come outside with him. We arrived very late and slept at the hotel. I went to see my sister as soon as I arrived and found the house full. I was with Adele all day, and we urged her to return with us after the funeral, for sickness and fever were raging in the town.

On 3rd. June the funeral took place. Mr. Thomas Bunbury, my Husband, three clergymen, and three doctors attended, and this scarcely a month after I had left them so happy with their child. The last service Robert Bunbury performed was christening his own child. The day after, the Bunburys left, and we began packing away everything in the house safely till she returned. Great sorrow was expressed by all at Swansea at the loss of their Vicar, and Mr. Warner preached a very good sermon on the occasion.

On 9th. June we went by sea to Bristol, Adele, Mr. and Mrs. Warner, and their little children with us. Mr. and Mrs. Warner became sea-sick at once, and the care of the children fell upon me, for which they were most grateful. We slept at Bristol, arrived next day at Selly Hall, where we stayed for one night with the Moilliets, and the next day Lucy, Adele, and I went to Claverdon. The next day, 12th. June, I met Edward at Rugby, and he drove me to Dunchurch, where we settled in.

[After various unsuccessful house-hunting expeditions, they took a house at Snitterfield, where they settled that summer.]

*

This autumn there began to be serious anxiety about the potato disease, which appeared again and was worse than in last year. When first dug up, the potatoes were perfectly good, but after a few days they became rotten and good for nothing. While we were at Dunchurch, my Mother sent us a basket of vegetables. The potatoes were good when packed, but when they arrived they had to be thrown away, smelling horribly. This was the beginning of the terrible famine in Ireland, where in spite of warning they had planted nothing but potatoes and all were bad.

In December, Francis returned from his foreign tour and came to my Mother at Claverdon, and we went to meet him. He had quite given up all intention of being a medical man, having sufficient income to be independent of practice, and he determined to devote himself to science. Emma decided to live with my Mother at Claverdon, and Adele, when she had finished all her affairs at Swansea, came to live in Leamington.

This winter was a terrible one in Ireland, and the accounts were heartrending, all potatoes gone bad, and nothing to take their place. There was not sufficient corn in England to spare enough for all Ireland, and the Corn Laws forbade foreign wheat to be imported. Every household, from the Palace downwards, was most careful to use as little flour as possible, that there might be more to send to Ireland. No pastry was made and no bread cut, but the loaf was sent up, that each might cut just what was wanted and no pieces left. In Ireland, numbers were dying daily from starvation, and often whole families were swept off. It was an awful time.

My sister Mrs. Moilliet sent me a letter from a lady in Ireland, describing the horrors the poor were going through, and requesting her to interest her friends in making and sending clothes, which were sorely needed. One could not read the letter without tears. I showed it to Mr. Cameron, our clergyman, and he read it from the pulpit the next Sunday, adding that I would receive and send any clothing that was sent to me. All our friends in Snitterfield and the wives of the principal farmers, set to work, and I was able to send a large packet to my sister, who forwarded it to the lady who wrote to her.

Some weeks after, one of the farmer's wives asked me whether I had heard from the lady acknowledging the parcel, naturally thinking we might have had some thanks. I wrote to my sister, who replied that the parcel had been sent and arrived safely, but not one word of thanks! And this was by no means a solitary instance of want of gratitude for what the English did for them. On 24th. March, 1847, we had a fast day all over the Kingdom on account of the famine, and the Government put an end to the restriction on corn and plenty came from America. [Knowing what we do now about the inadequate help which the Irish received during the famine – especially from the government of the day – this passage makes strange reading. Perhaps the ungrateful Irish lady was too busy to keep up the niceties – or she may herself have been a victim?]

We lived a very quiet life with two maids and a boy, Henry Horsman, who lived close by and took charge of the pony, &c. We set up poultry, pigs, and a swarm of bees, and took much interest in our garden and orchard. My husband qualified as a magistrate and went every week to attend the Warwick Petty Sessions.

My sister Emma came to stay with us, and on 21st. April my first child was born at six o'clock in the morning. I made a good recovery, but it was so cold a spring it was some time before I could go out of doors. On 19th. June, Lucy and four children and Emma Wheler came to stay, and on Sunday, 20th. June my baby was christened Lucy Elizabeth by Mr. Cameron. In this month I began to visit a district in the parish, which Mr. Cameron had allotted to me, and in which I took great interest.

On 4th. September we went to stay with the Sitwells at the Parsonage at Leamington Hastings, where we stayed till the 18th., my husband shooting with Captain Wilmot and Mr. Sitwell. We always enjoyed our visits there, and seeing our friends and relations in the neighbourhood. They had a custom in the village, that no one was allowed to go in the fields to glean till a bell rang about eight o'clock. The object was to enable the married women to dress their children and give them their breakfast, and start at the same time as the unmarried girls.

*

On 3rd. December a person came to question me about a letter I had sent to one of my sisters-in-law, outside of which was written, "A used stamp, twopence to pay". There had for some time been complaints about letters with stamps apparently taken off and charged double, and one of the men at the Post Office was suspected. When my letter was delivered, my sister took it at once to the Post Office, knowing that I should not think of putting an old stamp on. The Authorities took it up – a man was sent from London to see me, and the letter was traced through the Stratford and Leamington Post Offices to Kenilworth, and it proved to be the man who delivered the letters, and who had been for some time taking stamps off newspapers and then charging double postage and pocketing the money, and he was sent to be tried. On 3rd. January, 1848, I was summoned to appear at the Quarter Sessions to give evidence against the postman, which was not pleasant. The trial did not come up till the next day. I was afraid I should have to stand in the witness box and was much relieved to find I might sit with Edward and Emma Wheler. The oath was administered, and I was merely asked whether I had put a fresh stamp on the letter. The man was found guilty and sent, I think, to jail for some months.

Old Mr. Ellis was the Clergyman at Wootton Wawen, an excellent old man, very fond of his garden. He was a widower. His daughter and her husband lived with him, also his sister-in-law, who looked about sixty or more. She so disliked that her age should be known that, when a census was taken, and every householder had to mention the age of every person who slept in his house on a certain night, she hired a fly and drove in it the whole night, and so escaped telling her age.

*

On 25th. May I went with little Lucy to Selly Hall to see my sister Lucy, who was ill. We had been rather anxious about her for some time, but when I now saw her and heard Mr. Hodgson's opinion, I knew she was very seriously ill and in great danger, symptoms of dropsy appearing. She was very anxious to go to the sea, which had always done her good, and on 9th. June, James and the six children went to Brighton, to take a house ready for my sister. We had settled a day for her going, when Mr. Russell, who attended her, recommended our putting it off, as there was expectation of a rise of the Chartists, who were coming in immense numbers to present a petition to Parliament, and disturbances were expected.

This took place on the famous 10th. April, when the Duke of Wellington managed so skilfully to make preparations without any show, and hundreds of citizens, Members of Parliament, Noblemen, &c. enrolled as Special Constables, among whom was Prince Napoleon. The Chartists, seeing they had no chance, gave up and dispersed quietly. [Perhaps not quite the verdict of history?] It was said the preparations cost London two millions. The Duke had ordered small parties of soldiers to drop quietly down the areas of the houses which the Chartists would pass by, but not to show themselves till ordered, so that the whole way was defended.

On the 19th., Lucy and I set off for Brighton, she lying down the whole way. When we arrived in London, Emma met us and went on with Lucy, while I returned with a heavy heart home.

On 5th. August, old Southall died in his ninety-ninth year, having been sixty years in the Galton service, and much respected by the family – a thoroughly honest, hard-working labourer. He was a very strong man, and it was said a heavy cart wheel once drove over his body without injuring him. He used to show off to the servants how he could eat crockery without harm, and pretended he liked it!

On 6th. August, I heard that Lucy wished I could come to her: accordingly on the 8th. I set off with my husband to Brighton. My sister was anxious to find a good governess, with whom she could feel at her death her children would be properly managed and cared for. A lady applied and seemed likely to suit; I wrote to a particular friend of ours, who knew her, requesting she would tell us honestly what she thought of her, and mentioning my sister's health. Although this lady knew Miss X was most unfit, she wrote giving her a most excellent character. She was engaged and came a few days after, and while I was there pretended to be everything we could wish, but she did much mischief, and my brother-in-law sent her away soon after my sister's death.

I stayed with my very dear Sister till the 18th. September, and left her with a very heavy heart, knowing I should never see her again. She became worse, and my Mother and Emma set off for Brighton and took lodgings near her. Erasmus also went and was of great use in lifting my poor sister, who was very heavy with dropsy. My sister rejoiced to see them, but gradually got worse and died quietly on 5th. November. My Mother, Emma, Erasmus, Francis, and James Moilliet were with her at the time.

It was a terrible break in the family – we were all much attached to her, she was so loving and sweet-tempered. She left six children, the eldest only fifteen, and the youngest not four years old. She was buried in the old Churchyard at Abberley. Her servants were devoted to her. Hannah Best, her maid, was like a Mother to the children after her death, and Ann Croft (Mrs. Hinsley) was brought up in her School and was then cook, and had been some years with her and a devoted servant. My Mother and Emma returned home the day after her death. I felt her loss greatly. She was nearest me in age and we were much attached to each other, and I had been with her in all her illnesses. She was always cheerful even when in pain and always trying to make others happy.

James gave up Selly Hall and moved to a house at Abberley [The Elms] near his Mother.

*

On 11th. November, 1848, my Uncle Robert Darwin of Shrewsbury died. He was half-brother to my Mother and was eighty-two years of age. He had been some time in declining health. He was a cheerful, kind-hearted man, whom we all liked, full of anecdote, and had a large practice among the nobility around Shrewsbury. I will relate one of his amusing tales. He was sent for to Mrs. I. of H., in North Wales, a beautiful place, far from a town. Dr. Darwin recommended her to try a particular wine and asked if she had any. She replied, "No, but Lord L., who lives near, has, and I will send to him." She rang for a servant and told him to send one of the men, who could speak English, to Lord L. and say that Dr. Darwin recommended her to take such a wine and to ask if he would kindly send her a bottle. Dr. Darwin, much surprised, said, "I thought you and Lord L. had quarrelled and did not speak?" "Quite true, Dr. Darwin, but we both live so far from any town that we find it convenient to do neighbourly actions of this sort." Soon after, the man returned with <u>two</u> bottles of wine from Lord L. Soon after, Dr. Darwin was sent for to Lady L., and recommended something to her which she had not got, but she would send to Mrs. I., who she knew could supply her. A message was sent by a careful man, for they would not write to each other, and a supply was sent. Some time after, one of the ladies told Dr. Darwin that they had met by accident in a shop and, after looking at each other, burst out laughing and shook hands!

*

On 23rd. January, 1849, Admiral Maling died, to our sorrow. His first wife was my Aunt, Harriot Darwin, who died in South America [see p.52]. His second wife was my first cousin, Jemima Bromley, by whom he had four children. The son married and went to New Zealand and has a large family [and descendants living today]. Admiral Maling was a very handsome agreeable man, whom we all liked. He was also a good officer and had seen much service.

[According to the sketch of his life which was written by his widow, and which we have found quoted in Abberley Manor, by the Rev. J.L. Moilliet, Elliot Stock, 1905, Admiral Maling had twenty years of active service, during which he captured a Spanish frigate of 28 guns, three privateers of from 16 to 20 guns, and about twenty sail of enemy merchantmen. "And what is really far more important, his endeavours were always supported by his example in promoting reverence, morality, and good conduct on board his ships."]

*

I had engaged a new cook, who had a bad cough when she came, owing, she said, to her late mistress when dying requiring her door and window opened night and day, and the cook had helped to attend her. She suddenly became very ill and we sent her to the Hospital at Leamington to undergo an operation, but when there it was found she was in the last stages of consumption and had begged to go home to die, which she did.

In March I became very poorly suddenly and had to go to bed and be kept quiet. We had invited a party to dinner, the Attyes and

Andersons, and Emma kindly came to do the honours for me. On Sunday morning, when the maids went to get the baby's milk and tea for me, they found the larder had been robbed in the night and everything eatable gone! Luckily they took nothing else, or they might have gone into the hall and carried off greatcoats &c. We had to send to our neighbours to beg for meat, bread, butter, milk, and everything for breakfast and dinner. There were many robberies after in the village.

On 8th. August Mrs. Phillips gave a grand archery party to all her friends. There were one hundred and seventy guests, and it was a beautiful day and a very enjoyable party. Darwin made excellent arrangements for the servants and horses. His coachman presided at a good supper for the visitors' coachmen, and another man presided over the cabmen's supper, and care was taken that they should not drink too much. Cricket was also provided for them and kept them out of mischief, and all returned Darwin thanks for his care of them. We went to Edstone in the afternoon: first we had archery, and when that was over there was a grand supper in a large tent. Two men cooks came from London, and everything was well done. We then adjourned to the house, and dancing was kept up till a late hour. My Uncle Howard Galton and his two sons were among the guests, and we all agreed it was a delightful party.

On 18th. September, 1849, my Mother took little Lucy to Claverdon while we went to Derby to visit the Robert Sitwells at Morley. We called on Mrs. Hadley on our way through Derby, and the next day we went to the dear old Priory, to call on my Uncle and Aunt, Sir Francis and Lady Darwin. I had not been in Derby since my dear Grandmother's death and it was a very painful pleasure seeing the Priory again without her. I went all over the house, gardens, wilderness, saw old Doctor's (the horse's) grave, etc., etc., but all was so changed, so different, I wished I had not gone. I went to Church at Breadsall, sat in the old pew, and saw all the Tablets to the family, but none of the old people I knew, all seemed changed! My Cousins were very kind and took me everywhere over the house and gardens. Georgiana, Violetta, Eliza and Millicent were at home. Fanny had just married her second husband, Mr. Huish, and was on her wedding tour.

We then returned home, saw my Mother, and brought back our child.

*

On 30th. March, 1850, my Mother took me in her carriage to Warwick to see Darwin, who was High Sheriff this year, bringing in the Judges. It was a pretty sight in those days, but not so grand as formerly. Some years before, I was in Derbyshire when my cousin Mr. Chandos Pole was High Sheriff. He had forty javelin men (his tenants) dressed in his livery and carrying long staves, walking to escort him. All the principal gentlemen in the county went to meet him on horseback and followed his carriage with the Judges to the Court House. During the Assizes, these javelin men were in Court and made a great show. The old custom before the railways came, was that the Sheriff, after the Assizes, should drive the Judges in state to the edge of the next County, where the Sheriff of that County would be ready to receive them, but latterly the Sheriff was accustomed to meet the Judges in their own carriage, a few miles out of the County Town only. On one occasion the Judge was much displeased with the Sheriff's conduct in some town, where he considered the Sheriff had not paid him proper attention; so after the Assizes, when he was in the carriage, he told the Sheriff he would insist on his driving him the whole way to the borders of the next county. The Sheriff replied, "Certainly, my Lord, I will do so if you wish it, but I must inform you the boundary is a river, and I must leave you in the middle of it." The Judge excused him!

In those days the expenses of the High Sheriff were very great, and never under one thousand pounds. It cost the Sheriff of York three thousand pounds, being so large a county. Now (1900) the Sheriff meets the Judge just outside the County Town, with no state, and hired footmen!

*

On 8th. June 1850 Emma came to stay with me during my confinement, which took place on the 12th., when my little boy was born at ten o'clock in the morning. Little Lucy was told a baby was coming, and when Mrs. Lomas (the monthly nurse) arrived, she would watch the whole time she was unpacking the clothes, thinking the baby was in the parcel. On 28th. August my little boy was christened Edward Galton Wheler*; Mr. Harvey Sitwell christened him in Snitterfield Church, Mr. Cameron being from home. Lucy stood by me during the ceremony and was much interested. From that time I generally took her to afternoon service at the Church, and she was very good. The first time she amused everyone by beginning to sing during the hymns, in her own childish way.

*

On 14th. February, 1851, I went with my Mother and Emma to London to Brown's for a few days' sight-seeing. The Crystal Palace was building and created great sensation, some admiring, some criticising and saying it would prove a failure, create a riot, the crowds of foreigners would capture London, &c., &c.

There had been a difficulty what the building should be, when Mrs. Paxton, the wife of the Duke of Devonshire's gardener, suggested why should it not be of glass like a greenhouse, and she drew a sketch, which was adopted. It was made in sections, every section alike, so would fit and could be put up easily. It had a great dome in the centre. There were some handsome trees in the way; as it was objected to cut them down, the dome was made high enough to cover them, and had a beautiful effect. We went to see the outside of the building and went to Bazaars, china shops, and in the evening to see the Panorama of the overland route to India.

Next day we went to see the Houses of Lords and Commons, the Panorama of the Arctic regions and various sights, and returned home at half past nine after two enjoyable days.

On 20th. March Mrs. Fox, my Mother's first Cousin, died. She was Mr. William Darwin's daughter and her brother William Darwin was

He took the surname of Wheler-Galton when he inherited Claverdon from his uncle, Darwin Galton. He died in 1935.

head of the Darwin family.

On 9th. May Emma went to London to the Gurneys. The Sitwells invited Edward and me to come to lodgings they had taken at 17 Dover Street, London, for some days to see the Exhibition, and on 19th. May we went, leaving the children at Claverdon with my Mother.

We went almost every day to the Exhibition and spent hours there. The sight at the entrance was almost overpowering! The grandeur, the size, the colouring, I cannot describe! It gave a feeling of awe and thanksgiving to the Almighty for the gift He had given to man to produce such wonders. Many told me they felt the same, no vanity, but wonder at the goodness of God to man. It was a sight never seen before, and every detail admirably planned. Even the flooring had been wisely arranged, the boards not touching by half an inch, so that the dust could be swept under them. All the best of everything of every nation was collected in that building and was interesting. One curiosity every lady went to see was in the artificial flower court: sprays of mignonette looking very real. It was thought most wonderful, and is now common in every milliner's shop! One thing struck us greatly: there were splendid pianofortes in the building, but in that great space they could be heard at a short distance only. There was a bed shown which, by setting an alarm at a particular hour, rang a bell and sent you out of bed. Everyone wanted to see it act, and the tinkling of that little bell was heard all over the building, while the pianos were not!

In the Dome, near the entrance, by the large tree, was a huge basin of water and fountain playing, with seats all round; it was the rendezvous of all parties walking round. There were courts upstairs and downstairs. The East India Court was gorgeous with shawls, elephant trappings &c. In the principal aisle was the Koh-i-nor diamond, uncut; it looked very like the stopper of a decanter. A Russian cloak, made of sables and costing more than one thousand pounds, was another wonder. It was quite a fairy scene, and one could hardly tear oneself away. Crowds of people, but all so orderly and quiet.

We went to the Royal Academy, water colours, dined with the Gurneys, and went one day to Kew Gardens. The last day we went to the Exhibition and saw the Queen and her Ladies and little Princess Alice there, walking round some of the Courts. We went to London on a Monday and left on the Saturday, greatly pleased, but dead tired.

*

My husband and I lived so quiet a life, with our children always with us, that I have little to tell. Our chief excitements were a swarm of bees or a hatch of chickens. At one of the poultry shows at Birmingham we sold several pullets at a pound each, sending some into Devonshire at that price. I remember one of my hives dying and a woman in the village telling me that the reason was, I had not told the hive of a death in the family. This was a common belief in the lower classes. They always tapped the hive, and then informed the Queen Bee that so-and-so was dead. Another belief was that it was unlucky to buy or sell a hive; they would give you a hive, and you would be expected to give a present to the wife of the seller of suitable value. When a hive swarmed, you followed it, beating on the warming pan with a key. The noise was supposed to induce them to settle, and also to show they were your bees, but if they settled on a dead tree it was no use to hive them: they would do no good and bring ill luck.

On 7th. April, 1852, we had the pleasure of seeing Francis on his return from South Africa. He had been away about two years, and it was a time of great anxiety to us. We were sometimes months without getting news of him, it was so difficult to send a letter. The Geographical Society were very kind in telling us if they heard anything of him. He had enjoyed his travels and had learned much of these countries. [This is rather an understatement: Francis Galton's expedition in Southwest Africa proved to be of considerable scientific value. It earned him the Gold Medal of the Geographical Society in 1853 and led to his election to the Royal Society in 1856. Numerous editions were printed of his books Tropical South Africa (1853) and The Art of Travel (1855). The latter was reprinted in 1971 by David and Charles, Newton Abbot.]

*

On 14th. September the good old Duke of Wellington died, after a few hours' illness, to the grief of the whole country. He was always called "The Duke," devotedly loyal to the Queen and his Country. His death caused as much sorrow as the death of a Sovereign would. The Queen felt it greatly and ordered he should have a public funeral.

On 17th. November, my Mother invited me to go with her and Emma to London, to see the Duke of Wellington's Public Funeral at St. Paul's. Francis, who was very out of health, went with us to Brown's Hotel. It was a fine day after the rains. On Thursday, 18th. November, we set off at seven o'clock in the morning to 88, Piccadilly, where we got seats at three pounds three shillings each. A very nice little alarm clock had just come out, and we had each bought one, and it seemed several people who had come to the Hotel had done the same, and we were much amused at hearing clock after clock going off in the different bedrooms.

The procession began to pass us at nine o'clock. It was a sad and most impressive sight, regiment after regiment playing the Dead March in Saul. All the principal Military Officers, and all looking grave and sorrowful, all shops closed, bells tolling, and everyone in mourning. The only thing that spoilt it was the funeral car, which tottered along as if it would come to pieces. It was very high and the Duke's coffin, perched at the top, looked as if it was a lid, instead of being the principal figure. Behind the car came the Duke's horse, led by his man, the boots hanging on and the man looking in grief; many of the soldiers showed grief in their countenances. It was a sight worth seeing but which I would not care to see again, it was so depressing.

We left London at five o'clock, an immense crowd of passengers, and had to wait till fresh carriages could be put on, and got home at half past nine. Francis, who had been suffering from a sort of low fever since he returned from Africa, was very poorly the next day. He continued so poorly my Mother determined to spend the winter at Dover, that he might be in a warm climate. She and Emma set off on 29th November and Francis joined them the next day. They found several friends there, and were introduced to Dr. Butler, Dean of Peterborough, whose Daughter became Francis's wife. Francis's health much improved, and they spent a very pleasant winter.

*

On 26th. April, 1853, we went to Claverdon to call and heard that Francis was engaged to Miss Butler, the daughter of the Dean of Peterborough. [She was Great-aunt to Mr R.A. Butler, later Lord Butler.]

On 4th. May we all went to stay at The Elms, in Abberley, with James Moilliet. We called at Abberley Hall on old Mrs. Moilliet, and I took the girls one day to call on old Lady Ward at Witley Court, an old Show Place [now a ruin] which used to belong to Lord Foley. We saw the new Church the Moilliets had built at Abberley. The bells were rung in a new manner by a person playing on a sort of pianoforte, each note striking a hammer on a bell, and requiring no strength. [This local wonder was, alas, destroyed by fire in 1873, and was not replaced when the church was rebuilt a few years later.] I visited the old Church, now in ruins, and saw my dear Sister's grave, and the graves of my Uncle Bromley and Uncle Maling.

This month the Dean of Peterborough died suddenly. He was sitting at dinner, and was saying how pleased he was at his daughter's engagement with Francis, when he suddenly fell back dead.

On 1st. June, Francis married Miss Louisa Butler at Peterborough, a quiet wedding, being so near her Father's death, Emma and Cameron Galton present.

*

On 24th June my Mother left Claverdon, and she and Emma went to live at Leamington, where she would be near a Doctor and have many comforts which they would not have in the country – bath chairs instead of a carriage and horse, &c. She took lodgings in Landsdowne Place, while she looked out for a residence, and finally took No. 5 Bertie Terrace.

Bertie Terrace, Leamington

Mrs Samuel Tertius Galton (née Violetta Darwin) in her drawing room at Bertie Terrace, 1867. Note the contrast with the sketch shown on page 3.

In October Mr. Robert Barclay of Leyton died. He was Head Partner of Barclay Bevan and Tritton's Bank in London, and Brother to my Aunt Hubert Galton. He was a very friendly pleasant man and we all liked him. He had several children, one Ann married Mr. Fowler, whom we met some years after at Cromer, with a large family. His son Gurney was a partner in the Bank.

In November we stayed with my Mother in Leamington. The Hubert Galtons were then in lodgings there. I enjoyed seeing my old friends, the Miss Manners Sutton, Nat Phillips, the Miss Bilbies-Le Blancs, Mat Wises, Woods, Charles Earles, Swynfens, Vyners, Carnegies, etc.

*

I am ashamed to go on with this journal, I have so little worth telling. We lived so quiet a life with our children, who were now very companionable and took much of my time teaching them. Little Edward was devoted to horses and enjoyed going with his papa to the stable; Lucy was very fond of chickens. We went nearly every week to see my Mother at Leamington and to old Mr. Wheler at Kenilworth, and the Powletts, Whelers, and Sitwells often came to us for a few days.

*

The 26th. April, 1854, was kept as a day of humiliation on account of the Crimean War, which was now going on, and in which we were much interested. I have not kept any particulars of this war in my diary. It was our first war since the Battle of Waterloo and was remarkable that the French and English should fight together against Russia, our former ally. It was always hoped that the Exhibition of 1851 would tend to cement peace among nations, yet in less than three years this war broke out.

On 1st. May, 1854, my Great Uncle, Captain Barclay Allardice, died at seventy-five. He was heir, through his mother, to the titles of Earl of Strathearn, besides the two Earldoms of Airth and Menteith, being lineally descended from Robert II of Scotland. At his Mother's death he put forward his claim, and though there was no doubt on the matter, it was not settled during his life and dropped through, and his successor had not enough money to go on with it. Captain Barclay was a noted pedestrian, and [once] walked a thousand miles in a thousand [consecutive] hours, and many other feats. He and his father were great Agriculturists, and did much to improve land and the breed of cattle in Scotland.

I had some trouble with my servants and parted with them all in May and got a new set. The new housemaid, Jane Parsons, had been maid to Mr. Bree, father of Archdeacon Bree. He was fond of collections, and Jane had learnt how to set butterflies, &c. and was an excellent help to my children, taking great interest in their museum.

On 9th. July, Lucy complained of sore throat and the next day began with scarlet fever. She went on pretty well till the 17th., when she became dangerously ill. She continued so ill the next day we sent for Dr. Jefferson [Jephson?] from Leamington, and his remedies took effect. We had Mr. Croft the surgeon to sleep in the house, in case she got worse, and to our great annoyance we were woke up in the night by his man knocking at the door to say he was wanted. Lucy began to recover, but did not go out of bed till the 23rd. It had been an anxious time to her father and to me. The nurse, housemaid, and I had never had the fever, and I dreaded their taking it. The housemaid took charge of little Edward, and with taking every precaution it did not spread. I did not hear till many months after that the new cook came from a house where the children had the Fever, and she must have brought it with her clothes.

*

My Mother very kindly invited us all to go to Tenby for some weeks with her, Lucy being very delicate after her illness. My Mother engaged a house for us next door to hers and we were to set off on the 4th. October. Little Edward, who was a very helpful child, helped to carry my winter clothes for me to pack up. They were in a drawer which had been locked up for some months, and when Lucy was ill she slept in my room, her bed near this drawer. The following day Edward looked ill, and next morning broke out with scarlet fever, three months after Lucy's attack. My husband went off at once to tell my Mother we could not leave home. She kindly offered to take Lucy with her till we could come, so the next day her Papa took her with her doll and a basket with her dinner and met my Mother and Emma at the station.

Little Edward had the fever mildly. I emptied the nursery of all furniture, carpet, and curtains to prevent infection remaining in the room and he soon recovered. To amuse him I had Viper, our dog, upstairs to play with him. The dog caught the fever from him and was never the same dog after.

On the 26th. October the child was so much better that we set off about six in the morning with two maids to Leamington, and got into the Great Western Railway for Tenby. Little Edward had a toy railroad and would stand at the window to watch the different parts of a real railroad. He seemed to get better every hour. At Narberth we left the railway and went by coach to Tenby, and arrived very tired about eight o'clock at No. 2, Castle Square. Emma was there to meet us and had ordered a good supper and a maid to help us, and very glad we were to go to bed. Our house was close to the sea; in front was the harbour and at the back the South Sands. The children were out all day long, collecting shells, cleaning them and putting them in a drawer I gave them. In the evening, when they were gone to bed, I went to supper at my Mother's.

The London papers did not arrive till six, at which time my husband went to the Reading Room and afterwards joined us to tell us the news from the Crimea, and the Battles which were being fought there. My cousin, Herman Galton, was employed in the trenches, and the sufferings of our troops were sad to hear of.

At Tenby, women from the country used to go from house to house offering poultry and eggs, to the amusement of the children. They were very cheap, a couple of fowls and a goose for six shillings! Rather than take them back they would sell them for anything.

The women wore tall hats and men's jackets, and mob caps under their hats, which were very becoming to the young women, but not to the old. In Tenby they talk English, but all out of the town talked Welsh. A colony of Flemings settled in Tenby years ago and speak English.

We took very long walks on the sands to pick up shells, and we found a clever man who went with us to St. Katherine's Rock, and showed us where the live shells were buried, and helped us to name the shells. He often went out with Conchologists. His wife kept a donkey, which we hired sometimes. The woman brought it into her kitchen to saddle and bridle for the children. Even little Edward got very knowing about shells. We took him and Lucy to see a gentleman's collection, and he good-naturedly gave little Edward a valuable one. Edward looked at it and exclaimed in disgust, "Why, it is a broken one." It had a small hole. The gentleman was much amused at this remark.

At first everyone looked shy at us, fearing scarlet fever, but soon seeing we were safe, we made many pleasant acquaintances. Frances Jane Fox [a cousin] had married the Rev. Mr. Hughes of Penally, and we saw them often, spending mornings with them in their pretty house. The Henry Wedgwoods and Mackintoshes (related to the Darwins of Shrewsbury) called and were agreeable. A Worcestershire family consisting of Mr. and Mrs. Isaac and four children of the ages of mine called, and their children and ours played and walked together every day. One day we went in a boat to Saundersfoot, where there are different sorts of shells to those at Tenby, especially the beautiful Pholas. My sister Emma used to walk with us sometimes, and when the children's backs were turned would drop a Pecten (a shell they were very fond of), and they thought the sea had washed it up and were delighted.

Among the shopkeepers we found Mrs. Morgan [or Morris?] the grocer, who remembered us when we were children, and Betty Tucker, who sold us shells, now sold them to my children. She was a dirty old woman, smelling of drink, and my husband did not appreciate her as I did, for auld lang syne.

We remained at Tenby till the 23rd. January, 1855, the children improving in health. We had many pleasant little parties, at the Wedgwoods, Mackintoshes, and Isaacs.

We took Jenkins the Conchologist with us to Gilter Point and other places, and learned much from him, and he packed up the children's shells, which arrived safely.

One great amusement to Eddy and Lucy was a fine dog belonging, to Mr. Morris [or Morgan?] the grocer, who generally sat on a chair in the shop. They gave him a penny, when he walked gravely to the confectioner, a few doors off, and brought back a bun in his mouth, but he always expected the bun to be given back to him.

We were grieved to leave the sea, we had enjoyed our stay so much. There were several curious customs at Tenby. At Christmas and the New Year little boys went to every house as Mummers. They acted a play, but without speaking, something like St. George killing the dragon, and they would come night after night and repeat the performance. Another custom was a sailor dressed up and carried about, high enough to look in at the windows, and everyone was expected to give him a trifle. On New Year's Day boys went round knocking at every door, and when the maid opened it, with a brush in some water, squirted it in her face for good luck.

An old woman, a beggar, came to our cook, and said if she did not give her something to eat she would bewitch her, and this frightened her very much. The people were very honest; it was not necessary to lock the door at night – they would cheat you, but would not steal.

*

On the 22nd. June, we went to a pic-nic at Wellesbourne. There was one every year, and they were very pleasant gatherings; all the neighbouring families attended. There was archery and a luncheon, every lady providing one dish. Miss Ryland's butler, who for many years had been in Mrs. Kemble's service, knew me and amused us much by whispering, "It is amber pudding, Ma'am, and very good." It was brought by Miss Ryland and quite deserved Denton's commendation.

On 23rd. July we were all invited by Mr. Staunton to come and drink syllabub under the cow, in the hay field. It was a lovely day, hay-carrying everywhere. When we got about a mile from

Longbridge, a heavy pelting shower came down in torrents. We put the children under the apron to keep them dry and went on to the Stauntons and had luncheon there. It rained the whole time, so the hay field and syllabub were out of the question. On our return, when we had gone a mile, the road was quite dry. It had been heavy from Longbridge to Warwick.

On 2nd. September Erasmus came from Aldershot and had the afternoon with us. I do not think I have mentioned that, when Erasmus commanded the militia, a young man, Mr. C., joined, and his mother begged Erasmus to see he was not persuaded to drink, as it was a failing in the family, the father being given to drink. Erasmus promised he would, and that evening announced to the mess that he meant to be a teetotaller and invited others to join him, which this young man did and was saved.

All the spring and summer we had been very anxious about the War. Lord Raglan had died from overwork and grief at having failed to take the Redan on 18th. June. Every day the first question was "What news is there?" Herman Galton, who had been for some time working in the trenches, was invalided home. I talked to my children, and made them interested in all that was going on at Sebastopole, that they might remember the War, so that they were as eager for news as we were. On 9th. September, I was in my bedroom when little Edward (five years old) rushed into the room saying "Sebastopole is taken," and capered about. I ran downstairs and found the news had just arrived. The bells rang all the evening.

On 5th. December Mr. Charles Barclay of Bury Hill died; his son Arthur, at my Uncle Barclay Allardice's death, became head of the Ury Barclays. My Uncle having no son, Ury was sold, to our regret, to Mr. Baird, after being some hundreds of years in the Barclay family. Mr. Baird blew up the old house with gunpowder, it being too strong to pull down any other way, and he has built a large house in its place. Ury is about a mile from Stonehaven, in Kincardineshire.

On 16th. December, my dear Great-aunt, Mrs. Hudson Gurney, died after a long illess. She had been a very kind Aunt, and we regretted her [death] much. She was never told that Ury was sold, it would have distressed her so much.

Our friend Mrs. Foley, who was Miss Wyndham, lost five of her little children in one fortnight at this time from scarlet fever.

On February 8th, 1857, old Mrs. Moilliet died at Abberley; she was Mother to James Moilliet, and only Daughter of Mr. Keir of the Lunar Society, and a great friend of my Grandfathers, Galton and Darwin.

*

We had for some time felt that the children required more education than I had time to give them. Eddy was not strong enough to go from home, so we determined with great regret to leave Snitterfield and live in Leamington, and put the children to day schools. It was a great trial, we were all so fond of the country, but their education was imperative. [They moved to No. 3, Bertie Terrace, near her mother, in September, 1857.]

Chapter 12

Final Entries (1857 - 1865)

[From here on the reminiscences become more and more a series of disjointed jottings about births, marriages, and deaths, or about minor comings and goings. The following extracts may, however, be of some interest.]

On 6th. June, 1857, Miss Anna Gurney of Northrepps Cottage died at sixty-one. She was half-sister to Mr. Hudson Gurney, and a very remarkable woman. She was paralysed in her legs from infancy and could not walk, but wheeled herself about in a chair. She was remarkably gifted and clever, understood Greek, Hebrew, and early Saxon languages. She spent her life doing good: took great interest in Missions, but her chief interest was in the fishermen at Cromer. She set up a lifeboat and all appliances for saving life. When a storm arose, she would be wheeled to the cliff, gave all directions, and saved many lives. She and her cousin Miss Sarah Buxton, who lived with her, travelled to the Holy Land and elsewhere, in spite of their infirmities. Miss Buxton was very asthmatic, but their energy carried them through everything. They were most agreeable and interesting women.

On 14th. June Francis bought 42 Rutland Gate for £2,500.

This was the year (1857) of the terrible mutiny in India. General Francis Wheler arrived in the spring for a long leave in England; before he had been a month in this country, he was recalled to India. On 13th. January (1858) we had intended to go to The Hunt Ball, but heard that morning that poor George Biddulph had been shot dead in Lucknow; we therefore did not go.

*

On 14th. June, 1858, Queen Victoria and the Prince Consort came to stay at Stoneleigh Abbey, and great preparations were made. The Abbey was illuminated with lamps round each window. It was fine warm weather, and the Queen went out in front in the evening to show herself to the crowds which had come to see her. Very early next day she drove quietly with Lord Leigh to see the Parks, and then went to Birmingham to open (I think) the Aston Hall Grounds. Birmingham was splendidly decorated for the occasion. The manufacturers, one and all, put out their fires for the day, that there might be no smoke, Many of the flags were of velvet, and the posts were gilt. The devices most loyal: one which amused the Queen was

"God bless Prince Albert, the pride of the Nation.
May he come to no harm when he goes from the Station."

The Queen was most gratified with her reception. The next day she left Stoneleigh to lunch at Warwick Castle on her way home and was to pass through Leamington, where great preparations were made. The town was covered with flags, devices, and flowers. The Shopkeepers emptied their windows of goods and placed rows of seats for visitors – some threw out balconies. Campbell of Monzie in York Terrace hung out little flags like eagles, holding a device in each bill, such as "And will ye no come back again?"

At the top of Lansdowne Place a scaffolding was put up for all the schoolchildren, who had been drilled for some days to sing the National Anthem together. We had seats at the Charitable Repository, and little Edward carried his flags there early in the morning. I took the children and all the maids there in good time, my Mother and husband remaining to take care of the houses. It was an intensely hot day. At one o'clock, we heard the guns fire at Stoneleigh, as a sign Her Majesty had left. Soon after, the procession arrived, first the High Sheriff in a carriage and four, coachman and footman with large nosegays. The Queen and Prince were in a carriage and four; Lord Leigh, as Lord Lieutenant of the County, rode close to her carriage. There were several carriages following, and those families who were invited to the Castle to meet her, all very gay.

The Queen bowed more like a person bowing to her friends, in the kindest and most pleasant way, and we were quite sorry when it was over. After seeing Warwick Castle, the Royal party went to the Station for London. Just after they left, a tremendous storm of thunder and lightning began, and lasted some hours. I never saw a more magnificent sight than that storm; fireworks were let off in honour of that day, but they looked so poor in comparison to the lightning. Several of the principal families were invited to Stoneleigh one evening to meet the Queen. Dr. and Mrs. Jephson were asked by the Queen's desire. The Doctor was ill and could not go, but Her Majesty spoke to Mrs. Jephson and asked after her husband.

*

On 15th. July, my Mother made us a present to enable us to go to the sea, and we went that day to Rhyl and took lodgings near the sea. There are capital sands and good bathing, and plenty of donkeys for children to ride. We found Miss Eliza Sitwell in lodgings, and she told us she always took the rooms under and over her bedroom, that she might have no noise. On the 26th., Mr. and Mrs. Carill Worsley came to Rhyl; she was Sir Francis Darwin's eldest daughter [i.e. Elizabeth Anne's first cousin]. They left on 17th. August, and on the 19th. we left. After seeing Chester, we went to Platt, near Manchester, to visit the Worsleys. [Platt Hall, now well inside Manchester, in Platt Fields Park, and near Platt (Unitarian) Chapel, is perhaps best known now-a-days for its collection of old costumes.] They took us to see Sir James Watts' wonderful warehouse, full of all manner of goods. One place was full of silks of all kinds, another full of boys' caps, all wonderfully cheap, but could only be bought wholesale. They supplied shops everywhere. I remember a boy's cap was charged ninepence – at a shop they charged one and six or two shillings. It was an immense building. The next day we went to see the Blind Asylum. All were at work; one little girl, who was blind, deaf, and dumb, interested us very much. She was actually sorting printer's types and putting them in their right places by touch, and made no mistake. She was very intelligent and able to be taught many things. On 23rd. August we left the Worsleys and returned home.

*

On 14th. January, 1859, Dr. Booth died, aged eighty-one. He married my Aunt Adele Galton. He was a clever man, but his manners were very peculiar and against his having much practice. The Hibberts gave a grand ball at Bilton Grange. My Husband went to it, but out of respect to my Aunt I did not. It was a grand affair; one lady appeared in a dress covered with pearls looted in China!

On 26th. June Miss Mary Parker died at her house at Ashbourne at a great age. She was Sister to Mrs. Hadley, and was much respected by the Darwin family.

In November, my Uncle Sir Francis Sacheverell Darwin died at the Priory, aged seventy-three. He was buried at Breadsall Church and was the last of my Mother's brothers and sisters.

On 19th. November 1859 my Aunt Hubert Galton died at Worthing. She was Daughter to Robert Barclay of Clapham, Banker of Barclay Bevan Tritton and Co., all cousins. One of her Sisters married Mr. Birbeck, and the other two, Susan and Lydia, died single. Lydia was the stiffest of all stiff Quakers; the Brothers were Robert, Rawlinson, Ford and John. My Aunt was buried at Hadzor.

*

On 21st. June 1860 we all set off to Whitby. We slept at the York Station Hotel, visited the Minster, and were amused by a party who went round with us, not caring at what the guide told us of the history of the Minster and looking carelessly at the monuments, but rushing with eagerness when the guide showed the corner where the man hid himself, that he might set fire to the building, which happened shortly before.

We went through the beautiful Pickering Valley, and arrived at Whitby on the 22nd., and took lodgings on the West Cliff, where we had a beautiful view of the Abbey opposite. We drove to the Falling Fogs, and to Mulgrave Castle, through beautiful woods, and to other places in the neighbourhood. The children bathed in the sea and picked up ammonites and jet, which they got made into brooches and pins. On 18th July we saw an eclipse of the sun, and soon after came a violent downpour of rain. It was very amusing to see the sales of fish. When a boat came in a pile of the fish they had taken was put on the sands, a bell was rung and crowds collected to buy, and the highest bidder got the fish, packed it up there and then, and sent it off to London and elsewhere. It was chiefly Cod and Ling (an inferior sort of Cod).

One day we were startled to see a Fly dash up to the door, and Eddy got out. We feared he had been hurt. It turned out he had been walking out and saw a cab driver trying in vain to get a stone out of his horse's foot with a stone. Sir Trevor Wheler had given Eddy a knife full of useful implements, of which he was very proud; amongst others was one for taking stones out of horse's shoes. Eddy offered his knife, and the man was so grateful he said he should like to take the young gentleman a drive round the town in return, which he did.

We enjoyed our stay in Whitby very much, the air was so bracing, and there was so much that was interesting to see. We left on 26th. July.

On December 1st., 1860, the Empress of the French arrived and went to the Regent Hotel [Leamington]. Erasmus, who was staying there, took Lucy in and placed her where she could see the Empress. The landlady had much difficulty in trying to walk backwards before Her Majesty, and after a few steps turned suddenly round and walked with her back towards the Empress, much relieved. The French Royal Standard was hoisted on the Hotel, and crowds tried to get a glimpse. Very early the next morning, the Empress and one lady went quietly out to Clarendon Square, where they asked someone they met to tell them which house the Emperor lived in the winter he was at Leamington. They were told it was No. 6, and I think they asked to be allowed to go in, but no one found out who she was. At one o'clock the French flag was taken down, and the Empress vanished quite quietly.

*

On 12th. March, 1861, we heard that Darwin was very ill with diphtheria; not knowing what it was, he did not call in a doctor till it was so bad it was only by using the strongest medicines that his life was saved. The whole household caught it, one after another, but taking it in time, they did not have it so severely. The Doctor came a hundred times, and I forget how many bottles of brandy were taken. On 11th. April, Mr. Middleton called to tell us that Darwin had been taken alarmingly ill with what they thought was an epileptic fit. He however soon recovered, and it proved to be not epilepsy, but that when he had diphtheria, his throat had been severely cauterised. Darwin, all his life, had been subject to frequent nose bleedings, which always relieved him. When his throat was cauterised, it prevented the usual nose bleeding and caused the seizure, which puzzled the doctors – though similar in some respects to epilepsy, it was very unlike in others. On 27th. May, Darwin and Mary came to stay with Emma Phillips, and on the 30th., he had another seizure. After a conversation with my Mother, who had found out from Darwin that he had no nose bleeding since the diphtheria, the Doctors found out the cause, and told him when necessary to put a leech to his nose, which would relieve him. On one occasion the leech was poisoned, and his face swelled enormously, He sent for the Doctor and in the meantime bathed his face in chloride of lime, which saved his life.

On 25th. July, my Husband took the children to see Blondin walk on the tight rope – a fearful sight.

On 19th. October I took Lucy to Bath and stayed with my Uncle Hubert Galton in the Royal Crescent, and left Lucy at the Miss Fournier's school, where I had been educated in my youth. I found them all alive, though aged. The next day, May and I went to the school to see the dancing. Miss Fournier took me all over the house, and I was much struck with the difference to what it was in my days, so many luxuries and comforts we never thought of. The next day I brought Lucy to my Uncle's to stay till the Monday to comfort her, she felt so much being alone with strangers. The next day I returned home, very low at leaving her.

*

It was a shock, on the 13th. November, that a notice was in the papers that the Prince Consort was seriously ill. It was known he was not well, but nothing was said as to danger till then, and it came like a blow and caused quite a consternation; everyone then felt how important he was to the country. The telegrams were less hopeful every time. The next day but one, Sunday, the first intimation that he had died late in the night of the 14th. was the clergyman leaving out his name in the prayers (the telegram having arrived just before Church time). It was like an electric shock, and many sobs were heard – the clergyman nearly broke down in praying for the Queen, for whom all felt deeply. There never was a more universal sorrow; one could think of nothing but the poor Queen and the irreparable loss to the country.

*

On 27th. January, 1862, I took the children to see the pantomime of Kenilworth. I had told them the history of Queen Elizabeth and Amy Robsart, which greatly interested them, and I was provoked to see the whole thing treated as a burlesque, Lord Leicester coming in on a child's wooden horse, and Amy after tumbling down through the trap door, jumping up laughing at the audience!

On 1st. May, 1862, the Grand Exhibition was opened in London, There was a melancholy feeling that the good Prince Consort, who had taken so much trouble about it and should have been there with the Queen to open it, was gone, and the Queen in deep sorrow. It was an excellent exhibition, but nothing like the beauty of the first, all glass.

*

On 21st. May I took a photographer with me to the Oaklands, where my Aunt Booth was staying with my Aunt Brewin. We were very anxious to have their photographs, and after much persuasion they consented, on condition I came and managed everything. They had never seen a photo taken! It was to have been done in their draw-

The photographs of Elizabeth Anne's elderly aunts taken outside in their bath chair

Above: Sophia Galton (Aunt Brewin)

Right: Adele Galton (Aunt Booth)

ing room, but the day became so dull, it must be done out of doors, and it was a cold day. I suggested they should be taken sitting in their bath chair, which was done. They were wrapped up warm and a shawl over their caps, which was taken off when all was ready, and put on again the moment it was done. They took no cold, and the result was most satisfactory and unique, being in a bath chair. My Aunts were much amused and had all the servants done. I returned in the evening, much pleased with my day's work.

On 22nd May, 1862, our very old friend Mrs. Leonard Horner died at Florence aged seventy-five. He, Mr. Horner was the most intimate friend my Father had and they had known each other ever since my Father had been at the College in Edinburgh. He and my father married about the same time, and their eldest girl, Lady Lyell, and myself were of the same age. Mr. and Mrs. Horner often stayed with us. He was most kind to us young people. Mrs. Horner was a Miss Lloyd – a relation of hers, an old Mrs. Lloyd, lived at Welcombe near Stratford. We all liked her extremely, and regretted her death. Mr. Horner lived some time longer.

*

On 6th. February, 1863, I took Lucy to Bath and slept at my Uncle Hubert Galton's, when to my sorrow my Cousin May told me she had entered the Roman Catholic Church, a great grief to Lucy, whom we could not allow to stay with May as she had done on holidays. I went with Lucy to the Miss Fourniers and left her there and returned home. We heard soon after that my poor Uncle Hubert, who was quite paralysed, had joined the Roman Catholics.

My sister Emma had been writing the little book called "Guide to the Unprotected," and she and I went to Birmingham to see Mr. Scott our broker, and Mr. Evans our solicitor, to ask them to correct any mistakes before she published it. They began to look it over without taking much interest, but as they went on were delighted with it, and said it was just what was wanted and took the greatest pains to make it correct.

*

On June 6th. we heard that my Aunt Brewin was very ill. My Sister Adele saw her and returned home. My Aunt Mrs. Booth arrived at the Oaklands. My Aunt Brewin continued getting worse every day till the 14th, on which day she died at eight o'clock in the evening. Emma was sent for and arrived ten minutes before her death. My Aunt was buried on the 21st. at the Quaker's Meeting ground. Adele, Emma, Erasmus, Cameron, Mr. James Lloyd, two Cadburys, and two Shorthouses attended. She had always been a kind and liberal Aunt to us, making us every year a handsome present. She left me two thousand pounds.

On 26th. June, Frederick and Emma Wheler came to us for one night on their return from abroad. About two months before, Lottie Wheler had planned an expedition abroad with her cousin Kate Plowden, and persuaded Frederick Wheler to go with them. But it was necessary they should have a chaperone, the two ladies being unmarried, and with some difficulty Emma Wheler, who did not at all wish to go, agreed out of good nature to go with them. They went to Switzerland, Paris, &c., and the result was that Frederick returned home engaged to Miss Plowden, and he and Emma came to tell us.

On 10th. February, 1865, [there was] great consternation in Birmingham at Spooner and Attwood's Bank stopping payment. It had always been considered so safe a bank.

On 28th. March J.L.Moilliet and Sons Bank agreed to merge with Lloyds Banking Company to form a Joint Stock Bank.

On 8th. August Keir and Lewis Moilliet called to see us before they went to New Zealand.

On 3rd. October Mrs. Nixon sent me the picture by Rollason of my Grandfather Darwin to my great pleasure. She had seen it at Bemrose in Derby and bought it for five pounds, which I insisted on paying her.

[The last entry in these reminiscences is dated 18th. December 1865.]

*

March, 1904. I am now ninety-six years of age and think it is time to stop continuing my diary. I have written the events in my life up to the time when my children were old enough to remember all that has passed since. I regret much not having written more about my Brothers and Sisters, what they did, and where they went, but not keeping much of a diary, and setting down those events which concerned ourselves only, I have not the dates to remind me.

My life has been a very happy one. My Children have given us no trouble, but have been a blessing to us, my dear Parents, Brothers and Sisters all that was kind, and my married life unusually happy.

For all these blessings, and for the health and strength vouchsafed to me in my great age, I feel most thankful to the Almighty. And since my children's marriages my happiness has been further increased by the affectionate kindness and love of my Son-in-law and Daughter-in-law. That God may bless them all is the daily prayer of their affectionate Mother,

Elizabeth A. Wheler

EPILOGUE

THE DIAMOND JUBILEE (1897)

[Mrs Edward Wheler to her sister, Miss Emma Galton of Leamington]

33 Jermyn Street, London S.W.
20th. June 1897

Dearest Emma,

You will have got my card. The beginning of our expedition was sad. The train ran over a boy at Claverdon and killed him. Aylmer [Mrs. Wheler's son-in-law, Colonel T.J.C. Aylmer Studdy] and Lucy felt a bump, as though going over something, and the train stopped to see what was the matter. They arrived at Leamington, and changed trains there. We were put in a third class train with only one man, the Head of the Police, and went through to London without a stop. Then got into a Station Omnibus, and arrived here, our heads out of the window looking at the decorations, everyone hard at work decorating. We have very nice rooms and no other lodgers as far as I know. Lucy has brought a whole larder with her, so we shall not starve. After dinner General Bishop came to talk over plans. Yesterday after breakfast Francis arrived, looking very well – he said Louisa was tired, but hoped to call. Just after he went, Edward arrived, and we all went shopping, and seeing all that was to be seen. Crowds of people, and crowds of vehicles of all sorts. After luncheon Colonel Henry Studdy arrived, also Percy Powlett and his Daughter. Aylmer got a carriage for me and Jane, and then he, Lucy, Edward, and Grace Powlett went off to Hurlingham, after directing my cabman to drive me all along the route the Queen will take, and most amusing it was. Some of the decorations were very handsome, especially Piccadilly, the grand houses, also the Strand, where they have large garlands like long skipping-ropes on the houses apparently of green leaves, but of course of paper, and these garlands hanging from post to post all along looked beautiful. The garlands across the roads of coloured paper (I suppose) looked like roses. Flags in profusion, and drapery on the balconies, immense quantities of seats everywhere, and a number on Constitution Hill for the School Children. It was slow work going, constant stoppages from the crowd; a man walking with a scarf, red, white, and blue, round his shoulders, selling similar scarves; also men selling penny opera glasses, which seemed to have a good sale. As it was time to return I came back a quieter way all along the Thames Embankment close by the river. I longed to go in one of the penny steamers going by.

On my return I found Louisa's card. Soon after, Sir Douglas [Galton] and my Lady called to know how we were. I sent word I should be glad to see them, but only Douglas came, looking very well and pleasant. He asked much after you and after Darwin (as did all who called). He was very pleasant and just after he went the maid came with a beautiful bunch of roses from my Lady. The Studdys did not return till I was gone to bed. Lucy says the dresses were magnificent at Hurlingham. We have not seen any foreigners about, except about ten men marching in a peculiar dress with hatchets in their hands, probably African.

This morning we all went to St. James Church, which looked just as it did sixty years ago, and I looked up at our old pew in the gallery. We had two verses of the National Anthem sung to begin with, and a splendid anthem appropriate to the occasion. Bishop Barry preached, and we are now reposing for tomorrow and Tuesday. We had a good deal of rain last night, which I fear will spoil some of the decorations. They were putting up illuminations yesterday, but have much to do yet. There are not many devices – a Crown and '1837-1897' was very general.

Tomorrow they lunch at General Bishop's, but I think I shall not go, as we have a party to tea – the Frank Whelers and Ted Wheler.

You can see nothing of the shops on account of the balconies. I wish you were with us. I hope you are better and free from pain.

Our love,

Ever your affectionate sister,

E. A. Wheler

P.S. Plenty of seats to be had everywhere. The maids are going tomorrow to try and get some cheap.

*

33 Jermyn Street, London, S.W.
22nd. June, 1897

Dearest Emma,

You will like to hear our adventures. We started at a quarter to eight this morning, and got to the United Services Club quite easily, through crowds of people, seats and balconies filling fast. We first had breakfast at the Club in a large splendid hall – tea, coffee, cucumber sandwiches and strawberries, and then went to our seats, which we were able soon to change for better ones, thanks to a friend of Aylmer's. We were in Waterloo Place – a huge stand opposite us – on the right some elevated seats for the Chelsea Pensioners who were properly cheered on their arrival. Behind the crowd were ambulance vans on one side for accidents. On their right, fire engines ready for fire, and five mounted police, so we were prepared for all emergencies. A little girl stood all the time half way up a lamp post near us, her brother holding her feet from slipping. I am sorry to say ladies did not regard Lady Galton's advice in respect of their hats.

We sat some time before the procession began, but when it did it was most interesting, especially the first part, the Colonials in their various uniforms – fine looking men. We were not near enough to see faces distinctly but the uniforms were clearly seen – very different from ours – some very handsome and some dark – the Japanese were curious and the South African. Our troops, the Scotch Greys and another regiment, lined the route. The Scotch Greys came too far, and had to back some way, and it was beautiful to see them back in a line, as even as when they came forward! After the Colonials came our troops, regiment after regiment, and your book (of which numbers were selling everywhere) enabled us to know who they were, and an officer near Lucy also told her the names as they went by. I ought to say the Colonials were well clapped by the lookers-on, and Lord Roberts very much cheered. It was a very long procession, so many of each regiment, and so many regiments.

At last there was a pause and the sun broke out suddenly, and at that moment bang went the cannon – a royal salute – to say the Queen had entered her carriage. First came aides-de-camp in splendid uniform, and others, then the grand royal carriage and four horses with red manes, grand trappings, hammer cloths, &c., with the Premiers of the Colonies. Then similar carriages with Ladies in Waiting, &c., &c., after them royal carriages with the royal children, after them the Royalties, Duchess of Teck, Empress Frederick and then Her Majesty with the cream coloured horses. She was followed by the Indian Escort in grand dress, nothing could be more orderly than the crowd.

When all was over we went into the large Hall and had a capital luncheon, and returned here highly gratified with all we had seen. Edward and M. L. called soon after. They were at the Duke's House with Lady Percy, and had just seen the Queen's carriage leaving the Palace after setting her down, so she did it all in about three hours. The little York children [the future Kings Edward VIII and George VI, who were three years and eighteen months old, respectively, at the time] were shown at the Buckingham Palace windows. Edward went on Sunday to Chelsea, and was much taken with the Colonials, who were put up there. He said they were remarkably fine strong-looking men, and their uniforms so business-like – made for work – and they were so pleasant to talk to.

There were one hundred special trains going all Monday night to bring up our troops. A policeman told Aylmer he had been on duty all yesterday, last night, today, and should perhaps be up again all tonight.

Yesterday we got an open carriage and went the whole of the Queen's route in the City, which was splendidly decorated, and many devices which I wish I could remember – "The best of Queens, Mother and friend" and a long one ending "an example to Princes." St. James's Street was beautifully decorated, garlands of green across the street and along the sides, interlacing each other – literally an avenue of green overhead, bunches of flowers hanging in the middle, with a dove flying in the wind. When we were at dinner we were startled hearing two fire engines rattle by, some decoration had taken fire in St. James's Street, but was put out at once before the engines arrived. Some of the houses in the City were preparing splendid illuminations. Marlborough House in Pall Mall will be splendid tonight. Yesterday Francis, Edward, M. L. and a host of Whelers came to tea.

Tomorrow I go to tea at Rutland Gate; Lucy and Aylmer are engaged elsewhere. They are just gone out sight-seeing, and now I must tell you something I meant to keep secret, but my children are like sieves. Lucy knows the Editress of the 'Queen' newspaper who wanted an account of the Coronation for the Jubilee paper, and Lucy, Edward, Aylmer and Mary, having seen my letter [c.f. Chapter 7] much against my will, would send her a copy of it which Lucy made, leaving out of course some parts, and it is in last week's 'Queen' paper, and Lucy is to have five guineas for it next month!

Our two maids got good places today for ten shillings each and saw well, I have enjoyed the whole extremely. Aylmer and Lucy take all the trouble, and I really feel very little tired. We sit at the window all day, looking out; I only wish you were here with us, It is very hot today. We return on Friday, and I do hope to find you have been able to go out and see something of what is going on.

Our love,

Ever your affectionate sister,

E. A. Wheler

Postscript
by her daughter, Mrs Lucy Studdy (née Wheler) written in about 1908

This Autobiography tells its own simple Family History recording the life led early in the nineteenth century, therefore little is needed from my pen, but a glance at her latter years. After her marriage, her life was a very quiet one. My Father and Mother were far from rich, and she devoted herself to her Husband and Children. She was an excellent manager, and made most of our clothes (and her needle-work was beautiful). I have the little babies' caps she made, and she spent much time on our education. She encouraged us to make collections, and we had a "museum" of which we were very proud. She illuminated well, as may be seen from the specimen [in the books of her reminiscences]. When we moved to No. 3 Bertie Terrace, Leamington, she visited her Mother and Sister Emma daily at No. 5. My Grandmother was a charming old lady – an excellent conversationalist – quite a picture, with a snow white fichu in her dress. She invariably had a black basket at her side. After her death, this was daily used, first by my Aunt Emma, afterwards by my Mother, and it is now in my possession. This basket contained everything we could want, pen, pencil, pins, scissors, &c., to all of which we were welcome, as long as we put them back. My Grandmother could just recollect being taken to a play with Penelope Boothby, the child immortalised by Sir Joshua Reynolds, and by the sculptor Banks. Mrs. Galton clearly remembered being told by her Father, Dr. Erasmus Darwin, of the unhappy life led by Sir Brooke and Lady Boothby, and of their final separation at Penelope's grave. Dr. Darwin was Sir Brooke Boothby's most intimate friend, and had strongly protested against his making a marriage for money.

My dear Grandmother took the liveliest interest in all our pleasures and concerns, helped in a large measure to pay for our education, and loaded me with presents, and showed her affection in every way. She was very dignified – no one could take a liberty with her. Aunt Emma lived with her and had a mine of fascinating books, (I still have the History of Cock Robin) and her sugar candy was excellent. We were in and out constantly, and always happy at No. 5. Some of us can remember her old butler Harwood, who stayed with her until he could work no longer.

It is a curious fact that since I first knew Bertie Terrace in 1857 it has been noted for the age of its inhabitants. Three have died at the age of ninety-seven, others were 92, 90, 86, 81, 79 and 75, and there are only eight houses. An old Derbyshire neighbour of my Grandmother's, Mr. Sitwell of Stainsby, Derbyshire, and late Squarson of Leamington Hastings, who had married my Aunt Sophia Wheler, and whose Mother was Lucy, daughter and heiress of Sir William Wheler, 6th Bart., and of Lucy Knightley, spent the last Winters of his life at No. 4 Bertie Terrace after his wife's death, to be near us. My Grandmother's health was visibly failing in 1873, and on 12th. February, 1874 she passed away at the age of ninety. Mr. Sitwell, who though far from well, had exerted himself to go to Derbyshire to record his vote at the General Election, was taken seriously ill at Stainsby, and died the following day, 13th. February, aged seventy-nine.

After my Grandmother's death Aunt Emma spent one thousand pounds in improvements on No. 5, and to the end there was daily intercourse between the two houses, and when weather or illness prevented this, a continual exchange of three cornered notes occurred. Aunt Emma was a great letter writer, and kept in touch by this means with all cousins and nephews and nieces. These letters were passed on to No. 3 and were of much interest to the two houses. The intercourse between my Mother and her Sister Emma was daily – almost hourly.

My Uncle Darwin Galton visited his Sisters every week. He was a man of strongly marked characteristics and of an autocratic nature.

Emma Sophia Galton
(1814-1903)
Elizabeth Anne's sister

Darwin Galton
(1814-1903)
Elizabeth Anne's brother

Erasmus Galton
(1815-1909)
Elizabeth Anne's brother

Sir Francis Galton FRS
(1822-1911)
Elizabeth Anne's brother

Yet there was never any friction between these three strong personalities – a fact which I attribute partly to the almost ceremonious courtesy which they observed to each other, and also to my Mother's resolute avoidance of disputed points and irritating topics.

My Uncle Erasmus spent his time between Leamington, Ryde and his property at Loxton, in Somerset, in which latter he took immense interest, getting up in the small hours of the morning to superintend his labourers, and living in a hut copied from those at Aldershot, and looking into every detail of the Estate. Each Sunday when at Leamington he was sure to be at No.5 to see his Mother and Sisters, always finding something amusing and interesting to tell them. He is still living and in his ninety-fourth year, still clear and bright in mind.

My Uncle Francis Galton frequently came from London to visit at Bertie Terrace, and when he was abroad his letters were an immense pleasure to them. They entered heartily into all his travelling experiences, and even into his scientific work. His "finger print" researches interested them greatly. My Mother (at ninety-six years old!) was seen looking into a dictionary for the exact meaning of the word "Eugenics". She was expecting a visit from my Uncle Francis, and did not wish to be ignorant of a work in which he was then engaged. She had a book full of notes and notices of his career from his earliest days. These [last] are the only two of the family who survive her.

In both Sisters the Quaker element was decidedly present – showing itself in a certain precision, politeness and punctuality which gave a quaint and old world charm to their household arrangements. In my Mother this Quakerism was blended with the strongest Jacobite feeling. "Prince Charlie" was an ever-present romance to her. I remember being much amused when, having been told that an acquaintance claimed descent from Oliver Cromwell, she remarked, "Well, my dear, it's very shocking indeed, and he had better say nothing about it"!

In her youth my Mother spent much time among the Gurney family, and her religious views were influenced and deepened by this intercourse. To the end of her life she read and re-read a volume of Joseph John Gurney's Sermons. The only modern religious writer she admired in her closing years was J.R. Miller. His book "Silent Times" was a great favourite with her.

My Mother did not often leave home, but always enjoyed a visit to the sea, which seemed to put new life into her, and which she loved. Visits continued to be paid by her to Dunchurch, Stainsby (which the Sitwells inherited), Claverdon, Hadzor, and when at the latter place, she had the delight of a visit to her dear Cousins the Miss Bromleys at Bewdley, and when at Stainsby, near Derby, of seeing her cousins, Mrs. Woollett Wilmot (née Darwin) and Mrs. Nixon (née Gisborne). One year she was ordered to Buxton after a terrible attack of rheumatic gout, from which she afterwards suffered at intervals, but in a much milder form.

There were usually about twenty families of relations within fourteen miles of Leamington – many of whom constantly dropped in to lunch. At one time there were as many as five different families of Whelers in Leamington, and at the Hunt Ball we usually got up a set of lancers comprised of Whelers and Wises!

In 1877 she was much grieved at the death of Mrs. Howard Galton of Hadzor. She had for so many years enjoyed her visits there, and was warmly attached to her Aunt.

My Brother was appointed Under Agent in 1875 to the Honourable Mark Rolle, and lived near Torrington, and she was delighted with that beautiful country, which she had last visited on her honeymoon. Another visit in 1872 was to her old friend and school fellow, Mrs. Sykes, at Grassmere; the latter died in 1878, as also did her brother-in-law, Mr. James Moilliet.

The death of my Father occurred on November 15th, 1879. He had been for some time in failing health, and was obliged to discontinue his duties as Magistrate and in County business. Directly afterwards we went to stay with my Brother, who had been appointed Agent to Colonel Cornwall Legh and to Captain Egerton Leigh, of High Legh, near Knutsford, Cheshire.

In 1882 she lost her third Sister Adele, Mrs. Bunbury, who died at Launceston after some months' illness, aged seventy-three, and the next year the death occurred of her old friend, and Sister-in-law, Emma Wheler, who died at Rugby in 1885, aged seventy-nine.

In 1888 my Brother was appointed Chief Commissioner to the

Duke of Northumberland, after which she almost yearly made the long journey to Alnwick, the last visit being in 1902. I think it was during this visit she enjoyed a two hours' drive in a motor car, then a novelty. She told me afterwards how she longed to examine its mechanism. Another Sister-in-law, Elizabeth Wheler, who had since 1870 lived in Grove Street, Leamington, and had been for years a terrible sufferer, passed away aged eighty-one.

My marriage with Colonel T.J.C.A. Studdy, Royal Artillery, nephew to the wife of Sir Francis Wheler, 10th Baronet, took place in September 1889. We took a house at Stoke, near Coventry, so as to be within easy reach of my Mother, and the year following my Brother married Mary Louisa Dugdale, daughter of Mr. Dugdale of Wroxall Abbey.

In the year 1893 Mr. and Mrs. Frederick Wheler came to live at 7 Bertie Terrace, he having resigned the Living of Dunchurch, near Rugby, where he had been many years. They, with Mrs. Herman Galton and my Aunt Emma, made four sets of relations in the Terrace. The second Mrs. Darwin Galton, née Fanny Arkwright of Willersley, died in 1894 at Claverdon.

During this year my Mother and Uncle Francis went to Birmingham to drive round their old Haunts – Duddeston, Ladywood, and The Larches but returned much disappointed at finding so few traces of the places they once knew so well. All now built over, and the beautiful House at Duddeston, with its Pools and Garden, now turned into a Lunatic Asylum!

They were also rather horrified when it transpired that at their age they had hired a hansom for the occasion!

[Note by Francis Galton. "Ladywood is now by the Crescent, to the right of the road from the Town Hall to the Five Ways. Duddeston is located by St Andrew's Church, and The Larches by Sparkbrook. The River Rea, once sparkling, subsequently filthy beyond compare, and finally distorted into a sewer, fed the Duddeston Ponds".]

1895 found her again at Alnwick. After her visit there she returned to her beloved Scotland, staying a few days with my Brother at Edinburgh.

Just at that time her Nephew, Admiral Powlett, was in command of the Channel Squadron, and to her intense delight took her round the Fleet in his Steam Launch. She was deeply interested in comparing the modern fleet to the wooden walls of old England of her youth. She said the only drawback to the excursion was its shortness! The next day she went to the Forth Bridge in a Steamer, which she examined thoroughly.

It was during this year that we moved to Clifford Chambers, near Stratford on Avon, and she went with us to inspect the old Manor House with which she was charmed. Just as we were moving she became very ill, and for many weeks was confined to the house.

My Mother lost another Sister-in-law in 1896, Mrs. Powlett, of Rugby. Mrs. Powlett retained her vitality and unimpaired memory to the end of her life.

1897 was the year of Queen Victoria's Jubilee. My Mother was of course one of the few survivors who had seen the young Queen crowned. My Husband and I took her to London for a week, to see the Procession. No one entered into it more than she did, and she would not move from her seat until the very end. I sent the letter she wrote on the evening of the Coronation in 1837 (which the editor of the Queen Newspaper said was by far the best he had read on that subject) to one of Her Majesty's Ladies in Waiting. She read it to the Queen who was greatly interested in it, and asked for a copy.

Later in this year, my Mother heard of the death of her Brother Francis's wife, daughter of Dr. Butler, Dean of Peterborough, and Sister of the present Master of Trinity. She died at Royat, in France.

The Reverend Frederick Wheler died in Bertie Terrace in 1898 at the age of eighty-six, and the following year Sir Douglas Galton died. In 1900 Mrs. Frederick Wheler died suddenly, aged seventy-five, and my Mother undertook another journey to Alnwick.

During the year of 1901 my Aunt Emma fell and fractured her thigh, and it was a long time before she could walk, and then only with a stick.

The Coronation this year (1901[?]) was of great interest to my Mother, and she was out on the Terrace on the morning of the day by eight o'clock, superintending the arrangement of her flags.

In 1902 she lost her kind friend and next door neighbour for thirty years, Lady Cartwright, who attained the great age of ninety-seven.

There were several events in 1903. She had a decided attack of Influenza, which caused us much anxiety, and her eldest Brother, Darwin [Galton] of Claverdon, who had been an invalid for some time died at eighty-eight.

As our house at Clifford Chambers was sold over our heads, we went to see one near Ashby de la Zouche. My Mother came to stay at the Hotel with us, and thoroughly enjoyed the outing. The house, however, would not do, and we bought The Avenue House, Bishopton, near Stratford on Avon. Whilst at Clifford some of our friends dressed in the time of George II, and danced the Minuet, Pavanne, &c. Mother came to stay for it, and took the keenest interest in all details. After Uncle Darwin's death Edward left Northumberland and settled at Claverdon.

In 1904 my Mother experienced a great blow. Her Sister Emma, who had lived next door but one to her since 1857, died after much suffering, aged ninety-two – for four hours before her death my Mother never left the sick room. After the Funeral at Milverton she came to us and was very ill, keeping to her room for some days. On her return home she resolved to move to No. 5, which had been left to her by her Sister, and as much as an attack of lumbago allowed her, superintended the move herself.

She paid us one of her usual visits in April 1905, and also went to Claverdon to stay, but whilst there was very ill with congestion of one lung. This year I exhibited a doll whose clothes she had made; all its garments took off, and each was knitted in a different stitch; even the socks, boots and handkerchief – it was Highly Commended. She knitted it when ninety-three.

My Husband and I spent Christmas with her as usual and a few days before Mr. Streatfield gave her the Holy Communion at home with me. She was very bright and seemed "as usual", but lay down a great deal and walked with much difficulty. She entered into all the Christmas Festivities and enjoyed games of Patience and Halma with my Husband, and did her accounts as neatly as ever. On the 26th we heard of the death of my Husband's Brother and returned home. Aylmer caught a bad chill, and was unable to attend the Funeral. On the 29th my Mother had a bad attack of bronchitis, but knowing my Husband was ill made light of it to me, and on January 2nd 1906 wrote me a Post Card saying she was doing well and it was Bronchitis. On going over that day I found her in bed, and her breathing very distressing, though she kept assuring me it was not as painful as it sounded. My Brother and his wife arrived that evening. Next day she was rather better, but the Doctor gave little hope. However on the 4th she again rallied, and he thought recovery possible. She thought of everything and everybody. On the 5th she fully realised her condition, and said Aylmer was on no account to attend her Funeral, as she knew he was ill. She asked for her Bank Book, and put on her spectacles to look at it. On Sunday at 3.15 a.m. she passed away peacefully from heart failure. She died, as she had lived, bravely, thinking of others to the last. She was buried in the Family Vault at Claverdon on the 11th. The service was taken by Archdeacon Bree, her Great-nephew, and the Vicar. A Memorial service was held at St. Mark's Church, Leamington – the Church she had so long and constantly attended, to which many of her friends came.

My Mother had a strong personality and excellent common sense. Many a one came to ask her opinion, knowing it would be kindly and just. She was most generous and helped many in an unostentatious way. No one ever saw her idle for a moment, the amount of knitting she got through was extraordinary, large quantities being constantly sent to the Parish, the Deep Sea Fishermen, Dr. Barnardo's, and the Ragged Schools, and all faultlessly done. She read with extreme rapidity; several times I watched her reading through letters so quickly, thinking it impossible she could have grasped the contents, but she always had done so. She remembered endless games at cards, and would play one after the other without hestitating, so fast and well. Few could beat her at Halma. Her conversation was most interesting and amusing, she was very quick at repartee and thoroughly enjoyed a joke. She read The Times and many books, and particularly enjoyed biographies.

My Mother and Aunt had a nice Kitchen Garden, as well as a flower garden, which was an immense pleasure to them and interest. Her only infirmity was deafness, but she learned to read from the fingers and was very quick at it, also at watching our mouths. Her loyalty to her Family was very strong, and she greatly enjoyed the visits of her Cousin Fanny Wilmot, who, living in Derby, was able to talk about her Derbyshire relations and old Haunts. Her niece, Grace Moilliet, and her Cousin, Mrs. Herman Galton (the latter had for years lived at No. 4), were most kind in constantly visiting her.

Until a few years before her death she went down to the basement to order dinner and to put out the Stores. She attended Church whenever possible up to the September before her death. I fancy there are few people who would wish to change their house at the age of ninety-five!

There was a piano at No. 5, and soon after taking possession she sat on the music stool and played "God save the King" and other things.

She was very brave; I remember a large Medicine Chest that had been fastened to the wall for thirty years, suddenly falling and grazing her face, and she stood there the only person unconcerned. Once, when at Alnwick, the drawing room chimney was struck by lightning, and the soot and dirt covered her and everything in the room. She told me it was very awkward, for everyone would ask her if she was alarmed, and added "I could not say I was, as there was nothing to frighten me".

After she was ninety I showed her this riddle from the Queen Newspaper, which she guessed at once :

Twice two of us are six of us – And six of us are three,
And three of us are five of us – Whatever can we be?
If this is not enough for you, I'll tell you something more,
That eight of us are five of us – and five of us are four.

Only a few months before her death she said "I have never understood the meaning of 'The weight of years', but begin to do so now."

Of my Mother's wonderful memory I need say nothing. This biography tells its own tale. But it leaves unrecorded her works of love and charity, such as – in her earlier years – collecting round her the neglected children of Leamington to teach them of their Saviour. It does not hint at her endless deeds of kindness and generosity. They are written in a Book ruled with no earthly lines.

Those who knew her best in her later years, who saw her cheerful patience under declining strength, her unfailing sympathy with the joys and sorrows of others, her resolution to spare distress to those she loved, must have felt that,

"Stronger thro' weakness,
wiser men become
As they draw nearer to the Eternal Home".

It was indeed "the wisdom which cometh from above" which ruled her life and enlarged her heart, and which enabled her to say – not three months before her death, words almost identical with those I quote below

"I have lived, seen God's Hand thro' a lifetime,
And all was for the best".

Lucy E. Studdy

The answer to the riddle on page 211 is as follows:

Twice two of us are six of us
(TWOTWO contains six letters)
And six of us are three,
(SIX contains three letters)
And three of us are five of us
(THREE contains five letters)
Whatever can we be?
If this is not enough for you,
I'll tell you something more,
That eight of us are five of us
(EIGHT contains five letters)
and five of us are four.
(FIVE contains four letters)

INDEX

(Where we know that people were not called by their first name, we have underlined the name by which they were usually known. Dates of birth and death have been included in this index where these are known).

A

"Abberley Manor" by The Rev. John Lewis Moilliet 170
Abberley, Worcestershire 10, 57, 68, 153, 154, 157, 158, 169, 177, 185
Abberley, Worcestershire, Rector of 106
Abberley Church, Worcestershire 177
Abberley Hall, Worcestershire 57, 149, 154, 158, 177
Abberley Rectory, Worcestershire 158
Abbotsford, Roxburghshire 138
Abercrombie, Elizabeth (née Innes) 75
Abercrombie, Maggie – see Lyons, Maggie
Abercrombie, Mary (-1871) – see Galton, Mary (-1871)
Abercrombie, Mr. 75
Abercrombie, Robert (later Robert Duff) – see Duff, Robert
Aberdeen 75, 135, 137, 138
Aberdeen, Lord (George Hamilton Gordon) (1784-1860) 115
Aberystwith, Cardiganshire 99
Abyssinia, King of 34
Achnacarry, Inverness-shire 135, 138
Adelaide, Queen (1792-1849) 96, 115, 118, 143, 158
Airth, Earldom of 139, 142, 179
Albert, Prince (1819-1861) 187, 192
Aldershot, Hampshire 184, 205
Alderson, Amelia (1769-1853) – see Opie, Amelia (1769-1853)
Alice, Princess (1843-1878) 175
Alnwick, Northumberland 207, 208
Alston, Mr. 53
America 30, 81, 139, 165
Amiens, Peace of (1802) 56
Amphlets, The Misses 104
Anderson family 171
Anderton, Miss 80
Anglesea (!), Marquess of (1st) (Henry William Paget) (1768-1854) 125, 162
Anne, Queen (1665-1714) 14, 136
Antiquarian Society 115
Antwerp, Belgium 107, 108
"Apology for the True Christian Divinity Held by the Quakers, An", by Barclay the Apologist 5, 136, 137
Apperley, Mr. 106
Archbishop of Canterbury (1805-1828) – see Manners-Sutton, Charles (1755-1828)
Archbishop of Canterbury (1838) – see Howley, William (1766-1848)
Archbishop of York (1808-1838) – see Vernon Harcourt, Edward (1757-1847)
Aris's Birmingham Gazette 158
Argyll, Duke of (6th Duke) (George William Campbell) (1768-1839) 134
Arkwright, Alfred 103, 111
Arkwright, Frances Jane (Fanny) (1817-1894) – see Galton, Frances Jane (Fanny) (1817-1894)
Arkwright, Ferdinand 110
Arkwright, Miss 50
Arkwright, Peter 103, 111
Arnold, Thomas Dr. (1795-1842) 147
"Art of Travel, The", by Sir Francis Galton 175
Artesian Well 8
Ashbourne, Derbyshire 14, 50, 51, 56, 189
Ashby de la Zouche, Leicestershire 209

Assembly Rooms, Leamington Spa 131
Asthma 26, 40, 78, 91, 99, 143, 151
Aston Church, near Birmingham 89
Aston Hall Estate 2, 65
Aston Hall Grounds, Birmingham 187
Attwood, Mr. 32
Attye family 170
Atwood, (The Rev. Mr.) 142, 159
Aurora Borealis 133
Australia 68
Avenue House (The), Bishopton, Warwickshire 209

B

Baddesley Clinton, Warwickshire 130
Baird family 136
Baird, John (Sir) 137, 184
Baker, Mr. (of Birmingham) 15
Ballachulish, Argyllshire 135
Balloons 15, 56
Bangor, Flintshire 98
Banks, Thomas (1735-1805) 202
Barclay family 73, 148
Barclay Mausoleum 136, 137
Barclay the Apologist – see Barclay, Robert (1648-1690)
Barclay, Ann – see Fowler, Ann
Barclay, Arthur 184
Barclay, Charles (1780-1855) 184
Barclay, David (1682-1769) 5, 6, 76
Barclay, Ford (1795-1859) 87, 189
Barclay, Ford Mrs. 151
Barclay, Gurney (1786-1830) 179
Barclay, John (1797-1838) 189
Barclay, Lucy (-1757) (née Barclay) 5
Barclay, Lucy (1757-1817) – see Galton, Lucy (1757-1817)
Barclay, Lydia 189
Barclay, Mary (-1859) – see Galton, Mary (-1859)
Barclay, Miss – see Birbeck, Mrs.
Barclay, Rawlinson 189
Barclay, Robert (of Clapham) (1758-1816) 189
Barclay, Robert (1648-1690) (the Apologist) 5, 72, 136, 137
Barclay, Robert (1732-1797) (later Barclay-Allardice) 5, 73, 180
Barclay, Robert (1785-1853) 85, 87, 179, 189
Barclay, Susan 189
Barclay-Allardice, Margaret (1780-1855) – see Gurney, Margaret (1780-1855)
Barclay-Allardice, Margaret (1816-1903) – see Ritchie, Margaret (1816-1903)
Barclay-Allardice, Robert (Capt.) (1779-1854) (the "Pedestrian") 5, 6, 75, 105, 112, 137, 138 139, 142, 144, 179, 180, 184
Barclay-Allardice, Une Cameron (1778-1809) – see Innes, Une Cameron (1778-1809)
Barclay, Bevan and Tritton & Co's Bank, London 179, 189
Barclays Bank 52
Barford, Warwickshire 30, 162
Baron du Potes – see Potes, Baron du
Barry, Bishop 198
Barnet, Mr. 81
Barr, Dr. 1
Bath, Somerset 36, 37, 51, 60, 92, 139, 162, 163, 191, 194
Batt, Charlotte (née Wood) 91, 96, 142, 143, 144
Batt, Mr. 142, 143
Battle of Culloden (1746) 109, 135
Battle of Leipsic (1813) 15
Battle of Waterloo (1815) 17, 18, 141, 162, 179
Beddgelert, Carnarvonshire 98
Belgium 93
Belper, Derbyshire 55
Bemrose's, Derby 195
Ben Nevis 135
Bent family 14, 50, 84
Bent, Elizabeth 84
Bent, Emma Sophia (Sophie) (1844-1940) (née Moilliet) 84, 153, 154

Bent, William Theodore (c.1836-1890) 84
Beresford, Agnes (1783-) (née Fitzherbert) 50
Berkeley, Gloucestershire 163
Berkswell, Warwickshire 104
Berry (or Bury), Mr. (school) 79, 82
Bertie Terrace, Leamington Spa 177, 178, 185, 202, 203, 205, 207, 208
Best, Hannah 169
Bettison's Verandah, Leamington Spa 151
Betts, Miss 101, 141
Bevan, Miss – see Galton, Mrs. Lincoln
Bevan, Mrs. 76
Bewdley, Worcestershire 156, 157, 206
Bicton, Devon 160
Biddulph, George (-c.1757) 186
Biggs, Lucy Amelia (Amy) (1833-1867) (née Moilliet) 98, 147, 158
Bilbies-le-Blancs, The Misses 179
Bilsborough, Miss – see Hughes, Mrs.
Bilston, Staffordshire 28, 93
Bilton Grange, Warwickshire 189
Bingham, Miss – see Pole, Mrs.
Bingley 2, 30
Birbeck, Mr. 189
Birbeck, Mrs. (née Barclay) 189
Birmingham 1, 2, 18, 26, 44, 52, 60, 61, 62, 70, 81, 82, 84, 88, 89, 93, 97, 104, 141, 162, 175, 187, 194, 195, 207
Birmingham and Liverpool Railway 110
Birmingham Music Meeting 33
Birmingham Riots 30, 33, 68
Birnam Wood, Perthshire 138
Bishop of Chester 142
Bishop of London 124
Bishop of Peterborough 103
Bishop of St. Asaph – see Shirley, Archdeacon
Bishopton, Warwickshire 209
Bishop, Gen. 197, 198
Black Country 93
Blair, Alexander (Dr.) 26, 28
Blair, Alexander Mr. (senior) 28
Blair, Miss 149
Blenheim Park, Oxfordshire 40
Blondin, Charles (1824-1897) 191
Blucher, Gebhard Leberecht von (1742-1819) 16
Boki, Madame 42
Boki, Monsieur 42
Bolivar, Simon (1783-1830) 38
Bonaparte – see Napoleon Bonaparte.
Bonetta, Victoria Forbes 129
Bontine, Master 142
Booth, Adele (1784-1869) (née Galton) 5, 64, 67, 103, 105, 111, 140, 157, 162, 189, 192, 193, 195
Booth, John Ray (Dr.) (1777-1859) 67, 103, 111, 119, 141, 162, 189
Booth, Johnny (-c.1835) 103
Boothby, Brooke (Sir) (1744-1824) 202
Boothby, Lady 202
Boothby, Penelope (c.1786-) 202
Botany Bay, Australia 66
Boulogne, France 60, 78, 79, 80, 82, 91, 128
Boulton, Matthew (1728-1809) 27, 34
Boulton, Mr. 142
Boulton, Mr., Jnr. 27
Boulton, Matthew Mrs. 27
Boulton, Mrs. 142
Boulton's Manufactory 82
Braithwaite, Mr. 67
Braithwaite, Mrs. 67
Braybrooke, Lord (3rd Baron) (Richard Griffin) (1783-1858) 115
Breadsall Church, Derbyshire 14, 31, 52, 171, 189
Breadsall Priory, Derbyshire 13, 14, 29, 50, 52, 55, 70, 74, 87, 171, 189
Brebner family 75
Brebner, Miss – see Innes, Mrs.
Brecon, Breconshire 140
Bree, Archdeacon 180, 210
Bree, Mr. 180
Brenton, Augusta – see Galton, Augusta
Brewin, Charles 98
Brewin, Sophia (1782-1863) (née Galton)

5, 32, 45, 56, 58, 64, 89, 91, 98, 111, 140, 157, 192, 193, 195
Brighton, Sussex 156, 167, 168
Bristol 24, 92, 141, 163, 164
Bristol Channel 38, 161
British and Foreign School 106
British Museum 94
Brodie, Mr. 41
Bromley family 57, 86, 149, 156, 206
Bromley, Col. 10, 68, 70, 177
Bromley, Elizabeth Anne (née Pole) 10
Bromley, Harriet 16, 31
Bromley, Jemima (1796-1857) – see Maling, Jemima (1796-1857)
Bromley, Mercy – see Cocks, Mercy
Bromley, Mr. 10
Bromley, Sarah 16
Bromsgrove, Worcestershire 158
Brooke, Arthur de Capel (Sir) 93
Brookes, Mrs. 27
Brown's Hotel, London 173, 176
Brown, Jane (1746-1835) – see Darwin, Jane (1746-1835)
Bruges, Belgium 107
Brunel, Isambard Kingdom (1806-1859) 84
Brunel, Marc Isambard (Sir) (1769-1849) 84
Brussels, Belgium 107, 108, 141
Buckingham Palace 124, 200
Buckinghamshire 13
Budgen, The Misses 92
Budleigh Salterton, Devon 160
Bunbury, Millicent Galton (1846-) – see Lethbridge, Millicent Galton (1846-)
Bunbury, Millicent Adele (1810-1883) (née Galton) 14, 20, 31, 35, 36, 40, 41, 50, 58, 65, 74, 78, 99, 101, 102, 105, 107, 113, 117, 126, 128, 141, 144, 145, 146, 147, 148, 149, 150, 151, 152, 153, 154, 155, 160, 162, 163, 164, 165, 195, 206
Bunbury, Mrs. (née Shirley) 153
Bunbury, Robert Shirley (The Rev.) (1803-1846) 153, 154, 155, 157, 161, 163, 164
Bunbury, Thomas 155, 164
Burdett, Lady (née Coutts) 51
Burdett, Miss (later Burdett-Coutts) 51
Bury, Mr. – see Berry, Mr.
Bury Hill 184
Butler, Dr. 16
Butler, George (The Very Rev.) 177, 208
Butler, Louisa Jane (-1897) – see Galton, Louisa Jane (-1897)
Butler, Richard Austen (R.A.) (later Lord) (1902-1982) 177
Buxton family 73
Buxton, Catherine (1814-1911) (née Gurney) 106
Buxton, Derbyshire 56, 206
Buxton, Edward North (Sir) (2nd Bart.) (1812-1858) 106
Buxton, Sarah Miss 186
Byerley's, Miss 30
Byron family 86
Byron, Capt. (later Admiral) (7th Baron) (George Anson Byron) (1789-1868) 10, 37, 38, 42, 43, 55
Byron, Elizabeth Mary (c.1799-1873) (née Pole) 10, 37, 38, 42, 50
Byron, Lord (6th Baron) (George Gordon Byron) (1788-1824) (the poet) 38
Byron, Georgina (c.1823-) – see Morewood, Georgina (c.1823-)

C

Cadbury, Mr. 91, 195
Cader Idris, Merionethshire 98
Calais 41
Calcraft, Miss 114
Calcraft, Mr., M.P. 114
Caledonian Ball 74, 118
Caledonian Canal 135
Caledonian Schools 75
Callao, South America 38
Calton Hill, Edinburgh 138
Cameron family 108
Cameron, Ewan (Sir) (1629-1717) 109
Cameron, Miss 108, 134, 138
Cameron, Mr. 135

Cameron, Mrs. 138
Cameron, (The Rev. Mr.) 165, 166, 173
Campbell of Monzie 187
Campbell, Dr. 79
Capel Curig, Carnarvonshire 98
Carisbrooke Castle, Isle of Wight 94
Carlisle, Cumberland 138
Carlton Palace, London 41
Carmarthen 81, 82
Carnarvon Castle 98
Carnegie family 179
Caroline, Queen (1768-1821) 35
Cartwright, Lady (c.1805-1902) 209
Cartwright, Major 32
Castle Bromwich, Warwickshire 28, 68
Castle Square, Tenby 181
Castleton, Derbyshire 56
Catalani, Angelica (1780-1849) 69
Cato Street Conspiracy (1820) 32
Cawdor, Lady (Isabella Caroline Campbell) (1771-1848) 25
Cawdor, Lord (1st Baron) (John Campbell) (c.1753-1821) 25
Chalmers, Matilda (née Marsh) 131, 132, 141
Chalmers, (The Rev. Mr.) 132
Chance, William 83
Chandos-Pole – see Pole
Channel Squadron 208
Chantrey, Francis Legatt (1781-1841) 82
Chaplain to King William IV & Queen Adelaide 96
Chapman, David 87
Charles Edward Stuart, Prince (1720-1788) 135, 136, 138, 205
Charles I, King (1600-1649) 116
Charles II, King (1630-1685) 65
Charlotte, Princess (1796-1817) 26, 29
Charlotte, Queen (-1821) 40
Chartists 167, 168
Chatham, Kent 72, 79, 108
Chatsworth (House), Derbyshire 56
Cheapside, London 6
Cheddar Caves 92
Cheddar Cliffs 92
Chelsea Pensioners 199
Chelsea, London 200
Cheltenham, Gloucestershire 92, 142
Chepstow, Monmouthshire 92
Cherry Street, Birmingham 63
Chester 98, 188
Child, Miss – see Wood, Mrs.
Cholera 62, 87, 92, 93, 99
Christ Church, Birmingham 17
Clapham, London 189
Clarendon Square, Leamington Spa 128, 190
Claverdon, Warwickshire 112, 113, 150, 151, 152, 154, 156, 157, 158, 161, 163, 164, 165, 171, 173, 174, 177, 197, 206, 207, 209, 210
Clevedon, Somerset 92
Clewes, Mr. 81
Cliff (The), Warwick 30
Clifford Chambers, Warwickshire 208, 209
Clifton, Gloucestershire 158, 160, 162
Clinton, Lord (20th Baron) (Charles Henry Rolle Trefusis) (1834-1904) 160
Cocks, Mercy (née Bromley) 10
Cocks, The Rev. Mr. 10
Codrington, Edward (Admiral Sir) (1770-1851) 87
Colborne, Zerah (1804-1840) 63
Collins, Mr. 126
Colour top 6
Combermere, Lord (1st Baron & 1st Viscount) (Stapleton Cotton) (1773-1865) 16
Conneau, Dr. 128
Constitution Hill, London 198
Conway, Carnarvonshire 98
Cooper, Astley Paston (Sir) (Bart.) (1768-1841) 41
Copp's Hotel, Leamington 88
Corn Laws 165
Coronation of King Edward VII (1901?) 208
Coronation of Queen Victoria (1838) 114,

117, 119, 121, 122, 123, 201, 208
Cotton, Sgt.-Major 108
Count Persigny – see Persigny, Count
Coutts, Harriet (née Mellon) (later Duchess of St. Albans) (c.1777-1837) 51
Coutts, Thomas 51
Coventry, Warwickshire 97, 117, 145, 151, 152, 153, 207
Craig, The Rev. Mr. 132, 153
Cranstoun, Lord (10th Baron) (James Edward Cranstoun) (1809-1869) 89
Crawshaw, Miss 85
Crimean War (1853-1856) 179, 181, 184
Croft, Ann – see Hinsley, Ann
Croft, Dr. 180
Cromer, Norfolk 179, 186
Crompton, Mr. 53
Crompton and Evans Bank 53, 55
Cromwell, Oliver (1599-1658) 205
Cross, near Torrington, Devon 160, 162
Crystal Palace, London 173
Culloden, Battle of – see Battle of Culloden
Cumberland, Duke of (3rd Duke) H.R.H. William Augustus, 2nd son of King George II) (1721-1765) 135
Cumberland, Duke of (5th Duke) (H.R.H. Ernest Augustus, 5th son of King George III) (1771-1851) 75

D

Dandridge, Lucy (-1850) – see Wheler, Lucy (-1850)
Darley Dale, Derbyshire 55
Darwin family 7, 144, 182, 189
Darwin, Ann (1727-1813) 7
Darwin, Ann (1777-1851) – see Fox, Ann (1777-1851)
Darwin, Ann Eliza Thomasine (1828-) 171
Darwin, Caroline Sarah (1800-1888) – see Wedgwood, Caroline Sarah (1800-1888)
Darwin, Charles (1758-1778) 9
Darwin, Charles Robert, F.R.S. (1809-1882) 8, 9, 58, 69
Darwin, Charlotte Maria Cooper (1827-1885) – see Rhodes, Charlotte Maria Cooper (1827-1885)
Darwin, Edward (1782-1829) 10, 78
Darwin, Elizabeth (1702-1797) (née Hill) 7
Darwin, Elizabeth (1725-1800) – see Hall, Elizabeth (1725-1800)
Darwin, Elizabeth (1747-1832) – (formerly Pole) (née Collier) 9, 10, 13, 50, 52, 53, 55, 88, 89, 171
Darwin, Elizabeth (1790-1868) (née St. Croix) 7, 70
Darwin, Emma Elizabeth (1820-) – see Wilmot, Emma Elizabeth (1820-)
Darwin, Eliza(beth) Hill (1782-1804) 7, 69
Darwin, Emma Georgiana Elizabeth (1784-1818) 12, 13, 31
Darwin, Erasmus, Dr. F.R.S., (1731-1802) 5, 6, 7, 8, 10, 11, 14, 22, 41, 67, 72, 88, 103, 185, 195, 202
Darwin, Erasmus (1759-1799) 9
Darwin, Erasmus Alvey (1804-1881) 50, 51
Darwin, Frances Sarah (Fanny) (1822-1881) – see Huish, Frances Sarah (Fanny) (1822-1881)
Darwin, Frances Anne Violetta (1783-1874) – see Galton, Frances Anne Violetta (1783-1874)
Darwin, Francis (formerly Rhodes) (1825-) 7
Darwin, Francis Sacheverell (Sir) (1786-1859) 5, 10, 14, 51, 55, 171, 188, 189
Darwin, Georgiana Elizabeth (1823-) 171
Darwin, Harriot (1790-1825) – see Maling, Harriot (1790-1825)
Darwin, Jane (1746-1835) (née Brown) 7, 69, 70, 103
Darwin, Jane Harriet (1794-1866) (née Ryle) 10, 14, 51, 56, 91, 171
Darwin, John (The Rev.) (1730-1805) 7
Darwin, John (The Rev.) (1787-1818) 10, 53, 55

Darwin, Marianne (1798-1858) 33, 50
Darwin, Mary (1740-1770) (née Howard) 7, 9
Darwin, Mary Jane (1817-1872) – see Worsley, Mary Jane (1817-1872)
Darwin, Millicent Susan (1833-) 171
Darwin, Reginald (1818-1892) 128
Darwin, Robert (1682-1754) xiii
Darwin, Robert Alvey (1826-1847) 7, 70
Darwin, Robert Waring (1724-1816) 7, 22
Darwin, Robert Waring, F.R.S. (1766-1848) 7, 9, 39, 50, 58, 70, 75, 169, 170
Darwin, Sarah Gay Forbes (1830-) – see Noel, Sarah Gay Forbes) (1830-)
Darwin, Susan Elizabeth (1803-1866) 33, 50, 76
Darwin, Susanna (1729-1789) 7
Darwin, Susan (or Susannah) (1765-1817) (née Wedgwood) 9, 50
Darwin, Violetta Harriot (1826-1880) 56, 171
Darwin, William Alvey (1726-1783) 7, 69, 103, 173
Darwin, William Brown (1774-1841) 7, 69, 70, 173
Davies, Dr. 79
Davies, Mrs. 79
Davy, Humphrey (Sir) (1778-1829) 21
Dean of Durham – see Lake, (The Rev. Mr.) Dean of Peterborough 177, 208
Deep Sea Fishermen 210
Dee's Royal Hotel 83
Defoe, Daniel (1660-1731) 87
Delys, Dr. 26, 27, 63
Delys, Marquis 27
Delys, Mrs. (née Ledsam) 27
Denbigh Hall, Warwickshire 117
Deodand 61
Deptford, Kent 106
Deputy Lieutenant of Warwickshire 88
Derby 7, 8, 14, 21, 32, 39, 53, 60, 70, 84, 171, 211
Derby Music Meeting 50, 69
Derby Races 53
Devonshire, Duke of (6th Duke) (William George Spencer Cavendish) (1790-1858) 50, 173
Dewe, The Rev. Mr. 14
Diamond Jubilee of Queen Victoria 197, 198, 199, 200, 201
Diphtheria 191
Diss, Norfolk 73
Ditchley Park, Oxfordshire 40
Dogs, Isle of 78
Dolgelly, Merionethshire 98, 99
Dorchester, Dorset 100
Double entry book-keeping 149
Dovedale, Derbyshire 56
Dover Street, London 174
Dover, Kent 78, 80, 176
Dr. Barnardo's 210
Drayton 82
Duchemin. M. 65
Duddeston, Birmingham 2, 3, 4, 6, 20, 21, 28, 50, 56, 64, 65, 67, 68, 81, 86, 91, 207
Dudley Caves, near Birmingham 89
Dudson – see Duddeston
Duff, Anne (Lady) 115
Duff, Robert (Sir) (formerly Abercrombie) 75
Duff, The Misses 115
Duff, Wharton Mr. 115, 116
Dugdale, Mary Louisa – see Wheler, Mary Louisa
Dugdale, Mr. 207
Duke of Argyll – see Argyll, Duke of
Duke of York – see York, Duke of
Dumbarton, Dunbartonshire 133
Dunchurch, Warwickshire 163, 164, 206, 207
Dunsinane, Perthshire 138
Dunstaffnage, Argyllshire 134

E

Earl Marshal (17th Duke of Norfolk) (Bernard Edward Howard) (1765-1842) 123
Earldom of Airth – see Airth, Earldom of

Earldom of Menteith – see Menteith, Earldom of
Earldom of Strathearn – see Strathearn, Earldom of
Earle, Charles 179
Earle, Charles Mrs. 179
Earle, Mr. 41
Earlham, Norfolk 86
East India Docks, London 85
East India Station 70
East Indies 93
Eastnor, Lady – see Sommers, Lady
Easton, Mr. 146, 147
Eaton Hall, Cheshire 98
Eclipse of the Sun 190
Edensor, Derbyshire 56
Edgbaston, Birmingham 26
Edgeworth, Maria Miss (1767-1849) 150
Edgeworth, Miss – see Wilson, Mrs.
Edgeworth, Michael Pakenham (1812-1881) 150
Edinburgh 138, 194, 207
Edinburgh Castle 138
Edstone, Warwickshire 141, 152, 157, 171
Edward VI, King (1537-1553) 33
Edward VIII, King (1894-1972) 200
Edwards, The Rev. Mr. 99
Edymead, Somerset 92
Eglinton Tournament (1839) 133
Eglinton, Ayrshire 133
Eldon, Lord (1st Earl) (John Scott) (1751-1838) 23
Elizabeth, Queen (1533-1603) 192
Ellis, (The Rev. Mr.) 167
Ellis-Bristow(e), Marianne (or Mary Ann) (1800-1829) (née Fox) 7
Ellis-Bristow(e), Samuel (1800-1855) 7
Elms (The), Abberley 169, 177
Elston, Nottinghamshire 7, 10, 22, 69
Elstree, Hertfordshire 103, 156
Emperor Napoleon – see Napoleon Bonaparte
Empress of the French 190
English Channel 79
English Church, Ostend, Belgium 107
Episcopal Chapel, Leamington Spa 132
Erysiphelas 162
Esterhazy 124
Eugenics 36, 205
Evans, Capt. 81
Evans, Mr. (butler) 56
Evans, Mr. 194
Exeter Change, London 41
Exeter, Devon 160

F

Fair Hill (later renamed The Larches) 33
Falmouth, Cornwall 80
Farmer family 2
Farmer, Mary (1718-1777) – see Galton, Mary (1718-1777)
Farmer, Miss (c.1749-1827) – see Lloyd, Charles Mrs. (c.1749-1827)
Farnham, Juliana Lucy Lady (-1833) (wife of John Maxwell-Barry (1767-1838) (5th Baron Farnham) 90
Fassifern, Argyllshire 135
Feodora, Princess (1807-1872) 40
Ferrers, Miss – see Granville, Mrs.
Fetteresso, Kincardineshire 75
Fingal's Cave, Staffa 135
Finger prints 205
Fisher family 78, 79
Fisher, Capt. 72, 78
Fisher, Mrs. 79
Fishguard, Pembrokeshire 25
Fitzherbert, Agnes (1783-) – see Beresford, Agnes (1783-)
Fitzherbert, Miss – see Wright, Mrs
Five Ways, Birmingham 68, 207
Flemings 182
Fletcher, Rev. Dr. 56
Florence 194
Foley, Lord 15
Foley, Lord (6th Baron) (Thomas Henry Foley) (1808-1869) 158, 177
Foley, Mrs. (née Wyndham) 185
Forres, Elginshire 135

Forrest, D.W. Mr. 36
Forster, Mrs. Lizzie 76
Fort William, Inverness-shire 135
Forth Bridge 208
Fournier, The Misses 36, 39, 50, 51, 92, 162, 191, 194
Fowler, Ann (née Barclay) 179
Fowler, Gurney 179
Fowler, Mr. 179
Fox family 38, 50, 80, 94
Fox, Ann (1777-1851) (née Darwin) 7, 50, 69, 103, 156, 173
Fox, Frances Jane (1806-) – see Hughes, Frances Jane (1806-)
Fox, Marianne (or Mary Ann) (1800-1829) – see Ellis-Bristow(e), Marianne (or Mary Ann) (1800-1829)
Fox, Martha (née Strutt) 7
Fox, Samuel (1765-1859) 7, 50, 80, 103, 156
Fox, William Darwin, (The Rev.) (1805-1880) 69
France 56
Franklin, John (Sir) (1786-1847) 103, 104
Franklin, Lady 103, 104
French Ambassador 117
French Revolution 27
French, Miss 14, 50
Frome, Somerset 163
Fry family 73, 86
Fry, Catherine 84
Fry, Elizabeth (1780-1845) (née Gurney) 74, 84, 86, 151
Fry, Hannah 84
Fry, Joseph 84
Fry, Miss – see Reynolds, Foster Mrs.
Fry, William 84
Full Street, Derby 8
Funerals 61, 62

G

Galton family 168
Galton, Adele (1784-1869) – see Booth, Adele (1784-1869)
Galton, Agnes Jane (1813-1813) 14, 50
Galton and James Bank, Birmingham 2, 32, 35, 53, 54, 67, 87
Galton, Augusta (née Brenton) 207, 211
"Galton Book" 1
Galton, Darwin (1814-1903) 15, 43, 62, 65, 78, 92, 103, 104, 111, 115, 117, 118, 119, 126, 141, 142, 143, 151, 152, 155, 158, 161, 171, 172, 173, 191, 198, 203, 204, 209
Galton, Diana Erminia (1818-1840) 50, 117, 119, 140
Galton, Dorset 1, 100
Galton, Douglas Strutt (Sir), F.R.S. (1822-1899) 58, 198, 208
Galton, Emma Sophia (1811-1904) 4, 14, 39, 45, 50, 65, 69, 72, 73, 74, 78, 79, 84, 85, 87, 89, 92, 98, 99, 100, 102, 106, 107, 109, 111, 113, 117, 119, 122, 126, 128, 146, 148, 150, 151, 152, 154, 155, 156, 158, 161, 165, 166, 168, 169, 171, 172, 173, 174, 176, 177, 181, 182, 194, 195, 197, 199, 202, 203, 204, 207, 208, 209
Galton, Erasmus (1815-1909) 17, 56, 65, 70, 71, 72, 79, 81, 93, 94, 95, 100, 106, 108, 110, 111, 113, 141, 144, 152, 155, 168, 184, 190, 195, 204, 205
Galton, Ewan Cameron (1791-1800) 5
Galton, Frances Anne Adele (1834-) (née Moilliet) 99, 147, 158
Galton, Frances Anne Violetta (1783-1874) (née Darwin) 1, 6, 7, 12, 15, 16, 17, 20, 21, 23, 26, 33, 36, 41, 50, 51, 52, 56, 57, 67, 78, 79, 81, 86, 89, 93, 97, 98, 99, 101, 111, 119, 122, 139, 141, 142, 144, 152, 153, 154, 156, 157, 161, 163, 164, 165, 168, 169, 171, 172, 173, 174, 176, 177, 178, 179, 180, 181, 187, 188, 191, 202, 203
Galton, Frances Jane (Fanny) (1817-1894) (née Arkwright) 50, 103, 111, 207
Galton, Francis (Sir) F.R.S. (1822-1911) 21, 22, 35, 36, 41, 65, 78, 79, 82, 86, 87,

91, 103, 118, 121, 122, 126, 133, 134, 139, 140, 151, 152, 155, 159, 165, 168, 175, 176, 186, 197, 201, 204, 205, 207
Galton, Herman Ernest (1826-1876) 58, 75, 181, 184
Galton, Hubert John Barclay (1789-1864) 5, 18, 44, 50, 52, 56, 62, 87, 91, 92, 117, 119, 120, 122, 140, 152, 156, 157, 179, 191, 194
Galton, Isabella (c.1798-1877) (née Strutt) 32, 44, 50, 58, 106, 111, 117, 161, 206
Galton, John (1705-1775) 2, 65
Galton, John Howard (1794-1862) 5, 23, 31, 44, 50, 58, 67, 80, 91, 102, 103, 117, 118, 126, 138, 157, 161, 171
Galton, Lincoln, Mrs. 132, 152
Galton, Lincoln (The Rev.) 102, 132, 152
Galton, Louisa Jane (-1897) (née Butler) 177, 197, 198, 208
Galton, Lucy (1757-1817) (née Barclay) 5, 20, 29, 52, 73
Galton, Lucy Harriot (1809-1848) – see Moilliet, Lucy Harriot (1809-1848)
Galton, Marianne (Lady) (-1909) (née Nicholson) 198
Galton, Marianne (or Mary Ann) (1778-1856) – see Schimmelpenninck, Marianne (or Mary Ann) (1778-1856)
Galton, Mary (1718-1777) (née Farmer) 2, 67
Galton, Mary (-1859) (née Barclay) 18, 44, 50, 56, 117, 122, 140, 156, 179, 189
Galton, Mary Barclay (May) (1816-1900) 50, 191, 194
Galton, Mary Cameron (-1871) (née Abercrombie) 75
Galton, Mary Elizabeth (1822-1869) (née Phillips) 141, 151, 152, 155, 161, 191
Galton, Millicent Adele (1810-1883) – see Bunbury, Millicent Adele (1810-1883)
Galton, Robert Cameron (1830-1866) 99, 177, 195
Galton, Samuel (1720-1799) 2, 5, 65, 76
Galton, Samuel (John) – see Galton, Samuel, Jnr.
Galton, Samuel, Jnr. F.R.S. (1753-1832) 2, 6, 11, 32, 64, 65, 67, 68, 91, 185
Galton, Samuel Tertius (1783-1844) 1, 2, 5, 15, 16, 17, 19, 20, 21, 23, 25, 26, 27, 29, 32, 40, 41, 50, 51, 53, 57, 58, 61, 63, 67, 70, 71, 72, 73, 76, 78, 79, 80, 82, 84, 87, 88, 89, 91, 92, 93, 98, 99, 100, 101, 103, 104, 105, 106, 107, 108, 112, 113, 117, 119, 121, 122, 127, 133, 143, 145, 146, 147, 148, 151, 152, 153, 156, 194
Galton, Sophia (1782-1863) – see Brewin, Sophia (1782-1863)
Galton, Theodore (1784-1810) 5
Galton, Theodore Howard (1820-1881) 58
Galton, Violet(ta) (1816-1817) 20, 25, 140
Geldart, Miss – see Jephson, Mrs.
Geneva, Switzerland 92, 103
Genlis, Madame 39
Geographical Society 175
George William Frederick Charles, H.R.H., Prince of Cambridge (1819-1904) 96, 142, 143
George I, King (1660-1727) 6
George II, King (1683-1760) 6, 209
George III, King (1738-1820) 6, 32, 100
George IV, King (1762-1830) 16, 32, 35, 41, 74, 80, 82, 163
George VI, King (1895-1952) 200
Germany 151
Ghent, Belgium 107
Gibbon, Mr. 64
Gilter Point, Tenby 183
Gisborne, John 10
Gisborne, Millicent (née Pole) 10
Gisborne, Miss – see Nixon, Mrs.
Gisborne family 14, 55
Gladstone, John Mr. 95
Gladstone, Mrs. 95
Gladstone, William Ewart (1809-1898) 95
Glamis Castle, Forfarshire 138

Glassaugh, Banffshire 75
Glastonbury Abbey, Somerset 92
Glastonbury Tor, Somerset 92
Glastonbury, Somerset 92
Glencoe, Pass of 135
Glenfinnan, Inverness-shire 135
Gloucester 105
Godson family 143
Godson, Miss 142
Goff, Cameron (née Latour) 75
Goff, Mr. 75
Goil, Loch 134
"Golden Treasury" 115
Gordon, Christina (née Innes) 75, 76
Gout 143
Grand Exhibition, London (1862) 192
Grant, Master 142
Granville, Mr. 130
Granville, Mrs. (née Ferrers) 130
Gravesend, Kent 108
Great Barr, near Birmingham 28
Great Exhibition, London (1851) 174, 175, 179
Great Malvern, Worcestershire 15
Great Pulteney Street, Bath 162
Great Western Railway 181
Greaves, Mr. 30
Greaves, Mrs. (née Whitehead) 30
Greece 5
Greenock, Renfrewshire 133, 134
Greenwich Hospital 78, 106
Griffiths, Capt. (later Admiral) 56, 70, 81, 109
Griffiths, Mrs. 56
Grove Street, Leamington 207
Gubbins, Elizabeth Catherine (-1893) (2nd wife of 9th Duke of St. Albans) 51
"Guide to the Unprotected", by Emma Sophia Galton 194
Guildford, Lady (née Coutts) 51
Gumbley, Mrs. 150, 151
Gurney Banks (The) 52
Gurney family 73, 78, 84, 93, 109, 116, 117, 122, 143, 148, 150, 151, 156, 205
Gurney, Anna (1795-1857) 186
Gurney, Catherine (1814-1911) – see Buxton, Catherine (1814-1911)
Gurney, Daniel (1791-1880) 84
Gurney, Elizabeth (1780-1845) – see Fry, Elizabeth (1780-1845)
Gurney, Harriet Jemima (Lady) (-1837) (née Hay) 115
Gurney, Hudson, F.R.S., M.P. (1775-1864) 73, 74, 76, 84, 115, 122, 139, 144, 148, 150, 156, 174, 186
Gurney, Joseph John (1788-1847) 76, 86, 88, 89, 205
Gurney, Margaret (1780-1855) (née Barclay-Allardice) 73, 74, 75, 79, 84, 86, 105, 106, 114, 115, 116, 117, 122, 125, 144, 148, 150, 156, 174, 184
Gurney, Samuel (1786-1856) 86, 106, 148
Gurney, Samuel Mrs. (-1855) 86, 148, 151
Gutta serena (sudden blindness of unknown origin) 149
Guy's Street, Leamington 101

H

H.M.S. Bellerophon 17
H.M.S. Blond 42
H.M.S. Cambridge 38
H.M.S. Condor 55
H.M.S. Erebus 104
H.M.S. Favourite 100
H.M.S. Northumberland 18
H.M.S. Regent 87
H.M.S. Revenge 87
H.M.S. Shipley 52
H.M.S. Southampton 70, 72, 78, 79, 93, 94
H.M.S. Terror 104
H.M.S. Victory 87, 94
Hadley family 50
Hadley, Eliza 14
Hadley, Henry (c.1766-1830) 14
Hadley, Henry 14
Hadley, Susan (1772-1856) (née Parker)

14, 39, 56, 171, 189
Hadzor, Worcestershire 58, 67, 102, 104, 106, 111, 156, 189, 206
Hagley Road, Birmingham 18
Hall, Elizabeth (1725-1800) (née Darwin) 7
Hall, Thomas (The Rev.) 7
Hallam, Mr. 72, 115, 151
Ham House, London 106
Hamburgh, German 87
Hamstead Hall, near Birmingham 87, 150
Hanbury family 73
Handsworth Church 82
"Happiness Hall" – see Breadsall Priory
Harcourt – see Vernon Harcourt
Hardwick Hall, Derbyshire 56
Harwood, Mr. 203
Hay Asthma – see Asthma
Hay, Harriet Jemima (-1837) – see Gurney, Harriet Jemima (-1837)
Hay, Isabella (Lady) (-1868) – see Wemyss, Isabella (Lady) (-1868)
Hay Mackenzie – see Mackenzie
Haythrop Park 40
Hazelrigge, Maynard (Lady) 114
Heathfield 44
Hemming, Mr. 81
Hercules 51
Heritage, Mrs. 150
Hibbert family 189
Hibbert, Capt. 163
High Bailiff of Birmingham 15
High Ham, Somerset 38, 92
High Legh, Cheshire 206
High Sheriff of Warwickshire 172
High Street, Leamington 88
High Town, Boulogne 79
Highwaymen 63, 64
Hill, Elizabeth (1702-1797) – see Darwin, Elizabeth (1702-1797)
Hill, Rowland (1st Viscount) (1772-1842) 16
Hill Top, near Birmingham 67
Hilliard, Capt. 87
Hilliard, Mrs. 87
Hinsley, Ann (née Croft) 169
Hoare family 73
Hockley Abbey, near Birmingham 18
Hodgson, Joseph (Dr.) (1788-1869) 31, 78, 86, 145, 151, 162, 167
Hodson, Lady 128
Holland 93
Holland, Henry (Dr., later Sir) 144, 148
Holly Walk, Leamington Spa 141
Holte, Lister (Sir) 65
Holy Land, (The) 186
Holyhead 70
Holyrood Palace, Edinburgh 138
Horner family 72, 73, 86, 109, 129, 142
Horner, Francis, M.P. (1778-1817) 16, 20
Horner, Leonard (1785-1864) 16, 20, 194
Horner, Leonard Mrs. (c.1787-1862) (née Lloyd) 20, 194
Horner, Mary (c.1808-1873) – see Lyell, Mary (c.1808-1873)
Horsman, Henry 166
Hougoumont, Waterloo 107
House of Commons 84, 87, 123, 124, 131, 173
House of Lords 84, 87, 89, 173
Howard, Katherine (Lady) 90, 91, 92
Howard, Mary (1740-1770) – see Darwin, Mary (1740-1770)
Howard, Miss – see Wilmot, Lady
Howley, William (1766-1848) (Archbishop of Canterbury from 1828 to 1848) 124
Hughes, Frances Jane (1806-) (née Fox) 7, 182
Hughes, George 7
Hughes, John (The Rev.) (1794-1873) 7, 182
Hughes, Mrs. (née Bilsborough) 7
Hughes, The Rev. Mr. 99, 182
Huish, Frances Sarah (Fanny) (1822-1881) (née Darwin) 171
Huish, Marcus (1815-1868) 171
Hume, Mr. 158
Hundred House Inn, Great Witley, Worcestershire 158

Hunt, Henry (1773-1835) 32
Hunt, Mr. 38
Hurd, Mrs. 68
Hurlingham, London 197, 198
Hyde Park, London 121

I

Ilfracombe, Devon 160
India 68, 88, 132, 186
Indian Mutiny 186
Influenza 62, 99
Ingleby, Clement 23
Ingram, Winnington Miss – see Wood, Mrs.
Innes family 74, 75
Innes, Cameron – see Latour, Cameron
Innes, Christina – see Gordon, Christina
Innes, Elizabeth – see Abercrombie, Elizabeth
Innes, John 75
Innes, Mr. 75, 139
Innes, Mrs. (née Brebner) 75
Innes, Une Cameron (1778-1809) (née Barclay-Allardice) 75
Inverary, Argyllshire 134
Inverness 135
Inversnaid, Stirlingshire 133
Iona Cathedral 134
Ireland 162, 165
Irving, Edward (The Rev.) (1792-1834) 149
Irvingite 149
Isaac family 182
Isham, Charlotte (-1885) – see Wheler, Charlotte (-1885)
Isle of Dogs – see Dogs, Isle of
Isle of Man – see Man, Isle of
Isle of Mull – see Mull, Isle of
Isle of Wight – see Wight, Isle of
Italy 5, 102, 161

J

Jackson, John (or "Gentleman") (1769-1845) 144
Jaegier(?), Mr. 16
James, Olivia (née Lloyd) 2, 35, 67
James, Paul Moon 2, 35, 67, 91
Jenkins, Mr. 183
Jephson Gardens 109
Jephson, Henry (Dr.) 90, 95, 96, 105, 127, 140, 145, 180, 188
Jephson, Mrs. (née Geldart) 95, 96, 188
Jermyn Street, London 197, 199
Jersey, Channel Islands 103
Jeune, Francis (Dr.) (1806-1868) 22, 103
Johnstone, John (Dr.) 43, 91
Joint Stock Banks 53

K

Katrine, Loch 133
Keir, Amelia (1780-1857) – see Moilliet, Amelia (1780-1857)
Keir, James, F.R.S. (1735-1820) 67, 88, 185
Kemble, John (1757-1823) 95, 155
Kemble, Miss – see Siddons, Mrs.
Kemble, John Mrs. (-1845) 95, 155, 183
Kenilworth, Warwickshire 60, 139, 142, 156, 159, 167, 179, 192
Kent, Duchess of (wife of 2nd Duke) (Maria Louisa Victoria) (1786-1861) 40, 82, 87, 117, 119
Kent, Duke of (2nd Duke) (H.R.H. Edward) (1767-1820) 32, 116, 160
Kew Gardens 174
Kilby Railway Tunnel 117
Kiltanon, co. Clare, Ireland 162
King, Mr. 100
King Charles I – see Charles, I, King
King Charles II – see Charles II, King
King Edward VI – see Edward VI, King
King Edward VIII – see Edward VIII, King
King Edward's School, Birmingha, 22, 33, 103
King George I – see George I, King
King George II – see George II, King
King George III – see George III, King
King George IV – see George IV, King

King George VI – see George VI, King
King-Hele, Desmond (author of books on Erasmus Darwin) 5, 8
King Leopold I of Belgium – see Leopold I, King of Belgium
King of Abyssinia – see Abyssinia, King of
King of Saxony – see Saxony, King of
King Robert II (of Scotland) – see Robert II, King of Scotland
King William IV – see William IV, King
King's College, Cambridge 140
King's Norton, Warwickshire 33
Kinross, Kinross-shire 138
Knight, Amelia (Emily) (1802-1890) (née Moilliet) 67, 114
Knight, Samuel (1791-1829) 67
Knight, Philippa (1829-) – see Shirley, Philippa (1829-)
Knightley, Lucy – see Wheler, Lucy
Koch, Dr. 37
Koh-i-nor diamond 174

L

La Haye Sainte, Waterloo 107
Ladywood, Birmingham 1, 2, 26, 32, 33, 207
Laeken Palace, Belgium 107
Lake District 144
Lake, Capt. 147
Lake, Mrs. 147
Lake, (The Rev. Mr.) 147
Lanark, Scotland 22
Lancashire 153
Langholm, Dumfriess-shire 138
Lansdowne Crescent, Bath 37, 51
Lansdowne Place, Leamington 88, 89, 119, 154, 177, 187
Larches (The), Warwick Road, Birmingham 32, 33, 58, 59, 63, 90, 102, 207
Latour, Cameron (née Innes) 75
Latour, Cameron – see Goff, Cameron
Latour, Col. 75
Laughern House, Great Witley, Worcestershire 158
Launceston, Cornwall 206
Laurencekirk, Kincardineshire 138
Lawton, Mrs. 101
Leamington Spa, Warwickshire 19, 45, 56, 60, 61, 88, 89, 90, 91, 93, 95, 96, 97, 99, 103, 105, 106, 108, 110, 112, 117, 122, 127, 128, 131, 138, 139, 140, 145, 146, 147, 149, 151, 152, 153, 154, 156, 157, 165, 167, 170, 177, 179, 180, 181, 185, 187, 197, 202, 205, 206, 207, 211
Leamington Hastings, Warwickshire 103, 166, 203
Ledsam, Miss – see Delys Mrs.
Leeches 62
Legh, Cornwall Col. 206
Leicester, Lord (14th Earl) (Robert Dudley) (c.1532-1588) 192
Leigh, Egerton Capt. 206
Leigh, Lord (7th Baron Leigh, of Stoneleigh) (William Henry Leigh) (1824-1905) 187
Leipsic, Germany 15
Leopold I, King of Belgium (1790-1865) 26, 107
Lethbridge, Millicent Galton (1846-) (née Bunbury) 161, 163, 164
Leven Castle, Kinross-shire 138
Leven, Loch 138
Leveson Gower, Anastasia Miss 143
Leyton, Essex 85, 179
Lichfield, Lord (6th Viscount Anson) (Thomas William Anson) (1795-1854) 116
Lichfield, Staffordshire 9, 10
Ligne, Prince de 120
Linwood, Miss 148
Liverpool 98, 133, 147
Llanbadarn, Cardiganshire 99
Llandilo, Pembrokeshire 26
Lloyd, Agatha 30
Lloyd, Anne 30
Lloyd, Charles (of Bingley) (1775-1839) 2, 30, 67
Lloyd, Mrs. (c.1749-1827) (née Farmer)

2, 30, 67
Lloyd, James 91, 195
Lloyd, Miss – see Braithwaite, Mrs.
Lloyd, Miss – see Horner, Leonard Mrs.
Lloyd, Miss – see Wordsworth, Mrs.
Lloyd, Olivia – see James, Olivia
Lloyd, Susan 30, 67
Lloyds Bank 53, 106, 195
Loch Goil – see Goil, Loch
Loch Katrine – see Katrine, Loch
Loch Leven – see Leven, Loch
Loch Lomond – see Lomond, Loch
Loch Long – see Long, Loch
Lochiel, Inverness-shire 109
Lomas, Mrs. 173
Lomond, Loch 133
London 41, 60, 61, 64, 70, 71, 72, 76, 78, 80, 84, 96, 103, 104, 105, 106, 107, 109, 114, 115, 116, 117, 118, 139, 143, 148, 150, 151, 156, 168, 173, 174, 175 176, 179, 192, 197, 208
London and North Western Railway 110
London Bridge, London 41
Long, Loch 134
Longbridge, Warwickshire 184
Lord Lieutenant of Warwickshire 187
Loxton, Somerset 38, 92, 108, 141, 144, 205
Lucknow, India 186
Lunar Society 6, 8, 30, 67, 88, 185
Lunatic Asylum 122, 123, 207
Lunaticks 6
Lyell, Charles (Sir) (1797-1875) 20
Lyell, Mary (Lady) (c.1808-1873) (née Horner) 20, 194
Lyons, Col. 75
Lyons, Maggie (née Abercrombie) 75
Lyttleton, Lord (4th Baron) (George Fulke Lyttleton) (1763-1828) 18, 70

M

Macco, Mr. 37
MacConnell, Mr. 70
Mackenzie, Hay, Mrs 127
Mackenzie, John Hay 127
Mackintosh family 182
Mackworth, Derbyshire 10
Maclean, Miss 138
Mail Coaches 116
Maling, Anna Martha (1770-) – see Welsh, Anna Martha (1770-)
Maling, Anne (1830-1866) – see Mnizech, Anne, Countess Vandalin (1830-1866)
Maling, Catherine Julia (1772-) – see Ward, Catherine Julia (1772-)
Maling, Harriot (1790-1825) (née Darwin) (first wife of Admiral Maling) 12, 13, 38, 52, 68, 128, 170
Maling, Irwin (-1845) 68, 70, 71, 155
Maling, Irwin Major ("Tiger Maling") (1781-1825) 69
Maling, Jemima (1796-1857) (née Bromley) (second wife of Admiral Maling) 10, 68, 170
Maling, Jemima (1834-) -- see Morgan, Jemima (1834-)
Maling, Lydia (1776-c.1855) 147
Maling, Martha Sophia (1771-1849) – see Mulgrave, Martha Sophia (1771-1849)
Maling, Thomas James Capt. (later Admiral) (1778-1849) 10, 12, 13, 38, 52, 68, 128, 147, 170, 177
Maling, Thomas James (or Tom) (1836-1922) 68
Malta 5, 100, 108
Malvern Links, Worcestershire 15
Malvern Wells, Worcestershire 42
Man, Isle of 155
Manchester 98
Manchester, Duke of (5th Duke) (William Montagu) (1771-1843) 114
Manners-Sutton, Charles (1755-1828), Archbishop of Canterbury (1805-1828) 40, 131
Manners-Sutton, The Misses 130, 131, 179
Marcet, Mrs. 21
Margate, Kent 8, 108

Marlborough House, London 201
Marquess of Anglesea (!) – see Anglesea (!), Marquess of
Marsh, Catherine 131, 132, 141
Marsh, (The Rev. Dr.) 131, 132, 141, 152, 153, 155
Marsh, Matilda – see Chalmers, Matilda
Marsh, (The Rev. Mr.) ("The Beau") 131, 132
Marshal Soult (1769-1851) – see Soult, Marshal (1769-1851)
Mary, Queen of Scots (1542-1587) 138
Mathew, Theobald (Father) 44
Matlock, Derbyshire 55, 103, 111
McAdam, John Loudon (1756-1836) 70
McDougall of Lorne 134
McGregor country 133
McGrigor, Miss 44
McGrigor, Miss – see Watt, Mrs.
Meare, Somerset 92
Mellon, Miss – see Coutts, Mrs.
Melville, Leslie, family 138
Menteith, Earldom of 139, 142, 179
Middleton, Mr. 104, 191
Miguel of Portugal, Dom (1802-1866) 80
Milford House, Tenby 24
Miller, J.R. Mr. (1840-1912) 205
Mills, Arthur Mr. 162
Mills, Catherine Mrs. (née Mordaunt) 162
Mills, Frank (The Rev.) 162
Milverton, Warwickshire 209
Minchin, Mrs. 92
Minorca 13
Mivarts, London 121
Mnizech, Anne, Countess Vandalin (see Maling) 68
Moilliet family 20, 28, 67, 87, 89, 141, 147, 150, 156, 164, 166, 167, 177
Moilliet, Amelia (1780-1857) (née Keir) 67, 88, 140, 150, 153, 158, 169, 177, 185
Moilliet, Amelia (Emily) (1802-1890) – see Knight, Amelia (Emily) (1802-1890), see also Powys, Amelia (Emily) (1802-1890)
Moilliet, Emma Sophia (Sophie) (1844-1940) – see Bent, Emma Sophia (Sophie) (1844-1940)
Moilliet, Frances Anne Adele (1834-) – see Galton, Frances Anne Adele (1834-)
Moilliet, Grace (c.1838-1914) (née Shuckburgh) 211
Moilliet, James (1806-1878) 67, 87, 88, 89, 91, 140, 147, 152, 153, 155, 167, 168, 169, 177, 185, 206
Moilliet, James Keir (1836-1906) 106, 195
Moilliet, John Lewis and Sons, bankers 106, 195
Moilliet, John Lewis I (Jean Louis) (1770-1845) 5, 67, 91, 149, 150, 153, 154
Moilliet, John Lewis (II) (1803-1828) 88
Moilliet, John Lewis (III) (The Rev.) (1836-1909) 106, 170, 195
Moilliet, Louisa Joyce (1821-1908) (née Townsend) 68
Moilliet, Lucy Amelia (Amy) (1833-1867) – see Biggs, Lucy Amelia (Amy) (1833-1867)
Moilliet, Lucy Harriot (1809-1848) (née Galton) 3, 14, 19, 31, 32, 33, 36, 39, 40, 41, 50, 51, 52, 57, 58, 65, 67, 69, 78, 79, 86, 87, 88, 89, 98, 99, 105, 106, 130, 140 145, 147, 149, 153, 155, 157, 158, 164, 165, 166, 167, 168, 169
Moilliet, Tertius Galton (1843-1895) 147, 148
Moilliet, Theodore (1810-1886) 5, 68, 152
Molony, James (-1874) 162
Molony, Lucy (-1855) (née Wheler) 162
Money Market 52
Mont St. Jean, Waterloo 107
Montfort, Lord (1st Baron) (Henry Bromley) (1705-1755) 10
Montreal, Canada 139
Monument (The), Birmingham 43
Monymusk, Aberdeenshire 142
Mordaunt, John (Sir) 162
Mordaunt, Catherine – see Mills, Catherine
Morewood, Georgina (c.1823-) (née

Byron)
Morgan, Edmund (The Rev.) 68
Morgan, Jemima (née Maling) 68
Morgan, Mr. (or Morris, Mr.) 182, 183
Morgan, Mrs. (or Morris, Mrs.) 182, 183
Morley, Derbyshire 171
Morris, Mr. 37
Morris, Mr. (or Morgan, Mr.) 182, 183
Morris, Mrs. (or Morgan, Mrs.) 182, 183
Morse, Miss 73
Mortimer, Ann (née Wozencroft) 81, 82
Mortimer, Mr. 82
Moscardi, Signor 37
Mulgrave Castle, Yorks. 189
Mulgrave, Lady (Martha Sophia Phipps) (1771-1849) (née Maling) 12, 128
Mulgrave, Lord (2nd Baron) (Henry Phipps) (1755-1831) 13, 128, 147
Mull, Isle of 134
Mumbles (The), Glamorgan 161
Mummers 183
Mundy, Rodney Capt. 100

N

Napoleon Bonaparte (1769-1821) 13, 17, 18, 35, 56
Napoleon III (Louis Napoleon, Emperor) (1808-1873) 128, 168
Narberth, Pembrokeshire 181
National Gallery, London 41
Neapolitan Ambassador 120
Nelson, Lord (1st Baron) (Horatio Nelson) (1758-1805) 87, 148
Nemours, Duke of (Louis Charles Philippe Raphael d'Orleans) (1814-1896) 119, 124
Netley Abbey, Hampshire 87
New South Wales, Australia 75
New Street, Birmingham 63
New York 76
New Zealand 68, 170, 195
Newcastle(-on-Tyne), Northumberland 88
Newmarket, Cambridgeshire 8, 112
Newtown, Isle of Wight 73
Nicholson, Marianne (-1909) – see Galton, Marianne Lady (-1909)
Nixon, Mrs. (née Gisborne) 195, 206
Noel, Edward Andrew (1825-) 7, 70
Noel, Sarah Gay Forbes (1830-) (née Darwin) 7, 70
Noot, Mr. 140
Norris Castle, Isle of Wight 87
North, Lord (7th Baron) (Francis North) (1704-1790) 155
North Sands, Tenby 24
Northrepps Cottage, Norfolk 186
Northumberland 209
Northumberland, Duke of (8th Duke) (Algernon George Percy) (1810-1899) 207
Norway 93
Norwegian Kings 134

O

Oaklands 192, 195
Oban, Argyllshire 134, 135
Oddingley murderers 80
Oddingley, Worcestershire 106, 111
Opie, Amelia (1769-1853) (née Alderson) 76
Orange, Prince of 107
Orleans, Duchess of 13
Oscott, Staffordshire 28
Osmaston, Derbyshire 7, 39, 50, 69, 103
Ostend, Belgium 107
Ostler, Mr. 34, 35
Ouseley, Gore (Sir) (1770-1844) 115
Owen Glendower (c.1354-c.1416) 99
Owen, Edward Campbell Rich (Admiral Sir) (1771-1849) 70, 72
Owen, Robert (1771-1858) 22
Oxford 17, 40, 67
Oxford High Church movement 130

P

Palgrave, F.T. Mr. (1824-1897) 115
Palgrave, Francis (Sir) (1788-1861) 115
Palgrave, Lady 115

Pall Mall, London 119, 126, 201
Parade (The), Leamington Spa 90, 151
Paris 15, 102, 128, 195
Parker, Mary (1774-1859) 14, 56, 189
Parker, Mr. (The Rev.) 81
Parker, Susan (1772-1856) – see Hadley, Susan (1772-1856)
Parr, Samuel (Dr.) (1747-1825) 16, 43
Parsonage (The), Leamington Hastings 166
Parsons, Jane 180
Pass of Glencoe – see Glencoe, Pass of
Paxton, Mrs. 173
Peace of Amiens (1802) – see Amiens, Peace of (1802)
Pearson, Hesketh (author of "Doctor Darwin") (1887-1964) 5, 136
Peel, Robert (Sir) (2nd Bart.) (1788-1850) 82
Pembroke 24
Penally, Pembrokeshire 7, 182
Penny Postage 139, 140
Percy, Lady (wife of 9th Duke of Northumberland) (Edith Percy) (1849-1913) 200
Pershore, Worcestershire 115
Persigny, Count 128
Perth 138
Pest Field, Ladywood 1
Pettigrew, Mr. 116
Phillips, Emma 141, 191
Phillips, John Mrs. 141, 171
Phillips, Mary Elizabeth (1822-1869) – see Galton, Mary Elizabeth (1822-1869)
Phillips, Nathaniel (Mr.) 143, 144, 179
Phillips, Thomas (Sir) 115
Phipps, Col. 147
Phipps, The Ladies 128
Phrenology 21, 22
Piccadilly, London 119, 176, 198
Pickering Valley, Yorkshire 189
Platoff 16
Platt Fields Park, Manchester 188
Platt Hall, Manchester 188
Platt Unitarian Chapel, Manchester 188
Plowden, Catherine Emma (Kate) (c.1825-1900) – see Wheler, Catherine Emma (Kate) (c.1825-1900)
Plymouth Brethren 111
Plymouth, Devon 18
Pocklington, Col. 141
Pocklington, Mrs. 142
Pole family 14, 86
Pole, Anne 10
Pole, Charlotte 10
Pole, Edward (The Rev.) 10
Pole, Edward Mrs. (née Bingham) 10
Pole, Edward Sacheverel (Col.) (1718-1780) 9, 10, 88
Pole, Edward Sacheverel Chandos- (1792-1863) 172
Pole, Elizabeth (1747-1832) – see Darwin, Elizabeth (1747-1832)
Pole, Elizabeth Anne – see Bromley, Elizabeth Anne
Pole, Elizabeth Mary (c.1799-1873) – see Byron, Elizabeth Mary (c.1799-1873)
Pole, German 10
Pole, Mary (née Ware) 42
Pole, Millicent – see Gisborne, Millicent
Pole, Reginald (The Rev.) 10
Pole, Sacheverel (1769-1813) 10
Pole, Sacheverel Mrs. 154, 155
Portman Square, London 117, 118, 119, 122, 156
Portsmouth, Hampshire 87, 93, 94
Portugal, Queen of (Maria Isabel) (Maria II) (c.1819-1853) 80
Postage Rates 60
Potato Famine 156
Potes, Baron du 120
Potts, (The Rev. Mr.) 28
Powlett family 179
Powlett, Admiral 207
Powlett, Grace 197
Powlett, Isabella Penelope (-1896) (née Wheler) 208
Powlett, Percy 197

Powys, Amelia (Emily) (1802-1890) (née Moilliet) 67, 114
Powys, Charles Littleton (The Rev.) (- 1872) 67, 114
Powys, John Cowper (1872-1963) 114
Powys, Llewellyn (1884-1939) 114
Powys, Theodore Francis (1875-1953) 114
Press-gangs 56
Preston, Lancashire 138
Priestley, Joseph (Dr.) (1733-1804) 30, 33
Priestley, Marianne 30
Priestley, Sarah 30
Prince Albert – see Albert, Prince
Prince Charles Edward Stuart (1720-1788) – see Charles Edward Stuart, Prince (1720-1788)
Prince de Ligne – see Ligne, Prince de
Prince George William Frederick Charles, of Cambridge (1819-1904) – see George William Frederick Charles (1819-1904)
Prince of Orange – see Orange, Prince of
Prince Leopold – see Leopold, Prince
Prince Napoleon – see Napoleon III (1808-1873)
Prince Regent – see George IV, King
Princess Alice – see Alice, Princess
Princess Charlotte – see Charlotte, Princess
Princess Feodora – see Feodora, Princess
Princess Victoria – see Queen Victoria
Priory (The) – see Breadsall Priory
Pritchard, Dr. 102, 145
Probert, Mr. 38
Pry, Paul 35
Pump Room, Leamington Spa 45, 142, 154
Puzzle Letter 46, 47, 48, 49
Pym, Mrs. 76

Q

Quakers 1, 2, 17, 58, 67, 74, 76, 86, 88 91, 136, 137, 189, 195, 205
Quarter Sessions 167
Quatre Bras, Belgium 135
Queen Adelaide – see Adelaide, Queen
Queen Anne – see Anne, Queen
Queen Caroline – see Caroline, Queen
Queen Charlotte – see Charlotte, Queen
Queen Elizabeth – see Elizabeth, Queen
Queen Mary – see Mary, Queen of Scots
Queen Newspaper 201, 208, 211
Queen of Portugal (c.1819-1853) – see Portugal, Queen of (c.1819-1853)
Queen Victoria – see Victoria, Queen

R

Radbourne, Derbyshire 9, 10, 11
Ragged Schools 210
Raglan, Lord (1st Baron) (Fitzroy James Henry Somerset) (1788-1855) 184
Raemoir, Kincardineshire 75
Ramsgate, Kent 40, 41, 43, 78, 108
Randall, Miss 68
Rea, River 207
Rector of Abberley, Worcestershire – see Abberley, Rector of
Redan (The), Crimea 184
Reform Bill 73, 84, 87, 89
Reform Club (The), London 120, 121, 122, 126
Regent Hotel, Leamington 90, 190
Regent Street, London 41
Reynolds, Foster Mrs. (née Fry) 151
Reynolds, Joshua (Sir) (1723-1792) 202
Rhodes, Charlotte Maria Cooper (1827-1885) (later Darwin) (née Darwin) 7, 70
Rhodes, Francis (later Darwin) (1825-) 7, 70
Rhyl, Flintshire 188
Richmond, Duchess of (Caroline) (wife of 10th Duke of) (1796-1874) 115
Riddle 211
Rio (de Janeiro), South America 42
Ritchie, Margaret (1816-1903) (née Barclay-Allardice) 85, 106, 135, 136, 139

Ritchie, Samuel (-1845) (private soldier) 139
Robert II, King of Scotland (1316-1390) 74, 180
Roberts, Lord (1st Earl) (Frederick Sleigh Roberts) (1832-1914) 200
Robsart, Amy (c.1532-1560) 192
Robson, Mr. 108
Roderick Dhu's country 133
Rodil 38
Roeckel, Mr. 37
Rojet, Mr. 62
Rollason Mr. (portrait painter) 195
Rolle, Lady (wife of 2nd Baron) (Louisa Barbara Rolle) (1796-1885) 160
Rolle, Lord (2nd Baron) (John Rolle) (1756-1842) 160
Rolle, Mark George Kerr (The Hon.) 206
Romaine and Patterson's, Edinburgh 138
Roman Catholics 111, 130, 194
Roos, Signor 102, 103
Ross(-on-Wye), Herefordshire 92
Rossetti, Dante Gabriel (1828-1882) 73
Rossetti, Gabriele Signor (1783-1854) 73
Royal Academy, London 174
Royal Chaplain to King William IV 96
Royal Crescent, Bath 191
Royal family 123
Royal Hotel, Birmingham 16, 44, 82
Royal Leamington Spa, Warwickshire – see Leamington Spa, Warwickshire
Royal Society 6, 36, 175
Royat, France 208
Rugby School, Warwickshire 147
Rugby, Warwickshire 117, 139, 145, 153, 164, 206, 207, 208
Run on the Banks 52
Russell, Dr. 105, 128, 167
Russia 57, 151, 179
Russia, Emperor of 150
Russian Mountain, Geneva 92
Rutland Gate, London 186, 201
Ryde, Isle of Wight 17, 18, 94, 95, 205
Ryland, Louisa 68, 89, 97, 121, 183
Ryland, Mr. 68, 89, 97
Ryland, Mrs. 68, 89, 97
Ryle, Jane Harriet (1794-1866) – see Darwin, Jane Harriet (1794-1866)
Ryle, Miss 117
Ryle, Miss – see Wood, Mrs.

S

Sabloukoff, Gen. 114
Sabloukoff, Mrs. 114
St. Albans, Duchess of (1st wife of 9th Duke of) (Elizabeth Catherine) (- 1893) 51
St. Albans, Duke of (9th Duke) (William Aubrey de Vere Beauclerk) (1801-1849) 51
St. Andrew's Church, Birmingham 207
St. Anne's Well, Great Malvern 15
St. Croix, Elizabeth de (1790-1868) – see Darwin, Elizabeth (1790-1868)
St. Helena 18, 35
St. James's Church, London 198
St. James's Palace, London 74, 116
St. James's Square, London 73, 84, 85, 106, 114, 116, 122, 123, 125, 143, 144, 148, 156
St. James's Street, London 201
St. Katherine's Rock, Tenby 182
St. Leonards-on-Sea, Sussex 151, 152, 153
St. Mark's Church, Leamington Spa 210
St. Mary's Church, Leamington Spa 131, 155
St. Paul's, London 148, 176
St. Philip's Church, Birmingham 34, 129
St. Richard's College, Hadzor 111
Sandwich Islands (later Hawaii), King and Queen of the 42, 43
Saundersfoot, Pembrokeshire 32, 182
Saxony, King of 151
Scarborough, Yorkshire 144
Schelde 93, 94
Schimmelpenninck, Marianne (or Mary Anne) (1778-1856) (née Galton) 5, 105

Schofield, Mr. 32
Schofield, R.E. (author of "The Lunar Society of Birmingham") 6
Scotland 108, 133
Scott, Anne Miss 130
Scott, Joseph (Sir) 28
Scott, Mr. 194
Scott, Walter (Sir) (1771-1832) 36, 130, 133, 138
Scott, Walter (Sir), Jnr. 130
Scottish Kings 134
Sebastopole, Crimea 184
Sedan Chair 37
Selly Hall, near Birmingham 150, 153, 156, 157, 164, 167, 169
Severn, River 9
Shakespeare, William (1564-1616) 17
Sheerness 52
Sheriff of York – see York, Sheriff of
Shirley, Archdeacon (later Bishop of St. Asaph) 154, 155
Shirley, Miss – see Bunbury, Mrs.
Shirley, Mr. 154
Shirley, Philippa (1829-) (née Knight) 67
Shirley, Walter Waddington (The Rev.) (-1866) 67
Shorthouse, Mr. 195
Shoulder Straps 60
Shrewsbury 7, 9, 28, 33, 39, 50, 57, 58, 69, 70, 75, 110, 144, 169, 182
Shrewsbury Race Ball 58
Shrewsbury Races 58
Shrewsbury School 16
Shuckburgh, Grace (c.1838-1914) – see Moilliet, Grace (c.1838-1914)
Siddons, Sarah (née Kemble) 95
Sidmouth, Devon 160
Sierra Leone, West Africa 129, 155
Simeon's Trustees 131
Sitwell family 14, 50, 174, 179, 206
Sitwell, Eliza 162, 188
Sitwell, Hervey Wilmot (The Rev.) (c.1795-1874) 166, 173, 203
Sitwell, Lucy (née Wheler) 203
Sitwell, Margaret 156
Sitwell, Robert, family 171
Sitwell, Sophia (-1869) (née Wheler) 166, 203
Skene family 108
Slugg, J.T. Mr. 66
Smallpox 43, 110
Smethwick Grove, near Birmingham 89, 98, 99
Smethwick, Staffordshire 20
Smith, Sydney 72
Smyrna 5
Snitterfield, Warwickshire 164, 165, 173, 185
Snowdon, Mount 98
Snuff 62
Society of Friends – see Quakers.
Soho Bazaar, London 148
Soho, Birmingham 27
Solar Eclipse – see Eclipse of the Sun
Sommers, Jane Lady (c.1786-1868) (2nd wife of John Sommers Cocks (1st Viscount Eastnor) (1760-1841) 90
Soult, Marshal (1769-1851) 119, 124, 125
South Africa 175
South America 170
South Sands, Tenby 181
South West Africa 175
Southall, Mr. 168
Southampton 17, 87
Spain 5
Sparkbrook, Birmingham 207
Sparrow, Olivia (Lady) 149, 150
Spithead 69, 87, 94
Spooner & Attwood's Bank 195
Spring (The), Kenilworth, Warwickshire 156, 163
Springhill 50
Staffa 134, 135
Stainsby, Derbyshire 203, 206
Stanford Hall, Worcestershire 57
Staunton, Mr. 183, 184
Steelhouse Lane, Birmingham 2, 54

Stevenstone, Devon 160
Steward, Col. 96
Stock, Mrs. 21, 22
Stoke, Warwickshire 207
Stone of Scone 134
Stonehaven, Kincardineshire 135, 137, 184
Stoneleigh Abbey, Warwickshire 187, 188
Strand (The), London 198
Stratford(-on-Avon), Warwickshire 17, 167, 194, 208, 209
Strathearn, Earldom of 179
Streatfield, (The Rev. Mr.) 209
Strutt, Isabella (c.1798-1877) – see Galton, Isabella (c.1798-1877)
Strutt, Joseph 32
Strutt, Martha – see Fox, Martha
Strutt, Miss 19
Strutt, William 8, 19
Stubbs, Miss 104
Studdy, Henry Col. 197
Studdy, Lucy Elizabeth (1847-1928) (née Wheler) 137, 166, 167, 171, 172, 173 179, 180, 181, 182, 183, 190, 191, 194, 197, 200, 201, 202, 203, 207, 208, 209
Studdy, Thomas James Charles Aylmer (Col.) 197, 199, 200, 201, 207, 208 209, 210
Sunderland, co. Durham 87
Sussex, Duke of (1st Duke) (H.R.H. Augustus Frederick, 6th son of King George III) (1773-1843) 74, 116
Sutherland, Duchess of (wife of 3rd Duke) (Anne) (1829-1888) (née Mackenzie) 127
Sutherland, Duke of (3rd Duke) (George Granville William Sutherland Leveson-Gower) (1828-1892) 127
Sutton – see Manners-Sutton
Swansea, Glamorgan 157, 160, 161, 163, 164, 165
Swinfin (or Swynfen) family 91, 179
Switzerland 127, 195
Sydnope, Derbyshire 55
Sykes, Mrs. (-1878) 206
Sympson family 127
Sympson, Mr. 127
Sympson, Mrs. 127

T

Tarbet, Dumbartonshire 133, 134
Teck, Duchess of (Mary Adelaide) (1833-1897) 200
Temple Row, Birmingham 82, 83, 140
Tenby, Pembrokeshire 20, 24, 25, 32, 80, 140, 141, 180, 181, 182, 183
Tenby Church 25
Tewkesbury, Gloucestershire 51
Thames Embankment, London 198
Thames Tunnel 84
Thames, River 78, 140
The Priory – see Breadsall Priory
Thomason, Edward (Sir) (1769-1849) 34, 162
Thomason, Lady 34, 162
Thomason's Manufactory 82
Throckmorton, George (Sir) 56
Throckmorton, Lady 56
Throckmorton, Mr. 56
Thurtell, Mr. 38
Tilbury, Essex 78
Tintern Abbey, Monmouthshire 92
Titterington, Mrs. 157
Torre, Mrs. 104
Torrington, Devon 160, 206
Tottenham, London 76
Tower (of London) 2, 41
Townsend, Charles (The Rev.) 68
Townsend, Louisa Joyce (1821-) – see Moilliet, Louisa Joyce (1821-)
Townsend, Mrs. 68
Tritton family 73
"Tropical South Africa", by Sir Francis Galton 175
Trossachs, (The), Perthshire 134
Tucker, Betty 182
Turner, Miss 66
Turner, Mr. 66

U

Unitarians 58, 111, 157, 161, 188
Upper Gower Street, London 72
Urie – see Ury.
Ury, Kincardineshire 5, 75, 135, 136, 137, 138, 184

V

Valparaiso, South America 52
Valpy, Dr. 5
Vauxhall, London 41
Vauxhall, near Duddeston 15
Velocipedes 27
Vernon Harcourt, Edward (1757-1847), Archbishop of York (1808-1838) 40
Victoria, Queen (1819-1901) 31, 40, 55, 82, 87, 109, 110, 115, 116, 117, 119, 124, 125, 129, 150, 175, 176, 187, 188, 192, 198, 200, 208
Viper 181
Vivian, Capt. 100
Vyner family 179

W

Wakefield, Edward Gibbon (Mr.) 66
Wakefield, Priscilla (Mrs.) 66
Walcheren, The Netherlands 112
Wales 89
Walker, Miss (school) 104
Wallace, William 133
Walmer, Kent 108
Walsall, Staffordshire 93
Walthamstow, London 76
Ward, Amelia Lady (wife of 10th Baron Ward) (c.1797-1882) 177
Ward, Catherine Julia (1772-) (née Maling) 12
Ward, Lord 124
Ward, Mr. 41
Ward, Robert, M.P. 12
Ware, Mary – see Pole, Mary
Warley, Birmingham 18, 50
Warner family 164
Warner, Mrs. 164
Warner, The Rev. Mr. 164
Warwick 93, 172, 184
Warwick Castle 187, 188
Warwick Petty Sessions 166
Warwickshire Yeomanry 93
Waterloo, Battle of – see Battle of Waterloo
Waterloo, Belgium 107
Waterloo Bridge, London 41
Waterloo Place, London 199
Watt, James (1736-1819) 27, 28, 44, 82
Watt, James (Sir) 188
Watt, Mrs. (née McGrigor) 44, 91
"Waverley", by Sir Walter Scott 130
Weare, Mr. 38
Wedgwood, Caroline Sarah (1800-1888) (née Darwin) 33, 50, 69, 76, 110
Wedgwood, Henry Mr. 182
Wedgwood, Henry Mrs. 182
Wedgwood, Josiah (I) (1730-1795) 9
Wedgwood, Josiah (III) (1795-1880) 110
Wedgwood, Susan (or Susannah) (1765-1817) – see Darwin, Susan (or Susannah) (1765-1817)
Wednesbury, Staffordshire 93
Welcombe, Warwickshire 194
Wellesbourne, Warwickshire 183
Wellington, Duke of (1st Duke) (Arthur Wellesley) 16, 78, 82, 83, 107, 108, 109 (1769-1852) 120, 125, 167, 168, 176
Welsh, Anna Martha (1770-) (née Maling) 12
Welsh, Col. 12
Welsh, Miss 128, 129
Welsh, Mr. 128
Wemyss, Isabella (Lady) (-1868) (née Hay) 115
West Cliff, Whitby 189
West Indies 76, 127
Westminster Abbey 120, 122, 123, 124, 125, 126, 134
Weymouth, Dorset 99, 100
Wheler family 103, 127, 131, 156, 162, 179, 198, 201, 206
Wheler, Catherine Emma (Kate) (c.1825-

1900) (née Plowden) 195, 207, 208
Wheler, Charles John (1766-1856) 179
Wheler, Charlotte Miss 156
Wheler, Charlotte Mrs. (née Isham) (-1885) 163
Wheler, Edward (1798-1879) 131, 154, 155, 156, 158, 163, 164, 166, 167, 168, 174, 175, 181, 182, 187, 189, 191, 202 206
Wheler, Edward Galton (Eddy) (1850-1935) (later Wheler-Galton) 173, 179, 180, 181, 182, 183, 184, 185, 187, 190, 197, 200, 201, 206, 207, 209, 210
Wheler, Elizabeth (c.1807-1888) 152, 156, 158, 207
Wheler, Emma (c.1805-1885) 121, 131, 162, 166, 167, 195, 206
Wheler, Francis (Sir) (10th Bart.) (1801-1878) 186, 207
Wheler, Frederick (The Rev.) (1812-1898) 158, 195, 207, 208
Wheler, Henry Trevor (The Rev.) (1804-1860) 163
Wheler, Isabella Penelope (-1896) – see Powlett, Isabella Penelope (-1896)
Wheler, Lottie 195
Wheler, Lucy – see Sitwell, Lucy
Wheler, Lucy (-1855) – see Molony, Lucy (-1855)
Wheler, Lucy (née Knightley) 203
Wheler, Lucy Elizabeth (1847-1928) – see Studdy, Lucy Elizabeth (1847-1928)
Wheler, Mary Louisa (M.L.) (née Dugdale) 200, 201, 207, 210
Wheler, Sophia (-1869) – see Sitwell, Sophia (-1869)
Wheler, Lucy (Lady) (-1850) (née Dandridge) 160, 162
Wheler, Ted 198
Wheler, Trevor (Sir) (9th Bart.) (1797-1869) 160, 190
Wheler, William (Sir) (6th Bart.) (-1799) 203
Whitby Abbey, Yorkshire 189
Whitby, Yorkshire 144, 189, 190
Whitehall, London 120
Whitehead, Miss – see Greaves, Mrs.
Whitehead, Mr. 30
Whitehurst, Mr. 8
Whittier 137
Wicklow, Earl of (4th Earl) (William Howard) (1788-1869) 90
Wight, Isle of 17, 87, 94
Wilberforce, William (1759-1833) 114
Willersley, Herefordshire 207
William IV, King (1765-1837) 55, 82, 84, 96, 109, 115, 143
Williams, Jane 26
Williams, Mrs. 45
Wills, Mr. 161
Wilmot, Capt. 166
Wilmot, Emma Elizabeth Mrs. (1820-) 206
Wilmot, Fanny 211
Wilmot, Lady (née Howard) 7
Wilmot, Miss 10
Wilmot, Robert (Sir) 7
Wilson, Mrs. (née Edgeworth) 150
Windsor Castle, Berkshire 40
Windsor, Berkshire 151
Winnington, Edward (Sir) 57
Winnington, Henry (Capt.) 57
Winnington, Thomas (Sir) 57
Winthrop family 152
Wise family 179, 206
Withering, Mr. 33
Withering, William (Dr.) (1741-1799) 33
Witley Court, Worcestershire 158, 177
Wodehouse (or Woodhouse), Miss 115, 123
Wodehouse (or Woodhouse), Mr. 123, 125
Wolverhampton, Staffordshire 28, 60
Wood family 179
Wood, Charlotte – see Batt, Charlotte
Wood, John Ryle 96, 142, 143, 144
Wood, Mr. 91, 96, 157
Wood, Mrs. (née Child) 97

Wood, Mrs. (née Ryle) 91, 96, 117, 157
Wood, Mrs. (née Winnington Ingram) 96
Woolley, Mr. 67
Woolwich 108
Wootten Wawen, Warwickshire 141, 167
Worcester 80, 93, 105
Worcester Cathedral 99, 144
Worcester Yeomanry 93
Wordsworth, Mr. 67
Wordsworth, Mrs. (née Lloyd) 67
Worsley family 188, 189
Worsley, Charles Carill (1800-1864) 188
Worsley, Mary Jane (1817-1872) (née Darwin) 188
Worthing, Sussex 51, 87, 88, 109, 110, 189
Wozencroft, Ann – see Mortimer, Ann
Wright, Mrs. (née Fitzherbert) 50
Wroxall Abbey, Warwickshire 207
Wyndham, Miss – see Foley, Mrs.
Wynn, Mr., M.P. 115

Y

Yatton, Somerset 92
Yeeles, Mr. 158
York 189
York Minster 189
York Terrace, Leamington Spa 187
York, Duke of (11th Duke) (H.R.H. Frederick, 2nd son of King George III) (1763-1827) 32, 40
York, Sheriff of 172
Yorkshire Dales 144
Young, Mr. 148
Young, Mrs. 101, 103
Young, Thomas 6
Youngsbury, London 76
Yoxall, Staffordshire 10